EXPLORING CHRISTIAN ETHICS

EXPLORING CHRISTIAN ETHICS

An introduction to key methods and debates

CRAIG HOVEY

CASCADE *Books* · Eugene, Oregon

EXPLORING CHRISTIAN ETHICS
An Introduction to Key Methods and Debates

Cascade Books
An Imprint of Wipf and Stock Publishers
199 W. 8th Ave., Suite 3
Eugene, OR 97401

www.wipfandstock.com

PAPERBACK ISBN: 978-1-5326-4128-2
HARDCOVER ISBN: 978-1-5326-4129-9

Cataloging-in-Publication data:

Names: Hovey, Craig

Title: Exploring Christian ethics : an introduction to key methods and debates / by Craig Hovey.

Description: Eugene, OR : Cascade Books, 2018 | Includes bibliographical references and index.

Identifiers: ISBN 978-1-5326-4128-2 (paperback) | ISBN 978-1-5326-4129-9 (hardcover)

Subjects: LCSH: Christian ethics.

Classification: LCC BJ1261 H65 2018 (print)

For Charlie

Contents

Introduction   1

Part 1
WHAT MAKES CHRISTIAN ETHICS *CHRISTIAN*?

1 The Bible   13
2 Following Jesus   36
3 Some key theological themes   55

Part 2
WHAT MAKES CHRISTIAN ETHICS *ETHICS*?

4 Classical roots   77
5 Modern options   95
6 Contemporary challenges   114

Part 3
THE STUFF OF CHRISTIAN ETHICS

 7 Baptism and identity   137
 8 Mercy and peace   158
 9 Justice from above (order)   177
10 Justice from below (liberation)   198
11 Sexuality   218
12 Vulnerable life   237
13 Challenges posed by science and technology   257

Bibliography   276
Further reading   282
Index   287

Introduction

All ethics is haunted by the word *should*. This word is powerful since it tells us and others what to do – not as a suggestion or a recommendation, but as an obligation. There are lots of possible reasons that might be given for what people should do. There might be a reward or punishment in store for them. Or there might be some other benefit or detriment associated with doing something. These outcomes might be realized by the individual person or might be realized by others, and they might come soon or many years later. In addition to these reasons, many others can be given when it comes to thinking about *should*.

In this book, however, I set out an account of Christian ethics that tries to work within a much larger frame than ideas about what we should do. I make a constructive attempt to rephrase Christian ethics as an essential part of the good news, portraying Christianity's moral resources as aspects of the good news it celebrates. I explore the question: what is good about Christian ethics? Specifically, what kind of living is obligated, permitted, made possible and promised for Christians? In approaching Christian ethics this way, I am making and demonstrating a particular claim about ethics – that it need not be characterized primarily by negative prohibitions, limits and tiresome hand-wringing. Rather, I want to show how the way of living that the gospel commends is also permitted and enabled by everything that Christians proclaim to be good about God's life with us in Christ. Theologian Robert Jenson captures the way that this works: 'In the church, moral commands tell what we may reasonably do because Christ is risen, which otherwise could be thought irresponsible. Insofar as it is the gospel that enjoins us, we do because we may, not because we ought.'[1]

So instead of beginning where a lot of ethics begin – with *should* questions – I want to begin elsewhere. There is a much larger set of questions about those things that are simply *worth doing*, although they may not be things that we immediately think of as having something to do with ethics: working on the health of our bodies, playing with children, being neighbourly, enjoying good music. These are things that we may judge to be worth doing and therefore *good*. But they don't fall within the more

---

1 Robert W. Jenson, *Systematic Theology*, vol. 2: *The Works of God* (Oxford: Oxford University Press, 1999), 209.

1

limited circle that some ethics draw. Not only is it not always clear whether we should do these things; but also if these activities are done out of obligation, they actually lose some of their goodness, their enjoyment, spontaneity and leisure.

Having said this, I suspect that most readers will be most familiar with approaches to ethics that primarily ask 'What should I do?' This is a **decisionist** approach that begins with problems or crises, usually ones faced by individuals who alone bear the burden of making a tough choice. Whether the issue is poverty or death or crime or something else, the expectation is that ethics will play the role of responding to it. Here moral questions arise because the world is full of pain, difficulty and suffering. The most pressing and interesting ethical issues are likely to be those in which any decision or any course of action is less than ideal. The difficulty merely continues in the form of an ethical dilemma. But this is not the only flaw of this approach. With this kind of ethics, individuals are usually asked to endure these difficulties on their own, particularly when told to make up their own mind or follow their conscience, which is very personal.

The point isn't to avoid these realities about our world. But it is possible to start at a different place and ask different questions that don't originate with the problems of the world. Beginning with problems means that ethics will always play a repairing and reactionary role. A different place to begin asks 'What is the shape of the Christian moral life?' This way of asking the question takes the focus away from strictly individual decisions and actions and places it on types of life. Relatedly, asking 'How should the people called Christian live?' shifts the focus on to the community and off the individual. It has the advantage of recognizing the interconnectedness of people and especially the corporate quality of the Church as the body of Christ. Popular Christian piety asks individuals to be like Christ, to be Christlike. But it is the community rather than the individual that the Bible recognizes to be the many-membered body, full of many gifts and dedicated to continuing the ministry of Jesus in the world. Paul's image of one person being a hand and another a foot also hints at a division of *moral* labour in which no single individual is asked to be the complete and total embodiment of the kingdom of God. This is the role of the people as a whole.

At the same time, like everyone else, Christians are members of more than one community simultaneously. In addition to their membership in the body of Christ, they are also members of families, citizens of nations, members of ethnic groups, and participants in civic and other organizations. One of the Christian tasks is to learn to navigate these many communities as a representative of the one that transcends them all, particularly when loyalty to one community exerts pressure against loyalty to another. The claims of nationalism are a good example of this since nationalism can easily overstep what is owed to nations and ask the Christian to give to them what belongs to God alone.

Nearly every system of ethics works from the premise that we ought to do good and avoid evil. (This is a fundamental principle of natural law ethics, which will be discussed in Chapter 5.) It is a premise so basic and so widely accepted that it is hardly worth arguing for. We barely notice, though, that the subject 'we' is staring us in the face. Who is this 'we'? Who is asking the question about ethics? Is it simply humans asking how to live as human beings? Is it Christians asking as Christians about how to live as disciples of Jesus Christ? Do these two lead to different ethics or is the Christian ethic held up as being the highest form of a general human ethic?

It is also important to ask what is going on in this time and place that makes it seem natural to ask moral questions of some things rather than others. Introductory surveys like this one, written near the beginning of the twenty-first century, will include moral matters that are pressing now, such as preserving the environment and experimentation on human embryos. However, not so long ago, some of these topics either weren't pressing but should have been, weren't conceivable within the popular categories being used at the time, or simply didn't exist, perhaps because they arose as a result of new technology.

So what are we to do with the aspects of morality that aren't on our radar currently? What about those things that are crucial but are not being discussed on the surface? As two contemporary Christian ethicists write, 'Most of what is important to our moral existence is not what causes us problems, but what is behind those problems and never raised as a question.'[2] If this is true, perhaps the most appropriate response is to allow ourselves to be haunted by the thought that the most important topics genuinely might not currently raise questions for us. The theological focus of a lot of what follows in this book is meant to lay a broad network of images, convictions and practices that shape Christian existence in the hope that we won't be led astray by rigidly focusing only on the issues that currently seem important.

Furthermore, if ethics is about *doing* good and avoiding evil, we should ask whether it's right to limit ethics to actions – those things that we in

---

2 Stanley Hauerwas and Richard Bondi, 'Memory, Community and the Reasons for Living: Theological and Ethical Reflections on Suicide and Euthanasia', *Journal of the American Academy of Religion* 44.3 (Sept. 1976): 439–52 (443).

fact *do* and *don't do*. What if I do something bad by accident or based on misunderstanding? Do I need to *choose* good or evil in order for either my choosing or my choice to be considered good or evil? Or what if I do something good for a bad reason? Does that make my choice good or bad? Is discussing the choice itself the best way of focusing our moral attention in these cases? Addiction poses an interesting case. While addicts choose the substance or other thing to which they are addicted, their reality is also distorted by it. So are we right to think of their choosing as free and deliberate? It is free in the sense that no one else is pressuring them to choose one way as opposed to another. But it is not free in the sense of being completely clear of all constraint or duress. This is true even while the constraints and duress come from the addict's own body.

I have avoided using the language of sin until now. Sin is how Christians understand everything other than the good – the duress, the choices and the effects. One main Christian tradition has followed St Augustine (354–430) in discussing sin very much along the lines of addiction. Augustine's point wasn't that addiction is sin, but that sin is like addiction. How so? According to Augustine, no one makes us sin. (I cannot claim that the devil made me do it.) But we also freely choose sin in the same way that addicts choose whatever it is that is distorting their reality. The reason is that we mistake it for good, even though it isn't. Part of the Christian's moral development involves learning to call things sin that he or she used to call good. Loving one's friends and hating one's enemies is an example of this that we will return to at several points in the following pages. We need to be taught to identify and name sin since otherwise we would continue calling these things good.

At the same time, we would be mistaken to assume that this discussion of sin means that the Christian account of the good is basically a matter of listing and then avoiding sins. In fact, following Augustine, this is actually an impossible project on its own. In a very famous reflection on the nature of evil and sin, Augustine went on to argue that these things actually have no existence on their own.[3] Instead, evil and sin are simply what we call the absence of good. They are 'privations' of the good, instances of diminution or lack. This means that we need to acquaint ourselves with goodness in order to notice when we see or experience something that is less good. If you want to notice what is missing from a picture, you become an expert

---

3 Augustine, *Confessions*, trans. Henry Chadwick (Oxford: Oxford University Press, 1991), VII.xiii.

in the complete picture. The more a doctor has in mind a fully healthy human being, the better he or she will be at detecting what is not working properly, where health is diminished or lacking.

One feature of this Augustinian account is that nothing can be *purely* evil. Since it is a lack, it is always the lack *of something*, which is known by everything else that is left surrounding it. A hole in a sock differs from a hole in a piece of wood, but not because of what the hole *is* (it is literally nothing taken on its own). The holes differ because of what surrounds the hole: the rest of the sock or the rest of the wood. A 'pure hole' is meaningless. In the same way, Augustine argued that every privation of the good is dependent on the good that is reduced or lessened. The good is never completely gone. This has practical consequences for everyday life.

One consequence is the acknowledgement that even the worst person is still good in some sense. We may not be able to discern goodness in that individual's character or actions, unfortunately. But his or her very existence as a person is good because life is a good gift of God and is a reflection of God's very image. The diminution, rather than complete erasure, of that image is sin.

Another consequence has to do with what it takes to overcome evil and sin. Here, to be sure, there are a few different Christian viewpoints. But the Augustinian one that I endorse here and which is deeply traditional points in a clear direction. If sin is privation of the good, it doesn't need to be destroyed; it needs to be made better, the hole filled with goodness, we might say. The analogy of health is more helpful than speaking of holes. If a person is ill, he or she lacks health and needs health restored, or is weak and needs strength. (Notice that the Augustinian account wouldn't have us focus on an analogy with infections from pathogens that need to be destroyed by antibiotics!) In addition to Jesus' ministry of healing in response to sickness as a clear analogy to sin and salvation, the prophet Jeremiah expressed his lament in terms of sickness, and salvation in terms of restoration and healing:

> My joy is gone, grief is upon me,
> my heart is sick . . .
> For the hurt of my poor people I am hurt,
> I mourn, and dismay has taken hold of me.
> Is there no balm in Gilead?
> Is there no physician there?
> Why then has the health of my poor people
> not been restored?
>
> (Jer. 8.18, 21–22)

The balm referred to here appears in the nineteenth-century Christian spiritual, 'There Is a Balm in Gilead', essentially answering Jeremiah's exasperation and hopelessness by pointing to the good news of the gospel:

> There is a balm in Gilead
> To make the wounded whole;
> There is a balm in Gilead
> To heal the sin-sick soul.

Sinners need saving because our souls are sin-sick. Sin makes us ill and is our sickness. Salvation is the process of restoring health to our souls. The point is that ethics shouldn't be reduced to moral obligation since it is closely linked to what Christians proclaim as good news (and moral obligation seldom sounds like good news on its own).

One way this insight will be expressed in the following pages is through a recognition that Christian ethics has often emphasized **being** and **willing** in addition to doing. An ethic of being holds that it is more important to be good than to do good. For example, the Lutheran theologian Dietrich Bonhoeffer (1906–45) argued that it is better for a good person to tell a lie than for a bad person to tell the truth. His reason was that a person's relationship to the truth (his or her virtue of truthfulness) is a precious thing that is easily corrupted, and we can sometimes notice what this relationship is like in other people and in ourselves. A bad person has corrupted truthfulness. Perhaps he or she tells the truth only when it is personally advantageous, in which case we would call that relationship a cynical one. But a good person with a generally healthy truthfulness respects the truth. When such a person tells a lie, it is out of character, we would say. And even though the bad person who tells the truth also does so out of character, it is a bad character. In Chapter 4 we will encounter a specifically Christian version of an ethic focused on being rather than doing. The shift is away from specific actions (doing) and toward broader consideration of a person's or even a community's character (being).

Willing is related to this. Like being, willing takes the exclusive focus away from discrete acts. Instead, what is most important is what is *desired* or *willed*. We probably agree that in many cases in life, it's the thought that counts. By focusing on desire or will, we are admitting that we don't always achieve what we set out to achieve. And if we hope to be judged by others for our intentions rather than our actions, it would be hypocritical to hold others to a different standard, such as judging their actions solely based on their outcomes.

Despite all of this, it must be acknowledged that a lot of ethics has the character of law. Business ethics, for example, is generally presented in the format of codes, those things that are allowed and not allowed. These are tied to authorities and institutions, such as professional associations or governmental agencies, that will enforce them. People guilty of 'ethical violations' have broken one or more of the codes that society or a discipline or guild have laid out ahead of time. Ethics as we discuss it here points to a richer meaning that has to do with how Christians currently and historically *deliberate* over moral matters.

It will also be important to insist throughout that there is no single, consistent Christian ethic. Christians very often genuinely disagree with each other about all of the things discussed here. But however much there is disagreement, it is usually still possible to identify when and where Christian people are disagreeing *as Christians*. If two people disagree about how to interpret the Bible, for example, it is because they nevertheless still *agree* that the Bible is worth taking the time to interpret in the first place. If they didn't agree on this, it would be hard to call their disagreement a Christian disagreement (such as if one simply thought the Bible is irrelevant to the conversation). Whenever possible, then, we should notice different viewpoints against the backgrounds of everything that they share and have in common.

My approach in this book is to look at both those things that are widely shared among Christians who treat ethical topics and some of the most interesting places that they differ. I am not interested in cataloguing every disagreement, nor am I always going to stand at a distance when presenting rival points of view. Instead, my goal is to offer an account of Christian ethics that I judge to be the most true and constructive while avoiding idiosyncratically introducing readers to 'my' ethics.

In addition, I've wanted to do two things that compete against each other. On the one hand, I want to give readers a sense of how Christians think about a wide range of contemporary moral questions. On the other hand, I also want to give a sense of why we are talking about some issues more than others. I don't want to take for granted the list of topics I treat here. Often Christian ethics is in the position of responding to changes in our world, our societies and our cultures. New technologies such as *in vitro* fertilization, for example, raise fundamentally new questions such as what to do with leftover embryos. Legal changes such as the introduction of no-fault divorce in the United States in 1970 (there is currently no equivalent in the United Kingdom) led to demographic changes that pressed churches to address divorce and remarriage in new ways. As we have already noted, historical context usually determines which topics get discussed the most. This means that Christian ethics shouldn't be thought of as a static list of viewpoints on a number of controversial issues. Often Christians will be divided on an issue based on whichever convictions they consider more fundamental. We may not really know what we should think or do until we are confronted with the newness of a historical development that now seems to be pressing, often in ways that call for pastoral responses.

This book assumes some familiarity with Christianity, but is intended for newcomers to the study of Christian ethics. Then again, I don't automatically assume that readers will sympathize with what we are doing here. It is important to acknowledge some reasons people give for preferring not to study ethics at all.

For one, it can feel hopeless. This is a frustration with the fact that there are no clear-cut answers. Some probably take this attitude toward all disciplines in the humanities, wishing for more mathematical and scientific specificity. They ask how a person can know that he or she is right when so many others disagree. Maybe moral conclusions expressed with confidence are merely opinions dressed up in imposing language. In response to this impatience, I urge readers to consider the depth of the subject matter. It's true that the questions of ethics are not easily answered, nor are the answers out in the world waiting to be uncovered. In a famous debate from philosophy, what we *ought* to do doesn't easily flow from descriptions of the world – what *is*. We will look in Chapter 13 at what this is–ought distinction means for thinking morally about science.

Another objection is that doing ethics feels judgemental. This frustration is tied to the ways in which ethics seems to be about passing judgement on the actions of other people. The response to this frustration is twofold. First, while this frustration is a real feeling that some have, it misunderstands what counts as an ethic. If one thinks that ethics is all about producing statements like 'Lying is wrong' and 'It's better to marry for love than money', it's true that these can be used to judge people. Then again, 'Let's all stop judging each other so much' is also a moral statement that might arise from the deliberation we call ethics (in fact it's dear to Christian ethics specifically; see Matt. 7.1). At the same time, it's easy to see how this ethic of not judging might go on to be used by some people to, well, condemn people who judge too much. Of course we might then call those people hypocrites for failing to live by their own ethic of not judging, in which case we too would be guilty in exactly the same way. And so on. Second, it is better to think about judgement that is for action (looking ahead) rather than for condemnation (looking back). One needs to get into the actual content of Christian ethics to see that it actually has a lot to say about backward-looking judgement. The most genuinely Christian ethics will be used for the purpose of forgiving and restoring rather than condemning.

These are not the only objections to doing ethics. We will look at more in Chapter 6. The strongest objections seem to carry with them their own moral convictions, objecting to ethics for ethical reasons. This can have the very positive effect of expanding our ideas about what counts as ethics.

Part 1

WHAT MAKES CHRISTIAN ETHICS *CHRISTIAN?*

1

The Bible

The Bible is clearly extremely important to Christian ethics. But there are reasons that it's not possible for the Bible to be the sole source of authority. Martin Luther's famous insistence on the principle of *sola scriptura* – which says that the Bible alone ought to guide doctrine and practice – characterizes the aspirations of many Protestant groups, but it is only an aspiration. In fact, every way of doing Christian ethics also draws on other sources of authority as well.

One such source is the *experience* of pressing issues and realities that people face in a particular time and place: a community's experiences with power, poverty and wealth, labour, violence, oppression, discrimination, marginalization, persecution and so on. These experiences can shape questions at an often pre-rational level about what is most important for a given community. If the ones asking the moral questions also hold political power, their questions may have to do with how to use power appropriately for the sake of justice, for example. But if the question-askers lack political power, their questions about power and justice will be framed differently and will therefore be likely to lead to different answers. Their notions of power will more probably be 'from below', grassroots, collective, non-sovereign, people-power.

Bible-reading works the same way: it is impossible to remove oneself from one's political, economic, ethnic, linguistic and other experience and then approach the Bible (or any text) with a clean slate. Rich and poor communities, you can imagine, will inevitably respond differently to Jesus' statement 'Blessed are the poor.' Recent trends in **hermeneutics** (the science of how we read and interpret) seek to embrace and acknowledge who we are as readers rather than attempt to bracket it. Because bracketing one's own experience will probably never be entirely successful and will involve a lot of self-deception along the way, I think we should judge the recent trends to be superior to the alternatives. That said, they do generate their own challenges for Christians to articulate how moral authority then flows from any source *other than* experience. Asked plainly, are some experiences better suited to Bible-reading than others?

The American novelist and essayist Wendell Berry (b. 1934) borrowed an idea from Henry David Thoreau to talk about the Bible as an 'outdoor book', a book 'open to the sky'. To Berry, Thoreau could have been describing the Bible when he wrote about 'a hypaethral or unroofed book, lying open under the ether and permeated by it, open to all weathers, not easy to be kept on a shelf'.[1] Berry means this both metaphorically and literally.

Christians ought to be open to the Bible since it is itself an open book, constantly gesturing beyond its words and pages to a horizon of meaning that cannot be exhaustively contained by our 'walls'. It experiments with language and ideas, engages in internal debates, raises questions it can't quite answer. In short, for Berry, the Bible is like the people it seeks to create in its readers: spacious, fearless, full of wonder and hope. Its language is often poetic and playful, at or beyond the bounds of the ordinary meanings of words. And the Bible wants to be read by poets who are willing to use their own words at the boundaries of language. God won't be nailed down. This is how it is a book 'open to the sky'.

Berry also means something rather more literal. To speak of an 'unroofed book' is to say that some ways of living will be more aligned with the kind of book the Bible is than will others. Outside, we are met by wonders that more naturally exceed our expectations, wonders that our controlled, indoor environments intend to keep at bay.

Of course there are many ways to become better readers of the Bible; spending time outside is only one. The point is not only that where one stands influences how one reads, but also that some places to stand are better than others. Surely poor people will respond to 'Blessed are the poor' better than rich people will. (We know this from the Gospels. It is a rare but not impossible thing for the rich to respond faithfully to this declaration. The poor hear it and rejoice if they believe it.) Then again, while 'better' may describe a closer harmony between the kind of text the Bible is and the experiences of some readers, it is also worth noting that throughout the centuries and throughout the world, many Christians have not been able to read at all. Literacy, the production of texts and the copying of manuscripts tend to be decidedly 'indoor' activities, while the outdoor work of peasants requires no reading. This suggests that the answer

---

1 Diary of Henry David Thoreau, 29 June 1851, cited in Wendell Berry, *The Art of the Common-place: The Agrarian Essays of Wendell Berry*, ed. Norman Wirzba (Washington, DC: Counterpoint, 2002), 504.

to a key question explored below – who is the Bible *for*? – is not going to be simple.

Apart from the complexity of reading the Bible in the light of varied experiences, the text of the Bible itself presents its own complications. There are tensions within the Bible on important, current moral questions concerning marriage, the death penalty and war. It is seldom possible to give a single answer to any question that asks what the Bible says on any topic. This is as much the case with strictly theological topics such as God, sin, sacrifice and redemption as it is with moral themes. Furthermore, partly because it is a collection of ancient texts, the Bible is simply silent on many of the topics Christians confront today like environmental degradation, abortion and gender identity. More perilous are the times when the Bible seems at first to offer clear moral guidance, but then further study reveals a tremendous lack of clarity.

It is good to notice, though, that the kinds of problems mentioned in the preceding paragraph especially accompany a reading style that asks a moral question of the Bible and then looks for answers within its pages. This, admittedly, has a venerable history among Christians. But let it be said that the questions we bring to the Bible are not its reason for being. It is not only that modern people will ask questions not countenanced by an ancient text. It is also that the Bible often refuses to play our game of question-and-answer by reversing the process. The Bible turns around and asks questions of us: 'Do you not believe? Do you still not understand?' It throws us into confusion at exactly the points where we had hoped our confidence would be the highest. The Christian experience, therefore, of drawing meaning out of the Bible turns out to be much more than a scholarly one. It can be a vertigo-inducing task that demands the faith of readers but promises to save them from making idols of their own explanations and certainties. Because what I am describing is an experience and challenge of faith, it will be difficult to capture on pages of printed text; its home is in the person of the Christian and within the faith community. Even so, my goal is to return to this liminal experience of the relationship between reader and text in this section.

The Bible is the Scripture of Christians and its primary purpose is to form the life of worshipping communities. This is most obvious in the Psalms, although it is true of every text. The primary function of a psalm is to be sung; the other texts are equally liturgical and are given to us to be read aloud in corporate worship and to be revered and discerned as the word of God for today's Church. Christian receptiveness to the meaning of the Bible is also liturgical, requiring preparation of the soul of the individual believer as well as the soul of the community in order to hear the word that God will speak through it. The challenge is to prepare oneself and others corporately to receive the messages of an 'unroofed book'. But it is important to notice that the Bible itself is also one of the instruments the Church employs to ready the people to hear its message. This means that preparing to use the Bible is not independent of the Bible, which cycles the believing community through the formation to receive it, to its proclaimed message and back again.

The approach taken here is to describe the Bible's role in Christian ethics in a way that allows us to notice when and where it functions to form Christian thinking and living, while also allowing us to see the ways that other sources are also brought to bear on how Christians think about how they should live.

God's story

There are good reasons to avoid the idea that the Bible is primarily a source of information on moral topics (or any other topics, for that matter). Before it is this, it is crucially a source for formation. It shapes Christian people and Christian communities according to its story, inviting us to locate our lives within it by enlisting us as participants within its narrative. Christians not only read in their Scripture the stories of their forebears in the faith; they also learn to see these stories as stories that include themselves. The Bible gives Christians examples and instructions in how to pray and sing, and it promises to form communities into praying and singing communities that, over time, will come to understand their common life in terms of these practices. Miriam's song in Exodus 15.21 is a song for all Christians to sing:

> Sing to the LORD, for he has triumphed gloriously;
> horse and rider he has thrown into the sea.

The song recalls God's deliverance of the children of Israel from Pharaoh's armies as Moses led them out of Egypt. But because Christians have sung the song about it throughout the ages as though it were also their own song, they have been pressed to look for God's deliverances in their own times. Social movements for liberation of vast numbers of people (such as the abolitionist movement) have been cast in terms of God's rescue of Israel. Singing is only one way Christians use the text of the Bible liturgically. (Martin Luther King preached a sermon titled 'The Death of Evil upon the Seashore' on the second anniversary of the US Supreme Court's school desegregation decision.) But singing is a very powerful way of accomplishing the self-involving intention of the Bible in the lives of the communities that claim it to be their Scripture.

The point here is that we will go astray from the very beginning if we neglect the rich, formative use of the Bible in real communities in favour of the much flatter, isolated enterprise of hunting for a chapter and verse from the Bible when trying to answer a question. The whole sweep of the Bible's narrative is the one that, in the wisdom of the early Christians, was taken to be the definitive story of humanity – it's in the light of this story that they made sense of their lives and also determined that those who came after them would likewise locate their existence.

The Bible was written by numerous different authors in different languages and over hundreds of years. We would do well to think about the Bible more as a *library* than a single book. Every author has his own way of writing, his own preferred themes to highlight and burning questions to ask. Depending on the time they were written, the intended purpose and audience, and the dominant theology, literary training and temperament of the authors, the various texts display an astounding range of material. Yet for all of its great variety, Christians can nevertheless still think of the Bible as a book since it tells a single story: of God and God's relationship with ancient Israel, Jesus and the early Christian Church. It is ultimately a single story about God's love for the whole world and God's desire to be with the human beings he created and his actions to bring that about. The complexity of the Bible, it must also be said – especially how it is typically laid out non-chronologically – makes it difficult for many readers to grasp the big picture.

In what follows, I couldn't hope to retell the entire story of the Bible. But I gesture toward some of its most notable contours for our purposes.

God creates the universe out of nothing and because of no compulsion. It is therefore free from needing to make up for any supposed lack in God. As Christian theology has always maintained, God is sufficiency and fullness, meaning that God relates to everything other than Godself (that is, creation) through love. The goodness of creation, including the 'very good'-ness of humanity (see Gen. 1.31), is God's declaration and celebration of this love. As with any love, the beloved is free not to love in return, but rather to exercise that freedom for separation. According to the Bible, this is the situation of humanity which claims for itself the goods of creation, including its own freedom. While the Bible tells the story of Adam (Hebrew for 'humanity') and Eve ('living one') in a way that some have unfortunately thought demanded a literal reading in order to be responsible, one prominent Christian habit since at least the third-century theologian Origen of Alexandria has been to look for the deeper meaning:

> Now what man of intelligence will believe that the first and the second and the third day, and the evening and the morning existed without the sun and moon and stars? And that the first day, if we may so call it, was even without a heaven? And who is so silly as to believe that God, after the manner of a farmer, 'planted a paradise eastward in Eden' and set in it a visible and palpable 'tree of life' of such a sort that anyone who tasted its fruit with his bodily teeth would gain life; and again that one could partake of 'good and evil' by masticating the fruit taken from the tree of that name? And when God is said to 'walk in the paradise in the cool of the day' and Adam to hide himself behind a tree, I do not think anyone will doubt that these are figurative expressions which indicate certain mysteries through a semblance of history and not through actual event.[2]

Origen understood Adam and Eve to be **archetypes** of all humanity. Abandoning the promises of God is a characteristic human act that explains suffering, death, violence, shame and all kinds of enmity between creatures. Adam's and Eve's sin is disobedience and lack of trust in God who had warned of death for eating from the tree of knowledge of good and evil. In Chapter 6, we will discuss the ways the twentieth-century theologian Dietrich Bonhoeffer took this knowledge to be itself the creation of ethics (which hopes to know good and evil). In short, ethics only becomes necessary once humanity takes its leave of God. It replaces trust in God with knowledge of things other than God. God's intention was a world without the need of ethics, with humanity fully and completely trusting in God's provision, where human action flows from love rather than fear, and where the decisions that lead to harm (and therefore require 'ethics' to avoid) do not come to mind.

Some interpreters have pointed out something else instructive for us here. Adam and Eve do not, in fact, suffer death as punishment for their sin as they had been warned. Furthermore, the first sin is quickly followed by the first murder in which God nevertheless acts to save the murderer (Cain) from being killed by others. In these first few chapters of the Bible, God acts to *redeem* his wayward creation by mitigating punishment and ameliorating suffering and shame. God's strategy for redeeming individual humans then gives way to redeeming a whole people – first Noah's family and then (and from then on) Abraham and his descendants. God *elects* or chooses

---

2 Origen, *On First Principles*, ed. G. W. Butterworth (New York: Harper & Row, 1966), 288.

Abraham to be the ancestor of a numerous people called Israel (named after Abraham's grandson Jacob). God makes a **covenant** or promise with Abraham to bless him with a son when he and his wife Sarah were too old for children, and through their son (Isaac) to build a nation that will, in turn, be a blessing to the other nations (literally 'Gentiles').

One of the themes we have already encountered in this book is the fact that all ethics is collective. A Christian ethic is not only an ethic for individual Christians, but is the 'ethos' (from the Greek for custom, habit or character) of a whole community since it is primarily seen in its way of living as a community. Here in the story of the Old Testament, it is crucial to see that what we would call the moral expectations of Abraham and his descendants (spelled out in much detail with Moses generations later) are expectations for an entire nation. For now, the nation is being promised and established.

Yet the nation is also routinely imperilled. First, God asks Abraham to kill his son Isaac, the child of promise (and this was called off at the last minute). This threatens the very existence of the lineage. Then Isaac's son Jacob spends a considerable time away from the land that had been promised to his grandfather and his descendants. Jacob's son Joseph, the victim of his brothers' jealousy and hatred, is made to depart from the land and go to Egypt where his descendants remain for hundreds of years. The descendants of Jacob eventually re-enter the story at the point where their suffering under slavery leads God to hear their groaning and act to deliver them through the leadership of Moses, a Hebrew raised in the household of Pharaoh.

This story, the exodus ('exit') from Egypt, has been deeply meaningful for Jewish identity – God rescues his people from suffering – and for Christian communities throughout the ages. God must reconstitute Jacob's descendants, though, as a people who worship God, since it seems from the text that by this time their numbers had grown very large (as had been promised to Abraham) but they did not reside in the land and may no longer have been worshipping God (elements of the covenant to Abraham that needed to be fulfilled). God therefore acts to deliver them and also to constitute them as a worshipping community. This reconstituting process, the giving of the law to Moses for the people of Israel, delivers a hefty dose of moral content, including the Ten Commandments.

As emphasized above, the law is given to a community. It is not given to an individual (although it applies to individual Israelites due to their membership), nor is it given in a general way to all of humanity. The law comes to a particular nation which might conceivably adopt it as its way of life with God at its head. The Israelites settle in the land of Canaan (recovering this aspect of the promise) yet are quickly discontented with having God as their king. This ushers in a period of various reigning human monarchs who range from the relatively good, yet still quite flawed (David, Solomon), to the downright evil (Ahab and Jezebel). The story is showing that the tendency to abandon God's leadership continues to be part of the human predicament, only now that God has chosen to work with one nation out of the many nations of the world, the consequences of this nation's disobedience can be seen to flow from the distinctive set of especially moral expectations that the law had set forth. The **prophets** remind the people of both the law and the covenant, which are closely intertwined since law is set up as part of what is entailed in being included in God's covenant. Throughout, there is tension over whether and how the covenant exceeds law. God's promises are supposed to remain in effect even when the people disobey the law, but they are also punished for their disobedience, which calls this supposition into question.

The pivotal event in the Old Testament – Judah's destruction and captivity at the hands of the Babylonians – challenges the issues of law and covenant in the most dramatic way. Hebrew prophets leading up to this great event bore messages of warning and calls to repent. When these go unheeded, the prophets turn their attention toward the welfare of the Israelite community in exile. Exile was devastating for many reasons, some of them theological. Hundreds of miles from their home, the captives grieved for their suffering and asked where God was. God could no longer be in Jerusalem, they believed, since Babylon had destroyed the Temple where God had been dwelling. Prophets and teachers in captivity comforted their fellow captives with assurances that God had left the Temple in time (see Ezekiel) and that God indeed was with them in their captivity. Israel had to modify its concepts about God to accommodate this new experience: God is not necessarily tied to land or Temple.

Many scholars believe that much of the Old Testament was written down during and in response to the exile, including the stories of creation, exodus, the giving of the law, and Israel's conquest of Canaan. One reading strategy, then, asks what special meaning these other texts take on in the light of the experience of exile. Or put differently: how does telling the earlier history of Israel in certain deliberate ways help to make sense of Israel's suffering of exile? For example, if the prophets immediately preceding the destruction of Jerusalem remind the people of God's demand for exclusive worship, their warnings are validated when Moses and Joshua issue similar warnings to Israel in an earlier period when, incidentally, Israel was without land, east of the River Jordan. To be sure, a lot of scholarship has focused on when the early histories of the Bible were written. For our purposes, the possibility that they were written down in response to exile highlights the self-involving, liturgical character of the Bible as a whole in which members of communities appropriate these stories as their own in order to make sense of their lives.

Some of this sense-making was in response to urgent, deeper questions the exiles were asking about the suffering they were made to endure. Hadn't they suffered enough for their disobedience? How could they make sense of the fact that their suffering now seemed to be much worse than they deserved? Some of the later chapters of Isaiah have this tone:

> Comfort, O comfort my people,
>   says your God.
> Speak tenderly to Jerusalem,
>   and cry to her
> that she has served her term,
>   that her penalty is paid,
> that she has received from the LORD's hand
>   double for all her sins.
>
>   (Isa. 40.1–2)

Here God is acknowledging what the people suspected was true of the excessiveness of their suffering; they are offered comfort and then hope:

> Have you not known? Have you not heard?
> The LORD is the everlasting God,
>   the Creator of the ends of the earth.
> He does not faint or grow weary;
>   his understanding is unsearchable.
> He gives power to the faint,
>   and strengthens the powerless.
>
>   (Isa. 40.28–29)

Several texts recount God's active involvement in human affairs that leads to the eventual return of the exiles to the land. They are promised that they will be renewed and reconstituted, brought close within God's covenant again and set on a righteous path. But Israel's political power would never be the same. Israel existed without its own sovereignty, under the protection or thumb (depending) of various empires: Persia, Greece, Rome. Questions about God's relationship to Israel's hopes of being a sovereign nation increasingly took on a messianic quality during these years. The people yearned for a real-world saviour who would remind them of David (the most praised Israelite king of the golden era) and free them from the oppressiveness of their Greek and then Roman captors. Assurances that God is king over all nations and that there is some kind of vicarious purpose to their excessive suffering were therefore important themes by the time of Jesus. The obviously enormous influence of the story of Jesus on Christian ethics is the subject of the next chapter.

When the Bible is silent

Sometimes the Bible is quite simply silent on pressing issues. The large-scale destruction of the environment is an example of this. Both Protestant and Catholic traditions, though, have drawn on the language of environmental stewardship to understand the human relationship to the rest of the created world. As stewards, we are not owners who have creation at our disposal, but are caretakers whose negligence or malice might lead to its destruction. In Genesis, God's description of humans exercising 'dominion' over the other animals (Gen. 1.26, 28) has sometimes been understood in the much stronger sense of understanding them to exist for human use and at human disposal. But the pressing facts of environmental disaster as well as a wider understanding of the role God wants humans to play in other areas of life, such as our use of wealth (Luke 16), leads to a more refined understanding of dominion as tending and caring for the good creation that God has made alongside ourselves.

Technology presents seemingly endless challenges to anyone striving to think morally about the ways we live. A lot of the Bible's silence on ethical topics of our day has to do with technology that is unique to our time. To use an example already mentioned, only since the late 1970s has it been possible to fertilize a human egg outside the womb. *In vitro* fertilization (IVF) has been very popular since then as a form of assisted reproduction for those who are infertile. This practice of course raises new questions that the Bible doesn't answer, at least not directly. Furthermore, an inevitable feature of the IVF procedure is the fact that many more human embryos are created than end up being used since this drastically increases the success rate. But because of this, modern societies face a new moral question that others simply haven't faced before: what should be done with these 'doomed' embryos? We treat this topic below in Chapter 12. The point for now is to recognize that many of our modern moral quandaries are recent creations and often accompany advances in science and technology.

Appealing to the story of the Bible is one way to approach issues on which the Bible is silent. Because Christian ethics asks about what is good and how we ought to live, Christians understandably ask these questions of the Bible. As we have seen, much of the Bible doesn't seem to be telling us how to live or what to do explicitly. It is often telling the story of ancient Israel – sometimes aspects of the story are clearly instructive and carry moral weight (such as when David is punished for disobedience), sometimes not (such as the polygamist practice of the patriarchs). Historically, Christians have understood the whole of the Bible's story to have moral significance. Even the most casual Bible-reader cannot help but notice that the Bible tells a story.

On one level, the Bible tells the story of Israel in the Old Testament, and Jesus and the Church in the New Testament. On another level, this is really the cosmic story of all humanity, centred on specific events like the calling of Abraham, the exodus of the children of Israel from Egypt, the reigns of various Israelite kings, their defeat at the hands of enemy nations, their captivity in Babylon and so on. However, while not always diminishing the literal, historical character of these events, Christians since antiquity have looked for meaning that goes beyond them. In truth, Christians read the story of the Old Testament in particular in the light of Christ. They went back and reread in a new way the familiar narrative that it contains – as pointing to and leading up to Christ. But they only did this because they had been formed to read all of reality this way. After all, they believed Jesus Christ to be the meaning of history itself. Jesus makes plain God's love for humanity and God's determination to save us. Jesus is therefore the embodiment of God's saving acts throughout the Old Testament.

The New Testament talks about Jesus as the 'Lamb of God', a reference to the Passover in Egypt. It discusses the return of the Holy Family from Egypt (during the time Herod was killing the children in Bethlehem) in terms of Hosea's description of the exodus in which 'God's son' is both Israel (in Hosea) and Jesus (in Matthew's use of Hosea). In dozens more examples like this, the New Testament not only reads the Old Testament in the light of Christ, but also shows Christians how to do the same. When they read the Bible this way, Christians are not content to situate Jesus within the story of – and leading up to – the first century AD. They understand Jesus to be the lens through which every moment in history can be understood to be God's unique moment with the human beings and communities that he loves. So the Christian skill of reading the Old Testament has been enlarged throughout the centuries to a point where Christianity boldly attempts to read all of reality in the light of Christ.

Because of this conviction, Jesus Christ may be found at the beginning and end of the Bible's story of the whole world. The Bible begins in a garden (the Garden of Eden in Genesis) and ends in a city (the city of God in Revelation); but in both cases, God and humans dwell together. The city at the end, though, isn't simply a return to the innocence and abundance of the garden. The story of humanity departing from God's ways and being pursued by God at great cost to Godself has actually shaped the human future. The glory of God living unmediated with people in the transformed and renewed creation includes the remembrance of death and suffering from which God promises to redeem us. In the same way that the Gospels present the risen Christ with the scars of his crucifixion, the transformed world is a hurt but healed world. The end of the story isn't simply a return to the beginning.

A recent trend in philosophy that has influenced Christian ethics focuses on some general observations about narratives. One of the main ideas is that stories (not just the biblical story or history, but all stories, including works of fiction), because they are dynamic, situate elements found within them that we might otherwise consider static. Events are not random and disconnected but make some sense once situated in their narrative context. What events led up to this? What followed on as a result? Answering these requires knowing the plot. Deeper still, was a horrible event anticipated by intentional wrongdoing or neglect? Is it made right afterwards? Who benefits? Who suffers? Whose voices are heard when people talk about it? Whose aren't heard? Does the total story 'make sense' to some people more than others? Who comes out on top in the end?

One feature of thinking in a narrative mode is that it gets us thinking about the total sweep of things. For example, it's significant that stories have ends. True, some stories intentionally trail off in order to try to make the opposite point, that things always carry on and we shouldn't look to ends to make sense of it all. Then again, endlessness is also a kind of end in its refusal to offer closure; it is constantly postponing what will never come.

It's a question relevant to Christian ethics, then, when we ask whether the story of God with creation has an end at all. The Bible itself ends with an extraordinary vision of new heavens and a new earth in which all things are made new. The end is a new beginning, with the wrongs of history made right. Hebrew prophets concerned with God setting things right often spoke about the great and terrible day of the Lord in which God's judgement would be dished out on enemy nations and corrupt leaders. In this sense, the Bible's story has an end that has not fully come yet.

On the other hand, some of what parts of the Bible talk about as the end is treated by other parts of the Bible as being fulfilled in Jesus Christ.

For example, New Testament writers conceive of Jesus playing the role of Isaiah's 'suffering servant', probably originally a personification of Israel itself whose suffering at the exile seemed so excessive that a prophetic account needed to be offered. This became important for making sense of Jesus' Passion. Likewise, Jesus' own predictions about the destruction of the Jerusalem Temple were not only fulfilled in history when the Romans destroyed the literal Temple; the narrative of the gospel also took on a deeper literary and theological effect once the description of Jesus' death was mapped on to the prediction: his body replaces the Temple. 'End' in the Bible is often a matter of what is being fulfilled, which is something that must be discerned.

Let's look, then, at an example of a concrete moral issue that is in the Bible but that the Bible doesn't treat as a moral issue: polygamy. Some males in the Old Testament had multiple wives, and the law outlines some instructions regarding this custom (Exod. 21.10–11; Deut. 21.15–17). But polygamy is never spoken of approvingly, while its practice was sometimes tied to one wife's inability to bear children (e.g. Sarah) and the stories that involve polygamy often highlight the problems this causes.[3] By the time of Jesus, polygamy in Israel is believed to have become rare. In Hebrew, Genesis 2.24 ('and they become one flesh') doesn't specify 'two', although there was a tradition of inserting that word, which the Gospels and Paul both do. The first-century Qumran community at the Dead Sea, known for its rigorous moral practice, prohibited polygamy, partly based on how its members read Leviticus 18.18 ('And you shall not take a woman as a rival to her sister, uncovering her nakedness while her sister is still alive'). Rabbinic Judaism critiqued polygamy until the eleventh century when it was finally prohibited altogether.

Christian tradition has sometimes followed St Augustine who, in the fifth century, defended the practice of polygamy for the patriarchs in the Bible but not for Christian practice. In general, Augustine argued that an act may be contrary to nature, custom or law. The reason the patriarchs had multiple wives was for the purpose of procreation, he said, which does not violate nature. But he condemned the pagan polygamist practices since he understood them to be motivated by lust. By Augustine's own day, polygamy was not only out of custom but also against civil law, so polygamy would be wrong then for being in violation of these two, even though, since it can't be said always and everywhere to violate nature, it

---

3 See David Instone-Brewer, *Divorce and Remarriage in the Bible* (Grand Rapids: Eerdmans, 2002), ch. 4.

can't be morally condemned in all cases. At the same time, monogamy from early on was being held up as the ideal and was theologically understood to be analogous with God's exclusive faithfulness to his people. When the tradition has taken a dim view of human sexuality, the elevation of celibacy has contributed to negative attitudes toward all marriage. Polygamy can therefore serve for us as a good example of a practice or custom found in the Bible but without any teaching that ought to make it morally normative for today. In this sense, the Bible is silent on the *morality* of polygamy (except for some possible interpretations of passages such as Leviticus 18) even while it recounts polygamy as an ancient practice.

Today's Catholic Church, however, differs from Augustine. It teaches that polygamy is always a violation of the dignity of marriage as a 'unique and exclusive' relationship between one man and one woman, regardless of the norms of one's culture. The *Catechism* goes so far as to give instructions for polygamist converts to annul all but one marriage:

> The predicament of a man who, desiring to convert to the Gospel, is obliged to repudiate one or more wives with whom he has shared years of conjugal life, is understandable. However polygamy is not in accord with the moral law. '[Conjugal] communion is radically contradicted by polygamy; this, in fact, directly negates the plan of God which was revealed from the beginning, because it is contrary to the equal personal dignity of men and women who in matrimony give themselves with a love that is total and therefore unique and exclusive.' The Christian who has previously lived in polygamy has a grave duty in justice to honor the obligations contracted in regard to his former wives and his children.[4]

While Catholicism would have those in polygamist marriages break up their marriages upon conversion, and the Anglican Church Lambeth Conference of 1888 decided not to allow polygamists into the Church, others have advocated a different approach. Anglican priest and theologian John Pobee has mostly worked in Ghana where polygamy is sometimes practised for reasons of childlessness tied to economic concerns. While this is not the Christian practice, Pobee thinks it is important to acknowledge that these are not frivolous, but respectable, reasons. His suggestion is for no new polygamist marriages while the existing ones remain in order not to abandon the women and children in them.[5]

---

4 *Catholic Catechism* (New York: Image Doubleday, 1995), 2387; internal quote is from Pope John Paul II's apostolic exhortation *Familiaris consortio*, 1981.
5 John S. Pobee, *Toward an African Theology* (Nashville: Abingdon, 1979).

The point here is that prevailing cultural practices partly help to shape the ways Christians think about moral matters. This cannot always be either good or bad. Sometimes it may be right to look for God's providential work in culture for ways of enriching Christian practice. Other times Christians will want to resist cultural trends. We can also imagine variations and combinations of these two as they will be worked out differently in different moments in history and at different locations geographically and demographically.

There are, of course, many moral issues about which the Bible is simply silent in the stronger sense of their not being mentioned whatsoever. In these cases, the standard strategy is to appeal to some of the other sources of Christian ethics: **tradition** (what have others taught?), **reason** (what does thinking logically and with wisdom tell us?) and **experience** (how does our encounter with these issues in real life affect how we approach them?). All three of these locate us as moral agents within the world in which serious moral questions arise that threaten to set us both adrift and at odds with others. We should therefore add to these three sources a fourth: **faith**, which doesn't so much ask questions but hopes beyond what can reasonably be thought or said.

Recall the earlier discussion about the Bible being a story, or rather two stories: of Israel and of all humanity. God journeys with humanity rather than stands at a distance issuing commands. This active, dynamic picture of God and humanity provides us with a framework for the task of working out what to do by trying to be faithful to God in the moment. The Bible's two stories are meant to converge into one. Israel's election by God has the purpose of Israel becoming a blessing to all the nations of the earth (all humanity) so that all people eventually become children of Abraham. As Gentiles are included into God's family, it is by the giving of the Holy Spirit rather than the passing on of the law.

Likewise, one becomes Christlike by doing what Christ does and by obeying his commands. But the goal of obedience isn't pleasing God, but becoming like God, sharing in the divine life by going through this life exhibiting God's own qualities: compassion, forgiveness, integrity, truthfulness, inclusivity, justice and so on. This means that a short answer to what to do when the Bible is silent is to employ these qualities for new topics and in new situations. A longer answer, though, will eventually be necessary since it's not always clear what it would mean, for example, to be compassionate in every situation. Often we are in situations where we need to choose between compassion to one person and compassion to another. These kinds of scenarios can't usually be solved in advance of encountering them, but that doesn't prevent us from having something to say about them, which we will have plenty of occasion to do in Part 3.

When the Bible is hard to interpret

In many ways, this section is just a variation on the last. There are matters on which some Christians consider the Bible to be silent while others consider it not altogether silent, but still difficult to interpret. For example, it is generally agreed that the Bible is silent on one of the most contentious issues of our day, abortion (which we take up in more detail in Chapter 12). Yet sometimes hard-to-interpret Bible passages are brought into the debate. Depending on how they are interpreted, they may or may not be relevant to abortion. Is the Bible simply silent on abortion or are there some relevant texts that are just hard to interpret? To answer this question, we will consider one of the very curious passages in the Bible that may or may not be of use in the abortion debate. Before that, however, we need to look more generally at some of the difficulties of using the Bible in general.

Such difficulties fall into two broad categories. First is the question of what overall lens or set of lenses is most appropriate to bring to the text. This is the question of **hermeneutics** and applies to the Bible as a whole (for example, should readers approach the Old and New Testaments differently?) and to individual parts of the Bible (for example, is the Garden of Eden story in Genesis in any sense literal history?). The main tools to employ for this are the study of history and literary theory. Second is the question of odd-sounding, mysterious or opaque passages. This is the question of **exegesis**, which is an activity literally meant to 'draw out' meaning from the text. The main tool for this is the study of language.

These two tasks belong to the work of any serious scholar of the Bible. Beyond these, though, are problems specifically related to our purposes in this book: how to use the Bible as a source for Christian ethics. According to Christian ethicist Robin Gill, there are seven 'serious problems' posed by using the Bible in this way:[6]

1 Many very important Bible passages can be interpreted multiple ways. When Jesus teaches 'Turn the other cheek' when struck (see Matt. 5.39), is the text promoting a pacifistic ethic including an ethic against fighting in all war (as Tertullian believed)? Or is the text speaking figuratively

---

6 Robin Gill, *A Textbook of Christian Ethics*, 4th edn (New York: Bloomsbury Academic, 2014), 10–13.

28

about an internal attitude of the heart (as Augustine believed)? We will look at this specific text in Chapter 9.

2 When it comes to ethics, what role should the authority of the Bible play alongside other sources such as reason, experience and tradition? Christian history reveals a variety of views on this. Martin Luther's insistence on *sola scriptura* in which the Bible is the *only* authority is a view held by many in the Reformed traditions. Anglican and Catholic traditions tend also to look for God's hand outside the Bible, in human reason and conscience and in the natural order of creation. These are sometimes characterized as **general revelation** as opposed to the **specific revelation** of the Bible, since all people have access to it and not just those with access to the Bible.

3 Even those who want to abide by Luther and use the Bible as the sole source of moral guidance usually can't help but operate with a **canon within the canon**. In practice, they go to some parts of the Bible more than others for actual guidance. Among those who claim to be utilizing only the Bible for their authority, some gravitate more to Paul's writings or to the Gospels or to the teachings of Jesus; others emphasize some biblical themes (the kingdom of God or 'the gospel', perhaps) over others.

4 How important is the Old Testament relative to the New Testament? We will encounter this again in Chapter 9 in our discussion of warfare: there are many wars in the Old Testament, often fought without commentary or condemnation and sometimes with God's explicit approval; an ethic of pacifism comes much more plausibly from the New Testament. If one hopes to find a consistent ethic of war across both testaments, some account of this shift is necessary. It is possible to cite many other examples of similar shifts, such as with capital punishment.

5 Is Jesus in any sense a higher authority than the rest of the Bible? This seems to be implied in a relatively recent Bible-publishing custom of setting Jesus' words in red type. Theologically, some have argued that the 'Word of God' refers both to Jesus Christ and the Bible itself with the Bible pointing to Jesus – this makes Jesus the point of the Bible and not vice versa, hence elevating Jesus' authority. This can become useful if there is a contradiction. Gill gives the example of divorce and remarriage which, in Jesus' teaching in Matthew 5 and 19, is only allowed in cases of 'unchastity'. At the same time, there is great variety among the different Christian traditions on this topic. Eastern Orthodoxy allows up to three divorces and remarriages for a person but not a fourth. Scholarship on Jesus in the past century has often looked for layers within the text of the

Gospels, arguing that some of Jesus' sayings are more authentic than others. If true, what effect might this have on ascribing authority to Jesus?

6 With specific regard to the New Testament, how far is it possible to make the Gospels and the writings of Paul agree? In practice, this is an example of number 3 above – a canon within the canon – since some Christian traditions clearly give precedence to one over another. Reformed Christians tend to go to Paul while Catholics go to the Gospels. Is a certain amount of tension between Paul and the Gospels acceptable?

7 Many of the issues faced by today's Christians are not mentioned in the Bible at all. This difficulty was the focus of the previous section.

With these specific problems in mind, let's now return to the issue of possible biblical texts relating to abortion. Surely a most curious example comes from Numbers 5 in which a woman accused of unfaithfulness to her husband is brought before a priest to perform a kind of test or 'trial by ordeal':

> [The priest shall say to the woman] 'But if you have gone astray while under your husband's authority, if you have defiled yourself and some man other than your husband has had intercourse with you' – let the priest make the woman take the oath of the curse and say to the woman – 'the LORD make you an execration and an oath among your people, when the LORD makes your uterus drop, your womb discharge; now may this water that brings the curse enter your bowels and make your womb discharge, your uterus drop!' And the woman shall say, 'Amen. Amen.' (Num. 5.20–22)

This ordeal strikes modern people as very bizarre and the text raises a lot of questions. Is this a cryptic reference to induced abortion in response to infidelity? Certainly it underscores the seriousness of infidelity by presenting a test (rather than just a punishment), failure of which at least results in barrenness if not the actual loss of a child, depending on whether or not the woman was pregnant. Jewish scholars in the Middle Ages in fact debated whether the procedure should be carried out immediately if the suspected woman was pregnant or whether it could be deferred in order not to enact a loss for the husband. The contemporary Bible commentator Baruch Levine notes that whether a scholar agrees or disagrees with administering the ordeal during a pregnancy 'depended on whether the religious authorities supported or opposed abortion'.[7] But because the text is unclear about whether or not there is a pregnancy as well as whether or not the potion of water and dust destroys the womb or implies also

---

7 Baruch A. Levine, *Numbers 1–20: The Anchor Bible* (New York: Doubleday, 1993), 203.

destruction of a foetus, we are left with questions that cannot be answered on the basis of the text alone. Levine, for one, concludes that an unstated policy of 'pro-choice' was at work in this portion of the law, partly because of the implication that the community was making clear that it would not care for children of infidelity.[8]

We know that from very early on, Christian literature outside the New Testament condemns abortion, although the reasoning behind it is less clear. But what, if anything, does this text from Numbers contribute to attempts by modern Christians to think biblically about abortion? There are some questions about how much the Old Testament law is meant to be observed by (Gentile or non-Jewish) Christians. At any rate, Jewish tradition abolished the ordeal in the third century, but it was probably not practised after the Jerusalem Temple was destroyed in AD 70. What is being described seems to be an ancient practice with parallels in other ancient societies (there are similarities in Hammurabi's Code, for example), but one that bears very little relationship to the subject of abortion as we have come to know it today. For one thing, the contemporary debate is mostly over *elective* rather than *compulsory* abortion.

Even if Numbers 5 does have something to say to pressing issues of today, it seems to be on the opposite side from Christian tradition that has generally disapproved of abortion, even in cases of infidelity. Because surely no mixture of water and dust actually acts as an abortifacient, the text probably understands God to be acting as the judge, producing the appropriate effect through miracle. How does the traditional Christian belief in the sanctity of human life fare then? Is it better or worse if God is the one doing the work?

A text like this that is bizarre and frankly offensive to many modern people also prompts questions *against* the text. How should we take the patriarchal, even sexist, subordinate role that a woman plays here in which a test and punishment destroy her sex organs? One wonders what a woman suspecting her husband of infidelity was supposed to do. There is no equivalent text that relates to a man in a similar situation. It's true that modern ideas about male and female equality cannot be expected of ancient texts. At the same time, other biblical texts are often brought in to support such ideas. How then do those texts sit alongside this one? More troubling is the violence and violation of the ordeal, which few modern Christians would argue should be part of any sexual ethic. Is it acceptable to ignore texts like this one that, on this level at least, seem to go in such a terrible direction?

---

8 Levine, *Numbers 1–20*, 212.

We won't go further to try to answer these questions here. But the case of this text highlights the fact that there can be a fine line between the judgement that on a given topic the Bible is silent and that the Bible is unclear. The distinctions we bring to the text will contribute to what we find there. Does the Bible address abortion or not? Is Numbers part of a 'pro-choice' priestly law tradition, as Levine understands it? Or are we all like the Jewish interpreters who read differently based on beliefs about abortion that they already held apart from this particular text? When all is said and done, are interpreters still likely to side with interpretations that align with beliefs they have already formed based on other reasons?

Maybe the last question is worded too cynically. At the least, it is certainly very difficult to step outside one's moral convictions that come from many different sources. We are almost certainly better able to see this in the history of interpretation than in our own interpretations. One of the tasks of Christian ethics is to allow the Bible – as well as other sources of moral authority, but especially the Bible – to stand over us, our times and our cultures, and to hear its authentic guidance. True to our existence as embodied in particular times and places, though, at least part of the ways Christians will have already been formed, sometimes substantially, is itself Christian. Christian ethicists are, as we have said, in a circular hermeneutical relationship with our existence in the world and the Christian moral sources to which we look. This is our context, and it is a complicated one.

Reading and interpreting responsibly means attending to not only our own various contexts, but also the contexts that produced, shaped, interpreted and delivered the Bible to us. There is quite a range among Christians regarding the question of how much the study of history – the history of the Bible itself, the history the Bible recounts within its pages and the history of its interpretation – ought to help determine its meaning. To some, the Bible should be thought of as the unchangeable word of God for all time and all places. This is a conservative approach in which a word spoken to the ancient Israelites is the same word God is speaking through it today. This view has the appearance of rigour, but is difficult to hold on to in practice.

Biblical studies gained a lot of energy in the nineteenth century around certain *critical* tasks. It began to ask in earnest: what is the history of the main versions of the biblical texts that we have? How old, reliable and consistent are they across the manuscripts? Who wrote the Bible, especially the Pentateuch (the first five books)? What was going on when the texts were written? How do these events and cultural beliefs and practices affect the meaning of the text?

When the Bible condemns practices such as getting tattoos (Lev. 19.28), do we need to know what was going on in the culture at the time? What did tattoos signify? Does this matter? In fact, it does. An ancient custom practised by Israel's neighbours and enemies (like the Egyptians) involved making permanent marks or brands on captives of a god or of a ruler like Pharaoh.[9] The Jewish philosopher Philo of Alexandria noted that a brand of the name of a god meant permanent allegiance, implying that what is forbidden isn't tattoos per se but marking the name of a god other than the Lord. The standard Hebrew way of signalling allegiance to God, on the other hand, was through phylacteries worn on the arm or forehead. There may be internal disagreement within the Bible as to whether a slave could be marked for life (and thus made a slave for life). Other texts (Exod. 21.6; Deut. 15.17) involve marking slaves by piercing the ear.

Without a doubt, knowing some historical context for the prohibition in Leviticus shows it to have little to do with reasons people in our day get tattoos. But it can teach us something about how the Bible is addressing idolatry and slavery, and possibly even engaging in some internal disagreement with other biblical texts.

Here we have considered briefly two Old Testament texts – Numbers 5 and Leviticus 19 – in order to raise some additional questions about interpretation. When Christians read Old Testament texts, especially ones with moral content, there is always a question about how that content functions within the total context of the Bible. This is called the **canonical context**. The terminology 'Old Testament' and 'New Testament' is unique to Christianity. Judaism considers what Christians call the Old Testament to be part of its collection of sacred texts, but not all of it. The Talmud is a collection of later writings considered sacred in Judaism but which hold no authority in Christianity. Christians have tended to emphasize the ways the 'Old' and 'New' covenants or promises to which the two testaments bear witness are promise and fulfilment. This is avowedly a way of reading both parts of the Bible in the light of Jesus Christ who is anticipated in the Old Testament and disclosed in the New.

In making this crucial point, some have taken the novelty of the gospel too far and have ended up overemphasizing its differences from the Jewish scriptures and religion. Marcion of Pontus, a second-century heretic, so strongly stressed what is new about the Christian message that he even taught that the Jews and Christians worship different gods: the Jewish God is the creator who values law and judgement; the Christian God is the

---

9 Jacob Milgrom, *Leviticus 17–22: Anchor Bible* (New York: Doubleday, 2000), 1694–5.

saviour who values love and forgiveness. Even though Marcion was condemned as a heretic, he had many followers and even established churches. Marcion's way of reading the Scriptures reflected this disjunctive approach to looking at Judaism and Christianity. Rather than try to identify ways of uniting them such as through prophecy and fulfilment, he took both at face value and judged that the Jewish scriptures were too obsessed with law and not sufficiently concerned with grace.

Throughout the ages, Christianity has always found the need to give an account of how these two testaments relate to each other. Marcion's extremism showed how urgent it was for Christians to be very clear that the Jewish story was in fact their own as well, and this most certainly included the Jewish Tanakh (or Christian Old Testament). Some have suggested that Marcion even prompted the Church to begin the process of identifying a precise New Testament canon. What Marcion failed to do was to read the Old Testament in the light of Christ. Doing this often means offering figurative readings and looking for prophecy (in the Old Testament) and fulfilment (in the New Testament). There are other strategies as well.

In our own day, versions of these debates are still visible. Especially since the Holocaust and in recognition of centuries of Christian anti-Semitism, it is now common for scholars to warn of the dangers of **supersessionism** (also called replacement theology) or the view in which the Church has simply replaced Israel. Promises God made to Israel (such as through Abraham, David or the prophets) are thought by some to apply only to the Church now. Gentile and Jewish believers in Christ now constitute the 'new Israel', 'children of Abraham' and 'the people of God' based on conversion rather than biological lineage. While this language has some support in the New Testament, it becomes a serious problem when it edges out Israel, which is something Paul completely rejected in Romans: 'I ask, then, has God rejected his people? By no means! I myself am an Israelite, a descendant of Abraham, a member of the tribe of Benjamin. God has not rejected his people whom he foreknew' (Rom. 11.1–2).

It's true that Paul was led to this point through an elaborate argument both for why the gospel is available to Gentiles apart from needing to keep the Jewish law and also for what might be interpreted as God's rejection of the Jews for their disobedience. Yet he goes on to argue that in being made recipients of the gospel, Gentile Christians are 'grafted into' the olive tree of Israel. Paul uses an image that is at once organic and biological while also being somewhat artificial in the sense that someone must do the work of grafting the branches in. Paul's challenge was to account for several facts: that God's promises to Israel have been fulfilled in Christ;

that both Jews and Gentiles are now claiming Christ; that God's covenant with Israel still has its own integrity; and that many Jews of his time were rejecting Jesus as the Messiah of Israel. Paul's theology on this question is notoriously difficult and perhaps it's understandable that some read him as supporting supersessionism. But most modern scholars strongly caution against this.

A much milder contemporary impulse is to approach the Hebrew scriptures on their own, without imposing Christian readings back on to them. In some Christian settings, one will find an aversion to the term 'Old Testament' in favour of 'Hebrew Bible' for this reason. At one level, the reason for this is very good: to allow the texts to speak for themselves and to value the ways that Jewish thought and practice read and have read them. At another level, though, what is at risk of being left out are the ancient Christian reading practices (such as allegory) that actually worked to hold the two testaments together and so, ideally, also hold Israel and the Church together.

2

Following Jesus

Christians confess a number of unique things about Jesus of Nazareth. The first is his status as the Messiah of Israel. The Hebrew word *Messiah* and the Greek word *Christ* have the same meaning: anointed one. Even though Israel understood many people to be anointed (prophets, priests and kings), Jesus is uniquely identified by this title to be the fulfilment of God's promises to deliver not only Israel but all the other nations. In his fulfilment of the role of king, for example, Jesus fulfils God's wish to be the one sovereign source, which the people of Israel had rejected once they asked God to give them their own human kings (1 Samuel). Jesus is hailed and crowned by the Jews (ironically, it must be said), which provokes confrontation not only with Jewish leaders but also with Roman political figures. The Lordship of Jesus challenges all earthly powers.

Second, Christians follow John's description of Jesus as the Word of God (Greek: *Logos*, John 1) to highlight more than just his prophetic role. Prophets from the Old Testament bear the word of God to various audiences, but Jesus differs from this by simply *being* the Word of God himself. As God's Son (a title related to Word in the history of Christian thought), he is nevertheless eternally one with the Father, always 'sent forth'. The Son, Christians affirm, was the agent of creation which God created by his word, that is, by speaking it into being ('Let there be . . .'). In addition, it is not a contradiction that Christians also refer to the Bible as the 'Word of God' since, as we have discussed already, the custom of reading the whole Bible in the light of Christ arises from the belief that it is from start to finish a book about Christ. In fact, the Christian claim is even bolder than this. Drawing on the meaning of *Logos* as reason or logic in Greek, Jesus Christ is the key to everything, and not just the Bible. He is the interpretive principle of everything that exists and even those things that do not exist.

Third, unlike Socrates or another great teacher, Jesus asks his followers to do more than follow his teaching; they are to follow the person. Jesus himself gives and activates the ability to follow what he teaches, which means that he gives his very self – and not just his words – to us. This kind of following is creatively depicted in the Gospels; disciples (meaning 'followers') literally follow behind him around Galilee and then on the road to Jerusalem. When they are short on faith, the physical distance between Jesus and them increases; they stumble along. Even so, the primary way that Jesus differs from a great moral teacher is by his enduring presence as one who has been raised. He is therefore alive to those who follow him: today's disciples follow a living person just as the original 12 disciples did.

The teaching of Jesus

According to three of the four Gospels, Jesus Christ came announcing that the kingdom of God is coming and that its coming will be good news for many. His teaching about how to live has to do with how to live now in the light of the kingdom coming. What did Jesus teach? Jesus didn't focus primarily on doctrine and theology, but on ethics. 'Go and *do* likewise,' Jesus said at the conclusion of the parable of the Good Samaritan (Luke 10). When it comes to Jesus' teaching, the point isn't usually to teach people what to believe, but how to live. Where God reigns, life will be very different.

But before we look at what Jesus taught, let's first consider *how* he taught. It is widely agreed that Jesus was a creative teacher who often taught using parables or stories to help make his points. But rather than this being a strategy for making his meaning *clearer*, Jesus was often actually trying to make his meaning more obscure. In the synoptic Gospels (Matthew, Mark and Luke), Jesus teaches that his use of parables is to weed out his listeners. This is clearest in a parable, usually called the parable of the Sower, in Mark:

> Again he began to teach beside the lake. Such a very large crowd gathered around him that he got into a boat on the lake and sat there, while the whole crowd was beside the lake on the land. He began to teach them many things in parables, and in his teaching he said to them: 'Listen! A sower went out to sow. And as he sowed, some seed fell on the path, and the birds came and ate it up. Other seed fell on rocky ground, where it did not have much soil, and it sprang up quickly, since it had no depth of soil. And when the sun rose, it was scorched; and since it had no root, it withered away. Other seed fell among thorns, and the thorns grew up and choked it, and it yielded no grain. Other seed fell into good soil and brought forth grain, growing up and increasing and yielding thirty and sixty and a hundredfold.' And he said, 'Let anyone with ears to hear listen!' (Mark 4.1–9)

Listening is clearly important here – it's both the first and last word Jesus speaks. So it's safe to assume that not everyone will have 'ears to hear' what

Jesus means by telling the parable. Also, as the reader comes to find out, this is not a parable about the kingdom of God (which is the theme of nearly all of the others). This one parable is actually a parable about parables – it is a story about the effect that Jesus' teaching has on different people in his audience and how they respond differently. For some, the meaning of Jesus' teaching will remain a secret; as far as they are concerned, they will only hear a story about a farmer and then go home unchanged and unchallenged. But others will receive much more:

> When he was alone, those who were around him along with the twelve asked him about the parables. And he said to them, 'To you has been given the secret of the kingdom of God, but for those outside, everything comes in parables; in order that
>
>> "they may indeed look, but not perceive,
>>   and may indeed listen, but not understand;
>> so that they may not turn again and be forgiven."'
>>   (Mark 4.10–12)

And then Jesus concludes by saying, 'For to those who have, more will be given; and from those who have nothing, even what they have will be taken away' (4.25).

Those who ask Jesus what he means are told the secret. But for those who don't, the parables function to screen them out. Is Jesus serious that he doesn't want some people to 'turn again and be forgiven'? It seems that this is at least Mark's meaning: some are not ready to hear Jesus' message. This complicates simplistic approaches to understanding Jesus' teaching that assume that its content can be taken up by anyone. Mark is implying that not everyone really wants to know what Jesus is teaching, which means that *wanting to know* is more basic and more fundamental than *knowing*. The point of Jesus gathering followers and sharing a way of life with them isn't to make sure they are close enough to hear what he has to teach when inspiration strikes. It is to form and elicit a love for Jesus himself so that his followers will desire to live as he does. Also, since Jesus is announcing the kingdom of God, he is aware that not everyone will want God to be king, especially worldly rulers, or their loyal subjects.

As a teaching strategy, this reveals the close connection that Christian ethics holds between *being* and *doing*. The desire for God and the things of God is tied to the character of a person who is open to receiving more from God, including more knowledge. This kind of knowledge, though, permeates the whole person and one's whole life rather than enriching only the mind. Athanasius of Alexandria taught this in the fourth century:

[F]or the searching and right understanding of the Scriptures there is need of a good life and a pure soul, and for Christian virtue to guide the mind to grasp, so far as human nature can, the truth concerning God the Word. One cannot possibly understand the teaching of the saints unless one has a pure mind and is trying to imitate their life. Anyone who wants to look at sunlight naturally wipes his eye clear first, in order to make, at any rate, some approximation to the purity of that on which he looks; and a person wishing to see a city or country goes to the place in order to do so. Similarly, anyone who wishes to understand the mind of the sacred writers must first cleanse his own life, and approach the saints by copying their deeds.[1]

Listening and seeing are talked about in similar ways in the Gospels and in many other Christian writings. We don't listen by just opening our ears nor see by simply opening our eyes. Athanasius follows Matthew 5.8 in insisting that only the pure in heart will see God. Notice the interesting position this puts the reader in. He says that in order to understand what the Bible is saying, the reader must already be working to try and live the kind of life it values. Otherwise, it's too easy to be selective in our reading, noticing only those things that already align with what we believe and how we live.

This discussion is crucial for approaching Jesus' teaching, especially since so much of the plain meaning of Jesus' words is frankly ignored by many Christians. For example, how many Christians are fond of citing 'eye for eye', the retaliation taught in Exodus 21.24, but neglect to notice that Jesus explicitly overturned it in his teaching (Matt. 5.38)? It is not just that some people don't know that Jesus did this. It is that we will normally desire an ethic of retaliation more than an ethic that Jesus teaches in its place: not resisting an evildoer and turning the other cheek. This is one of the perilous realities for the study of Christian ethics. Our desires will potentially work against the study of our topic.[2]

Our point, then, cannot simply be to lay out Jesus' teaching on its own, nor any other teaching of the Bible. We also need to be aware of why we might tend to notice some things rather than others or emphasize some teachings at the expense of others. One prominent answer to this question comes from contemporary scholarship about the interpretation of any text, the activity of hermeneutics, as we have seen. Different readers interpret differently because we can't help but read from a particular place.

---

1 Athanasius, *On the Incarnation*, ch. 9, 57: <https://www.ccel.org/ccel/athanasius/incarnation>.
2 Glen H. Stassen, 'The Fourteen Triads of the Sermon on the Mount (Matthew 5:21–7:12)', *Journal of Biblical Literature* 122.2 (2003): 267–308.

We bring to our reading all of our experiences and identities, our hopes, wounds and prejudices. The ways people live – their **praxis** – form them to be interpreters of one sort as opposed to another. So when Jesus teaches 'Blessed are the poor' and 'Woe to you who are rich' in Luke 6, we shouldn't be surprised when poor people remember, tell and celebrate this teaching, or when rich people are quiet about it or offer interpretations that try to make it go away. This is what Athanasius meant, and recalls for us the reasons Jesus taught in parables.

As we have noted, instead of explicitly telling his followers what to do or how to act, Jesus often simply described a different reality: the kingdom of God. At the start of the famous Sermon on the Mount (Matt. 5—7), Jesus begins by describing the kinds of people who will rejoice when the kingdom comes: the meek, the poor in spirit, those who mourn, the pure in heart and those who are persecuted for righteousness. Jesus isn't trying to get his followers to *become* such things; he is recognizing that such people exist and they will be the ones who are overjoyed when God reigns. These teachings, in other words, aren't *prescriptive* (commanding), but are *descriptive* (describing). It is important to understand how this kind of teaching works.

Let's look at two examples. First, think about what it's like to be meek. Meek people are shy, aren't listened to very much and tend not to get their way in life. Our world seems to belong to the opposite kinds of people – those who are assertive, who insist on having their way, on being in control. That's how the kingdom of the world works; it's so normal that we hardly notice it, and we will have a very hard time imagining that life could be any different. But in God's kingdom, not only are the meek listened to; they inherit the earth (Matt. 5.5). The point here isn't to tell us to *be* or *become* meek, but to indicate the nature of things as God intends to bring them about, a reality in which meek people inherit the earth. Next, we can also consider what it's like to mourn, having lost something important or someone loved. To this, Jesus says, 'Good news! You are about to be comforted.' Again, the point isn't that Jesus is telling his followers that it's somehow good to mourn (would that make any sense?), but that mourners have reason to be glad when the kingdom comes, since they will be comforted.

Many interpreters have made the mistake of thinking that Jesus is giving pointed moral instruction to people: we should be more meek (but should we be more mournful?). This is an unfortunate mistake since it misses the key to the whole of Jesus' message about the kingdom of God. When God is king, there will be some people in the world who will experience the greatest relief and joy. These are the people who have generally been on the losing side of the status quo that God is going to reverse. When God's kingdom reigns, the mourners will laugh and the laughers will weep; the rich will bemoan it and the poor will celebrate it. We need only consider the various characters in the Gospels – some rejoice at Jesus (the sick, the oppressed) while some reject him or conspire against him (the rich, the religious and political leadership) or reject him in less dramatic ways.

A number of scholars have enriched our ability to understand this concept of the kingdom of God by showing that it is not a pie-in-the-sky concept for some future time, but a concrete reality that the believing community can inhabit now. These scholars have argued that the most important precursor to the kingdom of God was the Israelite celebration of the Jubilee year described in Leviticus 25.[3] The Jubilee was meant to be celebrated every fiftieth year. For the whole year, the entire nation would enact many of the same practices of the Sabbath day (seventh day) and the Sabbath year (seventh year). Since the Jubilee is the seventh seventh (the year following seven Sabbath years), it is even more dramatic and widespread. All debts will be cancelled and all lands will go back to their original owners. Those who were too poor to pay off a debt and therefore needed to sell themselves into slavery were likewise to be freed. It was a radical provision for resetting the economic reality of the nation.

Jesus's declarations that the kingdom of God has come in effect declare that the Jubilee year is here. Jesus begins his public ministry with an important proclamation that recalls the theme of Jubilee, citing Isaiah 61:

> The Spirit of the Lord is upon me,
>   because he has anointed me
>   to bring good news to the poor.
> He has sent me to proclaim release to the captives
>   and recovery of sight to the blind,
>   to let the oppressed go free,
>   to proclaim the year of the Lord's favour.
>
> (Luke 4.18–19)

Here 'the year of the Lord's favour' may be a reference to the year of Jubilee, the one year out of 50 that truly embodies God's will for how people should live, just as the Sabbath day is the one day out of seven that exhibits the original and intended relationships between humans and between humans and God. It's generally agreed that Israel never actually enacted the Jubilee

---

3 For example, see André Trocmé, *Jesus and the Nonviolent Revolution*, ed. Charles E. Moore (Maryknoll: Orbis, 2003).

year; all the more reason for Jesus to declare that it is long overdue. If Jesus is declaring that the Jubilee year has come, he is not just saying that the forgiveness of debts, the redistribution of resources and the trust that enables true rest shall be a reality for the next 12 months. Rather, Jesus' words indicate that this is now the new reality for all time.

Luke places this proclamation – sometimes referred to as the 'Nazareth Manifesto' – at the very start of Jesus' ministry since it defines everything that Jesus is going to do and teach. It is important to notice that those for whom the kingdom of God is 'good news' are the same people who would naturally rejoice when the Jubilee year rolls around: the poor and the captive. In our day, if credit card debts were routinely cancelled every 50 years, those with the most debt piled up by that time would most consider the year of the great cancellation of debt to be 'good news'.

Jesus explicitly taught this three chapters later in Luke:

> 'A certain creditor had two debtors; one owed five hundred denarii, and the other fifty. When they could not pay, he cancelled the debts for both of them. Now which of them will love him more?' Simon answered, 'I suppose the one for whom he cancelled the greater debt.' And Jesus said to him, 'You have judged rightly.'   (Luke 7.41–43)

The word 'gospel' means good news. But it is important to recognize that news that is considered good by some will probably be considered bad news by others. The credit card companies will not look forward to the Jubilee as much as their debtors will. If the gospel is 'good news for the poor', it will generally be considered bad news for the rich if they value their wealth more than the lives of those who could be helped or freed by sharing it. The rich, incidentally, are not excluded from the kingdom of God any more than they are excluded from the Jubilee. They have a role to play, which is simply to use their wealth for the good of the poor.

We see this on several occasions in the Gospels. After encountering Jesus, Zacchaeus, a rich, chief tax collector, promises, 'Look, half of my possessions, Lord, I will give to the poor; and if I have defrauded anyone of anything, I will pay back four times as much' (Luke 19.8). In another case, Jesus instructs a rich man who asks about how to be saved, 'You lack one thing; go, sell what you own, and give the money to the poor, and you will have treasure in heaven; then come, follow me.' The text goes on to say that 'When [the rich man] heard this, he was shocked and went away grieving, for he had many possessions' (Mark 10.21–22).

Jesus was certainly a radical teacher on the topic of wealth and poverty. But it is important to see that he didn't invent a completely new ethic.

Rather, he was fulfilling an ethic that already should have been known and practised in Israelite society. At the same time, he doesn't just reiterate it and urge the people to do what they have been neglecting for hundreds of years. What is new is that Jesus also acts to recreate a new society along these lines. Jesus recreates Israel, calling 12 disciples, which represents the 12 tribes of Israel. This will be a remnant society that comes to be called 'church' and whose members have God's covenant so written on their hearts that they joyfully share their wealth without the command of law, which Israelite society had neglected anyway. We simply see this new society, this new community, beginning to be itself as its rich members share with its poor members. Or, sadly, in the case of the rich young man who came to Jesus in Mark 10, we see some people refusing to join the new community of the gospel.

The example of Jesus

We know that Jesus primarily taught by example since, by calling followers, his focus was not only on those who followed his teachings, but also on those who might become followers of his own life. 'Follow me,' Jesus says, indicating that his movement is physical and dramatic. In all three of the synoptic Gospels, but especially in Mark, disciples leave their homes and jobs and journey with Jesus throughout the region. In Mark 8, Jesus makes a decisive and abrupt turn toward Jerusalem. From that point on, disciples follow him on the 'way' or road (in Greek). Jerusalem is a place of danger and death for the Jesus movement since it is the place where political and religious power is concentrated in Israel, the two powers that Jesus is famous for most upsetting. The disciples stumble along behind Jesus, usually confused about the nature of his mission – why he would set his sights on Jerusalem, what he intended to do there and what role they were to play. A space opens up between Jesus and his followers, and the space grows as they get closer to their destination. By the end, of course, all of his followers abandon him in Jerusalem.

So Christians have the narrative of the Gospels in which following the example of Jesus is clearly important. But it is also shown to be difficult, confusing and costly. In the Gospels, this quality of Jesus is called 'scandal', which causes many people to stumble. Jesus is a scandal when he doesn't turn out to be what people hope or expect. The biggest scandal for the early Christians was the fact of a crucified Messiah. Artefacts from this period show that Christians were mocked for this central element of their message. The Messiah (the new king of the Jews) was supposed to accomplish a lot of great things for Israel, but was certainly not supposed to die when he was close to taking the throne. By insisting that the crucified Jesus was indeed the Messiah, his early followers had to begin to tell a different story about what God's Messiah does. His resurrection, for example, is actually the act by which he is enthroned – and not only over Israel, but over the whole world.

Yet it is not only Jesus' death that was considered a scandal. There were plenty of aspects to the way Jesus lived that led to anything from raised eyebrows to outright hostility. Many of these have to do with his disregard for certain accepted norms of his culture, including the religious culture. For example, Jesus exemplified a radical disregard for social and economic status. He was unimpressed by the powerful and the rich. Instead, he routinely was found spending time with weaker members of society such as women, the ill and the poor. Jesus himself came into the world amid questionable circumstances: his mother was pregnant outside marriage and he was born in a stable surrounded by animals. Details like this are meant to show the contrast between the statuses of kings and Jesus' own humility, itself a way of radically reversing worldly expectations. In addition, Jesus had a reputation as a teacher and was called Rabbi on the basis of the content of the teaching itself, rather than on the basis of his credentials. This calls into question the usefulness of the credentials and the authority they are thought to carry.

Other characters such as Nicodemus the Pharisee are concerned with their own status, yet in this are contrasted with Jesus. For example, Nicodemus came to Jesus by night (John 3) when he was then instructed about being born again – born into a new status, one in which God delights but that may not really impress fellow humans. The Magi who pay homage to baby Jesus and worship him spurn Herod's kingship, demonstrating in a different way how political status is upended with the Messiah.

Jesus' disregard for pollution is well known and is most shown by his close association with people who were considered unclean. The statuses of **clean** and **unclean** were specified by the Old Testament law. Some of the conditions that make a person or thing unclean make sense to modern people within a medical context that focuses on hygiene. Avoiding contact with a leper, for example, or the bedding or clothing of a leper will help to stop the spread of the disease. Even the extreme measures of putting diseased people outside the community (Lev. 13.46) can be thought of as a way to quarantine disease from the rest of the population. However, the Bible's language of pollution and cleanliness is not actually related to medicine but to holiness. Because God dwells in and with the community, the 'separateness' of the community must be maintained. The phrase 'to make holy' means to keep separate. Unclean people and things were in a state of disorder and were therefore considered unfit for close association with the deity.

With this religious category of holiness in mind, it is that much more striking that Jesus transgressed boundaries between clean and unclean – in effect holy and unholy. As if to emphasize this point, Jesus goes out of his way to touch unclean people:

> A leper came to him begging him, and kneeling he said to him, 'If you choose, you can make me clean.' Moved with pity, Jesus stretched out his hand and touched him, and said to him, 'I do choose. Be made clean!' Immediately the leprosy left him, and he was made clean. (Mark 1.40–42)

Notice that this text is specifically designed to draw the reader's attention to the very holiness issues (touching, clean and unclean things) that Leviticus (especially chapter 13 dealing with lepers) is concerned about. The leper's concern is to be made clean and Jesus touches him, saying 'Be made clean!' This reverses the expectation of the Levitical law, which would certainly have made Jesus unclean too and done nothing to cleanse the leper. Mark is not only indicating that Jesus as a person is breaking these rules (although Jesus' enemies saw it only this way). Mark is also showing how Jesus embodies a new kind of dwelling of God with humanity that redefines holiness itself.

Touching those who are considered unclean is actually a theme throughout Jesus' whole life. He touches a corpse in Mark 5, an action that (according to Num. 19) made him unclean and worthy to be 'cut off' from Israel. He also touches a haemorrhaging woman (Mark 5.25–34; Luke 8.43–48). Leviticus 15 lists a number of strict rules for dealing with men and women who have unusual discharges from their bodies. In this case, not only was the woman unclean, but so is anyone who touches her.

We can think of Jesus' disregard of status as a form of *equality* – he treated people equally whether they were clean or unclean. But his example goes beyond this. He took the initiative to go out of his way specifically to be with people who, for one reason or another, were considered polluted by society: lepers, tax collectors, prostitutes and other 'sinners'. What he taught he also exemplified: that it is not the well who need a physician, but the ill (Mark 2.17); he came not to call the righteous, but sinners (Luke 5.32). This included tax collectors, whom devout Jews considered unrighteous in a more straightforward moral sense. In all of this, Jesus developed the reputation of being a friend of sinners (Matt. 11.19).

We can offer a theological reason for Jesus' behaviour. In Christ, God undergoes a fundamental change: God becomes a human (see 'incarnation' in the following chapter). In doing this, the divine nature and human nature are united in such a way that separateness and holiness must now be redefined. While God had in the past dwelt among the people, God now dwells among us as one of us. Holiness will now be a matter of turning the heart and soul toward God. As Jesus teaches in Mark:

> 'Do you not see that whatever goes into a person from outside cannot defile, since it enters, not the heart but the stomach, and goes out into the sewer?' (Thus he declared all foods clean.) And he said, 'It is what comes out of a person that defiles. For it is from within, from the human heart, that evil intentions come: fornication, theft, murder, adultery, avarice, wickedness, deceit, licentiousness, envy, slander, pride, folly. All these evil things come from within, and they defile a person.' (Mark 7.18–23)

Jesus redefines holiness in a way that also overcomes separateness. God has come near in Christ in order to save, to cleanse and to heal. In his homily on Leviticus 20 ('Be holy, for I am the LORD your God'), the third-century theologian Origen of Alexandria writes: 'we say to be set apart, not from places but from deeds, not from regions but from ways of life.'

Unlike Leviticus, modern people are accustomed to thinking one way about illness and another about sin. Illness is a *physical* failing and sin is a *moral* failing. Perhaps this distinction has Jesus to thank for undoing a close association between sin and illness. If we read Leviticus on its own, though, it is clear that its main concern is holiness – cleanliness and uncleanliness, which can be physical or moral (or ritual, for that matter). Yet if we have Jesus to thank for separating illness (which needs healing) and sin (which needs forgiving and saving), then we might ironically misunderstand the ministry of Jesus in which he preaches salvation and repentance but spends a lot of time healing people. We might miss that these are united in the text in order to make points that reinforce each other, even while the text is also working to separate them.

In the West, it can be easy to make the mistake of separating Jesus' mission to *save* from his mission to *heal*. This mistake is parallel to a problematic separation of humans into souls and bodies, where what really matters are souls. However, theology in the East (that is, what came to be Eastern Orthodox theology, largely written in Greek) has tended to hold these two together, preferring to use healing terms to talk about salvation. So lepers and tax collectors both need healing *and* saving. Our word 'salvation' shares a root with 'salve' which is a healing ointment (cf. *salvare* in Latin). Jesus is the great physician who offers to us the medicine of salvation or, thought of eucharistically, offers his body and blood as the medicine of eternal life for all who receive it.

In associating salvation and healing, we can make better sense of Jesus' healing ministry in Galilee. There he healed people of various illnesses and other distresses, giving sight to the blind, healing lepers and a woman who had been bleeding for 12 years (she had 'endured much under many physicians, and had spent all that she had; and she was no better, but rather grew worse', Mark 5.26). But the Gospels also depict Jesus as the physician of our souls in his deliverance of those who were both physically and spiritually oppressed, as in the example of the man with many demons who lived among tombs (that is, living as though dead) and whose body was constantly suffering injury from thrashing about in chains (Mark 5.1–20). There are also stories that strike readers as seeming to be about physical healing but that take a different turn: Jesus is presented with a paralysed man and declares his sins are forgiven (Mark 2), even though he goes on to heal the man's paralysis too.

In separating sin from illness, Christianity in the West has usually reached for other images to describe what is wrong about sin, how it affects us and what should be done about it. Without naming our 'sin-sick' condition as something that enfeebles us and needs the medicine of Jesus to make us whole again, these Western theologies sometimes preferred to conceive of the human problem primarily in terms of sin that must be punished. And if this is the problem, then the solution will require either forgiveness (forgoing punishment) or some kind of substitution (someone else is punished in our place). This set of images, which we shall unpack at length in later chapters, belongs to criminal justice rather than medicine.

Though these criminal and juridical images will be familiar to readers shaped by Western Christianity, they have the unfortunate effect of limiting the life of Jesus to an exchange between God and Jesus on our behalf whereby God either is now able to forgive us or doesn't have to (having vented his wrath completely on Jesus our substitute). This is only one version of the theology of **atonement**, one which today has brought forth many critics. But any theology of human salvation that focuses exclusively on Jesus' death (and possibly resurrection) has the effect of also shifting focus away from Jesus' life and ministry. If salvation of our souls comes through the cross, Jesus' healing in Galilee is perhaps only an optional prelude to his Passion. There might have been other ways for Jesus to spend his time before the main event – going to Jerusalem, being arrested, tried and killed.

A better way is to understand that the death of Jesus Christ exemplified his life. This doesn't just mean that Jesus' life culminated in his death, since in some sense this can be said of every person. It means that it was first and foremost his way of living that got him killed, that led to confrontations with the religious and political authorities, and that finally and tragically led to the disaffection of the crowds who wanted a deliverer of a different sort.

If Christian ethics is best described as reflection on the Christian life as one of following Jesus, then his demonstration of making a costly commitment to his mission is surely an important element. If his disciples had been equally committed to the mission, they would have shared in his fate, probably being crucified alongside him (spots occupied instead by robbers, Mark 15.27). Two conclusions follow.

First, following the example of Jesus is more likely to yield anger from those threatened by the coming kingdom of God, and this is very likely to include those people who are regarded as the most respected, powerful and religious members of society. Jesus' own prediction that 'You will be hated by all because of my name' (Luke 21.17) should not be limited to his first-century hearers. Indeed, this is the experience of many Christians throughout history and across the globe today. Theologian John Milbank (b. 1952) has written a wise and enlightening essay called 'Can Morality Be Christian?' in which the answer given is unquestionably 'no' because Christian morality is so different from what is called good by the world. In Milbank's words, 'Christian morality is a thing so strange that it must be declared immoral or amoral according to all other human norms and codes of morality.'[4]

Second, because of the incredibly high bar and high cost of Christian discipleship, forgiveness rises to the top of core Christian values and practices. The disciples all abandon Jesus (and Peter does so quite dramatically) yet the story doesn't end with their abandonment, but rather continues with their reincorporation into the Jesus movement. Even their abandonment is forgiven and the story of their failure is redeemed. John's Gospel concludes with an exchange between Jesus and Peter in which their mutual love is declared and Peter is brought back into the ministry (John 21). Mark's Gospel ends differently, but by making similar points. The risen Jesus is not seen, even by the women who witnessed the empty tomb, but the mission of Jesus is renewed and the call to follow is reissued. The young

---

4 John Milbank, *The Word Made Strange: Theology, Language, Culture* (Oxford: Blackwell, 1997), 219.

man at the tomb says, 'But go, tell his disciples and Peter that he is going before you to Galilee; there you will see him, as he told you' (Mark 16.7). There is hope for those who have tried and failed to follow Jesus' costly way.

The law of the spirit

We have been reviewing the very important topics of the teaching and example of Jesus and the roles these play in Christian ethics. Yet for the first several centuries, Christians did not *primarily* look to the moral teachings and example of Jesus. Instead, they foremost sought to be brought within God's family, alongside Jesus to God. This was the most important thing. God in Christ was reconciling the world to himself, sharing in our limits, our vulnerabilities and our infirmities, yet also uniting humanity and divinity together in his very body. The good news wasn't primarily a new message about how to live, but the joyous new reality of the cosmos in which God had rescued human creatures from the clutches of sin and death. This doesn't mean that our Christian forebears neglected moral questions; but they didn't start by asking what Jesus would do. Jesus is Saviour and Lord before he is a teacher or model of morality. At the same time, these Christians believed that their lives would be changed as they were drawn closer to the heart of God through Christ. Their first focus was not on doing, but being.

Christians have generally been realistic about the human struggle to choose the good. The reason is not that we aren't free to choose it, but that apart from the saving work of God, we lack the will to do so. The grace of God precedes every positive human response to God, just as Jesus taught: 'You did not choose me but I chose you' (John 15.16). One of the most important theological debates – between Pelagius and Augustine in the fifth century – centred on the role of the human will to choose to do good. Augustine argued against Pelagius that God's gifts of Christian devotional practices and the revelation of Christ's teaching were not sufficient on their own to lead people to follow them. What is needed in addition is God's gracious repair of the distorted human will that otherwise perceives evil and calls it good. Like knowledge, our will is useless unless it is reformed, repaired and healed. Only then will a person want to choose what is good, what brings true and long-lasting happiness rather than fleeting gratification. The Church sided with Augustine on this matter.

This idea was not altogether new to the early Christian movement. It had emerged in a different form centuries before in response to Israel's experience of exile and captivity at the hands of the Babylonian Empire.

Exile was a catastrophic experience for Israel that functioned to return God's people to a more devout righteousness. It was not going to be enough to have the law and sometimes follow some of it. God requires a constant, deep and abiding commitment to his ways, and not only in action, but in matters of the heart. The law therefore moves from being external to being internal.

Moses had received God's law for Israel and this was meant to guide Israel's life together as distinctive among all peoples of the earth. A very strong emphasis had been put on remembrance of the earlier captivity (slavery) in Egypt. The people of Israel were instructed to remember how they had been slaves in Egypt (Deut. 24.22), how God defeated Pharaoh (Deut. 7.18), how God had led them for 40 years in the desert and how they had rebelled there (Deut. 8.2; 9.7). The memory of God's deeds – that God had created this people to be his own – is the justification for the law: 'Remember that you were a slave in the land of Egypt; therefore I am commanding you to do this' (Deut. 24.22). Alongside the covenant with Moses and all Israel, the law was now also a thing to be remembered and passed down from generation to generation:

> You shall put these words of mine in your heart and soul, and you shall bind them as a sign on your hand, and fix them as an emblem on your forehead. Teach them to your children, talking about them when you are at home and when you are away, when you lie down and when you rise. Write them on the doorposts of your house and on your gates, so that your days and the days of your children may be multiplied in the land that the LORD swore to your ancestors to give them, as long as the heavens are above the earth.
>
> (Deut. 11.18–21)

In time, Israel's disobedience to the Lord came to be understood as a failure, not only on Israel's part, but also on the part of the covenant itself. The prophets, agents of God's memory, sought to remind the Israelites of their identity as partners in God's covenant with them. Their messages were almost universally ignored: return to the Lord, seek his holy ways, obey his commands, seek justice for the poor and righteousness for the vulnerable. After Israel was overrun by the Assyrians, and Judah by the Babylonians, a new covenant was needed – a new way of conceiving of law. This is what the prophet Jeremiah declared:

> The days are surely coming, says the LORD, when I will make a new covenant with the house of Israel and the house of Judah. It will not be like the covenant that I made with their ancestors when I took them by the hand to bring them out of the land of Egypt – a covenant that they broke, though I

was their husband, says the LORD. But this is the covenant that I will make with the house of Israel after those days, says the LORD: I will put my law within them, and I will write it on their hearts; and I will be their God, and they shall be my people. No longer shall they teach one another, or say to each other, 'Know the LORD', for they shall all know me, from the least of them to the greatest, says the LORD; for I will forgive their iniquity, and remember their sin no more. (Jer. 31.31–34)

Ezekiel, prophet to the exiles, spoke something similar to Jeremiah:

A new heart I will give you, and a new spirit I will put within you; and I will remove from your body the heart of stone and give you a heart of flesh. I will put my spirit within you, and make you follow my statutes and be careful to observe my ordinances. (Ezek. 36.26–27)

The focus here is on an internal transformation that God will enact through which the law will eventually become redundant. It is a vision of a future when Israelites will not have to teach the next generation about the Lord nor train them to remember the commandments they were meant to follow. Instead, God's spirit would guide their living by transforming their desires, their hearts, to want what God wants.

This is the classic tension between law and spirit that Paul discussed and which has also been the subject of a great deal of debate throughout Christian history. Where there is spirit, there is no need for law. It is not an overstatement to say that the goal of Christian ethics is not to identify and follow God's laws, but to surpass them and even render them unnecessary. This bold claim, which we will look at in more detail in the next chapter, is one of the key themes in the New Testament as Paul works out the relationship between law and gospel (especially in Galatians and Romans).

On the one hand, yes, God gave laws such as the Ten Commandments to his people and expected them to obey. The laws were usually given alongside stern warnings and detailed descriptions of the consequences of disobedience. The story of Israel is in fact quite a long recounting of various instances of disobedience, punishments and return. God's character as long-suffering and forgiving out of steadfast love is highlighted by these stories of disobedience. The law isn't all that there is, since the larger story is about God redeeming a wayward people, partly through law, but mostly apart from, around and in spite of law.

It isn't surprising, then, when Jesus is said to 'fulfil' the law and positively overturns some specific laws (such as 'eye for an eye' retribution), and Paul teaches that the law served only a temporary purpose. For Paul, the law was like a disciplinarian or tutor (or babysitter) who, one hopes, with maturity will be outgrown and rendered unnecessary. This is how he argues throughout much of Galatians. The law was necessary to get the people to the point where they no longer needed it. But does this new spirit come about in any way *through the law itself*, if only finally to surpass it? We can think of examples from everyday life.

We grow up with various 'laws' that we learn from our parents and that may even come attached to warnings and punishments or rewards for when we follow them. I remember that as a child I was told over and over to 'say "thank you"' when someone gave me something. I don't need to be told that any more, but it is crucial to see that the reason isn't that it's no longer important to say 'thank you'. In fact it's close to the opposite: by now I have so internalized its importance that there's no reason for that specific law any more. I don't say thank you to please my parents (or to get a reward or to avoid a punishment). I have come to value saying it for the same reason my parents wanted me to say it – it is good and right to feel and express gratitude upon receiving a gift. More interesting still is that no doubt one of the ways I came to the point of no longer needing the 'say thank you' law is that at one time I *did* need it, and responded to it.

It's the same with Paul's discussion of law and gospel. The point is not that the law was never necessary or was a mistake from the beginning. It's that it's possible to get to the point of internalizing the spirit of the law within one's own person so that it overtakes and therefore characterizes our deepest, most genuine desires. Once this happens, there is no longer the need for law.

If it's true, then, that Christian ethics has as its goal the surpassing of God's laws and commands, then what takes their place? Greek philosophers used the language of the development of good character to discuss this. Christians have spoken about developing the 'mind of Christ', of being 'Christlike', or, as we will see at length in Chapter 4, of possessing virtues. Christian accommodation of this focus on good character helped to shift emphasis away from objectifying the moment of decision that always calls for obedience to specific commands and focuses exclusively on acts and behaviour. Focusing on more subjective matters like the heart and internal dispositions is obviously more complex since actions we normally think of as bad can be carried out with good intentions and motives. But in the same way, having the mind of Christ gives Christians hope that they will be able to face an entirely novel and unexpected situation with confidence. Not every situation is anticipated by law.

In this, we are reminded of what we said above about times when the Bible is silent. Christians have often looked to the lives of the saints to instruct us in how to live. What they give to us is not a body of commands and laws, but a complete story of a life through which ordinary people can discern the work of God. The saints are simply other people who have so internalized the spirit of Christ that they have no need to receive direction about God's will in the explicit form of commands. At the deepest level, the Christian moral life is not about choices and decisions, but – astonishingly perhaps – about learning to live in such a way that we acquire habits and dispositions that actually close off choices. Some options will simply no longer come to mind as law is replaced by desire. In this sense, the more we grow in Christian virtue, the less choice we have. This is a situation worth contemplating for how deeply it runs counter to the spirit of our own time which always seeks to maximize our options and insist on more choices.

An even more important answer to the question about what takes the place of the law is 'spirit'. When Christians hear this word, they rightly think about the Holy Spirit, who Jesus promised would 'guide you into all the truth' (John 16.13). The Holy Spirit was given to the world at Pentecost, which Christians celebrate as the creation of the Church. This means that God actively and personally leads his people in real time, just as God led the children of Israel in the desert before they were given the law: by cloud during the day and by fire at night. The fourth-century theologian Gregory of Nyssa reflected on how God led in this way. Cloud and fire both lack fixed boundaries; it is unclear where they are, where they begin and end. They also both draw a person toward themselves, toward their uncertain boundaries. Like faith before the law, trusting God would need to be direct, day to day and ad hoc. Gregory praised the faith of Moses in contrast to the other Hebrews for continuing to respond in faith even when they reached the seemingly more solid Mount Sinai (which quickly disappeared in a surrounding cloud):

> A fire shining out of the darkness presented a fearful sight to those who saw it. It hovered all around the sides of the mountain so that everything which one could see smouldered with the smoke from the surrounding fire.[5]

But Moses knew that the invisible God cannot be beheld the way that ordinary things can. He trusted that God would be found beyond the visible realm and ascended the mountain, leaving the company of the Israelites and disappearing from their sight. To Gregory, Moses is the archetype of a faithful Christian disciple who responds with trust even before there is

---

5 *Gregory of Nyssa: The Life of Moses*, ed. and trans. Abraham Malherbe and Everett Ferguson, Classics of Western Spirituality (New York: Paulist, 1978), I.43.

a law to follow and obey. Like Moses, the Christian is called to follow the spirit of God, whose lack of fixed essences invites a different quality of faith from that possessed by those who must be told what to do.

At the same time, we can be misled slightly by Gregory's focus on a single person as an archetype of faith. Indeed, it is important that the Holy Spirit is given at Pentecost, the moment of creation of the Church as itself a distinctive, *collective* community of believers in Christ. The Holy Spirit does not primarily renew the hearts of individuals and set them on solitary paths of devotion. Instead, the very idea of the Church as the primary locus of Christian discipleship is that the Holy Spirit is in the business of initiating, animating and leading a new people whose way of life is common, shared and communal. This people demonstrates a new way of being in the world, not as individual people, but as a renewed and redeemed *polis*, the sojourning city of God whose collective life witnesses to God's creativity.

3

Some key theological themes

There is something absurd about trying to talk about Christian ethics in the light of only three theological themes (incarnation, crucifixion or sacrifice, and resurrection). We could easily go through the same exercise by appealing to a number of additional themes such as creation and redemption or humanity and divinity. My decision to discuss the three I have chosen partly comes from wanting to centre Christian ethics as much as possible on the person and work of Jesus Christ. Sometimes, as we saw in the last chapter, the specific words and deeds of Jesus have immediate application for Christian living. The focus of this chapter is a little different. It is structured thematically in an attempt to draw out something distinctive from the pattern of Christ with humanity.

Even though it will be the work of the more concrete chapters in Part 3 (Chapters 7–13) to spell out how these themes affect Christian thinking about specific issues, we can anticipate that work now in glimpses. For example, the doctrine of incarnation in which Jesus Christ shares human life identifies God with human suffering, locates God's concern with the good of the creation he has made, and communicates God's decision to redeem all of creation rather than leave some or all of it behind. Some Christian ethics have not always been true to the depths of all that is conveyed by the Incarnation, especially when the spiritual life of people has been unduly separated from their material existence, or where emphasizing otherworldly salvation has weakened concern for the environment. Going in nearly the opposite direction, where incarnation is one-sidedly made to legitimate and dignify material existence as it is while offering little in terms of deliverance from suffering, the fullness of incarnation is likewise lacking in depth.

Theology is everywhere. Everyone has convictions about things like the nature of reality, the meaning of life, the direction of history, the value of people and other living things, and the purpose of freedom. Even though most 'theologies' don't explicitly mention God, they shape how we see things and perceive the choices available to us. The approach taken here is to insist that Christian ethics should be no different, but should help to identify where theologies are at work and how they relate to Christian theological claims. More importantly, Christian theology is presented here as rich content that gives shape to everyday reflection on moral topics.

Incarnation

Christians believe that Jesus Christ is God *incarnate*. Literally (or close to it), he is God 'in the meat'. Charles Wesley's 1739 hymn 'Hark! The Herald Angels Sing' is richly theological when it comes to the Incarnation:

> Christ by highest heav'n adored,
> Christ the everlasting Lord!
> Late in time behold Him come,
> Offspring of a Virgin's womb.
> Veiled in flesh the Godhead see,
> Hail the incarnate Deity,
> Pleased as man with man to dwell,
> Jesus, our Emmanuel.
> Hark! The herald angels sing
> 'Glory to the newborn King!'

The idea that Jesus is 'our Emmanuel' means that he is 'God with us'. This idea is good news to a world that needs God but routinely turns its back on God. Incarnation actually begins and ends the Gospel of Matthew. From the beginning of the story when Joseph is told by an angel that Mary will bear a son who will be called Emmanuel (1.23) to the very last verse when Jesus leaves his disciples saying 'I am with you always, to the end of the age' (28.20), this theme is present.

Western Christians have become accustomed to focusing on how the cross saves us. Various doctrines of atonement belong to the theology of the West in order to make sense of the death of Christ as the thing that saves us. But the Eastern Orthodox Church focuses more on the Incarnation. The whole life of Christ – indeed the very *fact* of Christ – is what saves humanity. Because he is *fully God* and *fully human* (a belief powerfully articulated by the Council of Chalcedon in 451), the human nature that we all share has been united to God in the very person of Jesus.

Sin not only separates us from God; it is actually the name given to that separation. What then restores and unites us to God? Again, for Western Christianity, the answer has usually focused on the 'work' of Christ – his crucifixion and resurrection. But the main reason why early Christian debates about Christ's *person* were so intense is that the Church understood that getting it wrong could really change our salvation. It became clear that God and humanity must be united in Christ's person in a way that, on the one hand, doesn't have the divine overpowering the human (making Jesus, in a sense, *too divine* to be one of us). On the other hand, a Jesus who is, in a sense, *too human* also doesn't work since not being intimately united to God is precisely our problem. Jesus must enjoy this intimacy with God if we can hope at all to share in and benefit from it. This explains why incarnation is so important for our salvation.

Becoming human meant that God would have to get dirty. The Christmas hymn 'O Come All Ye Faithful' makes clear that God doesn't hold his nose at humanity: 'Lo, he abhors not the virgin's womb.' God was not put off by what many ancient people considered to be beneath and offensive to the gods: the physicality of material existence and what was widely thought to have been the supposed indignity and filth of human bodies, especially women's bodies and childbirth.

Instead, early Christians concluded that the Son of God genuinely needed to become 'fully human' in order to save us. He needed to share in everything that characterizes the human condition, including its greatest difficulties – temptation, loneliness, betrayal, forsakenness, hunger, pain and death. Their argument was not that there is something secretly or ironically good about these things. Just the opposite: these are the things from which we need to be saved. Incarnation shares in our struggle, weakness and vulnerability.

The German theologian Jürgen Moltmann (b. 1926) sees a problem with an understanding of incarnation that focuses solely on the *person* of Christ – the unique unity of human and divine natures in one person that in Christianity is known as the **hypostatic union**. He calls this a 'necessary' view of incarnation since it reasons from what is necessary for humanity to be saved.[1]

The problem is that if this necessity is met by humanity and divinity being brought together in Christ's person, it unwittingly still makes the life and ministry of Christ irrelevant. And it is precisely the life of Christ that is the point of the Incarnation in the first place, Moltmann says. He prefers what he calls a 'fortuitous' account of incarnation: God becomes human as the culmination of God's love for humanity and the highest and most concrete expression of his desire to be with us, even at great

---

1 Jürgen Moltmann, *The Trinity and the Kingdom: The Doctrine of God*, trans. Margaret Kohl (Minneapolis: Fortress, 1993), 114–22.

cost. Just as God walked in the garden with Adam and Eve, though they hid from him (Gen. 3.8), God resolves to be with the ones he has always loved. What is most important is not that Jesus *be* something in particular (divine and human), true as that is; but that he *be with* – as lover with beloved.

I like to illustrate Moltmann's concept of fortuitous incarnation using the film *Superman II*. As everyone knows, Superman is not human. He was born on the planet Krypton and was sent to earth as a baby and raised in Kansas by foster parents. He disguises himself as Clark Kent, an ordinary human, but quietly retains all of his superpowers, occasionally putting them to use for good when out of disguise. When he falls in love with Lois Lane and she discovers his secret, Superman decides to become human for real. He needs to become human in order to be with the human woman he loves. Through intentional exposure to powerful Kryptonian sunlight, he loses his superpowers and emerges as a bona fide human being. Lois Lane asks him, 'You did that for me?' I think this is a good illustration of how Moltmann sees the Incarnation of the Son of God. It flows from the desire of a lover for his beloved. 'For God so loved the world that he gave his only Son' to be human, to be with us (John 3.16).

Now, there are some obvious differences between Christ and Superman. Superman was sent to earth from the dying world of Krypton in order to save his life. It was only once he got here that he fell in love with Lois Lane. This contrasts strongly with the Christian story in which Christ's Incarnation is an expression of a pre-existing love. It is, from beginning to end, an act of love for humanity. Another difference takes longer to explain. And it involves thinking about how far 'down' the Son went in becoming human.

Orthodox Christianity has always insisted that Jesus wasn't just God in disguise (a heresy known as **Docetism**). He was, as the Council of Chalcedon declared, 'fully human'. But does this mean that Jesus could still, at any moment, act as Superman while looking like Clark Kent? Could he use his 'superpowers', unfairly drawing on abilities the rest of us don't have by pulling out the might of divine omnipotence? Or did he give up these qualities and abilities in the Incarnation? There is debate in the tradition on these questions.

Either we should think of Jesus as holding back, whether out of obedience or love, in the same way a father who wrestles with his children might not use his full strength. Or we need to understand the Incarnation in a stronger sense: that he truly shared in all of our fragilities. While

Moltmann's distinction between a *necessary* and a *fortuitous* incarnation shows that there is debate over the *reason* for incarnation, here we also see disagreement about the *extent* of incarnation.[2]

The important question here is what it means to still say that Jesus is 'fully divine'. In the comic book *Superman/Batman #3*, Batman makes the comment: 'In many ways, Clark [Kent] is the most human of us all. Then . . . he shoots fire from the skies, and it is difficult not to think of him as a god.' So is *this* what it means for Jesus to be God incarnate?

Sometimes it can sound as if Jesus *does* have special fire-from-the-skies powers at his disposal and just refuses to use them. (In the next section I'll discuss the specific passage from Luke 9 where Jesus' *disciples* themselves offer to call down fire to smite the Samaritan villages!) But it is crucial to see that even though Jesus performed miracles, these are not usually meant to be evidence that he is divine. He walked on water, multiplied fish and loaves of bread, healed the sick, raised the dead and turned water into wine. As extraordinary as these are, they do not prove his divinity. After all, Jesus told his followers that they would do greater things than he (John 14.12). Peter and John heal the lame (Acts 3) and Paul raises the dead (Acts 20) and no one thinks them divine. In a sermon, Peter summarized how Jesus 'went about doing good and healing all who were oppressed by the devil, *for God was with him*' (Acts 10.38, emphasis added). Jesus didn't do these things because of special powers that he possessed, but simply because God was with him as he promises to be with others.

In the account I'm giving here, it's a mistake to think that Jesus secretly harboured special powers that he could at any moment tap into at will. The reason is not only that he would not be playing fair among superpower-less humans (he would not genuinely be sharing our humanity) – this is the concern for the 'necessary' view of incarnation. Far more important is that a secretly powerful Jesus threatens the idea that God's love for us in Christ is a love that those who are 'in Christ' can also have for each other. There is no separate ethic for Jesus that only he can achieve. Rather, what

---

2 In theology, this debate has sometimes focused on the meaning of the Greek word *kenosis* which Paul uses in Phil. 2.7 to describe how Jesus 'emptied himself' of divinity's advantages. In her essay 'Kenosis: Theological Meanings and Gender Connotations', Sarah Coakley observes that some interpreters have understood this to refer to the Incarnation while others have thought it to be a reference to Christ's willingness to suffer death on a cross, making 'he emptied himself' in v. 7 parallel to 'he humbled himself' in v. 8. See *The Work of Love: Creation as Kenosis*, ed. John Polkinghorne (Grand Rapids: Eerdmans, 2001), 192–210.

we see is that the extraordinary life of Christ is now a life that God makes possible for every person. Isn't this the lesson of the apostles' own miracles? If Jesus did miracles because God was with him, the apostles show that God is with them too.

One consequence for a Christian ethic is simple but crucial. The same love that motivated God to send his Son to us, to be *with us* – Emmanuel, somewhat recalling Superman with Lois Lane – is not beyond us. Jesus showed us the Father's love, but his love was also human. And a characteristic of that love is to share his life with those who suffered, to be vulnerable to the same things that we are, especially death. This means that if we turn our backs on the weak, the hungry, the poor and the meek, we are failing to be true to what Christ has shown to be the meaning of our humanity. And what is that meaning? It is to offer a life completely to God and to one another by fully sharing our own vulnerable lives with them without holding ourselves back. It is to give up any well-being that comes at the expense of others for the sake of our own protection. Being fully human is something that Jesus both reveals and embodies. Jesus 'walks with us' as God did with Adam and Eve. And our world is a risky place to walk.

Even so, isn't there a difference between suffering alongside someone and rescuing them from their suffering? Humanity doesn't just need God's companionship, but also God's deliverance. Let's go back to Superman. In *Superman II*, the transformation that Superman undergoes in order to be with his beloved involves the loss of his superpowers. Now he is not just Clark Kent holding back superhuman abilities he really has; he is a fully human Clark Kent with no special powers at all. When he gets into a fight with a ruffian at a diner, he is surprised by his own weakness and the fact that he can be hurt. The sight of his own blood shocks him.

In that moment, the president of the United States appears on the diner's television with a message to the whole world. Under the careful watch of General Zod, the president begins to abdicate his power and urge the people to follow Zod in order to spare the lives of millions of people. But when he is suddenly emboldened to call on Superman directly to come to the rescue, Zod steps in and demands to know who Superman is. Whoever he is, even Superman must now bend the knee to Zod.

But having just become aware of his weakness and vulnerability, Clark Kent immediately understands that he is useless to the world as a mere mortal. His superpowers, which he gave up out of love for a human, are now required for the sake of saving the whole human race. He tells Lois Lane that he needs to go back and reverse the process. There is no question that his new vulnerability is now a liability. Even though Clark and Lois had both understood that the process of becoming human was irreversible, Clark was now determined to find a means of going back to the way it was before – to get back to being Superman again. In the end, Clark Kent manages to reverse the process, regain his powers and save the world.

Now, even though this is not widely talked about, Christianity teaches that the Incarnation *has never been reversed*. Jesus didn't stop being human when he rose from the dead or when he ascended into heaven.[3] Jesus is still fully human even though he has been exalted and now intercedes for us at the right hand of the Father. This is the biggest difference with Superman who apparently needed to shed his humanity (become *super-man* again), recover his powers and become invincible in order to save the world. Yet Jesus saves the world *as a vulnerable, suffering, bleeding man*.

Recall that Eastern Christianity says that the Incarnation saves us whereas Western Christianity focuses on the cross. As we have seen by now, both views risk downplaying the *life* of Jesus. In truth, the Incarnation is not just a one-time event. It is God's continuous act of being with us and his constant refusal to leave us to our rejection of him and his ways. In his ministry throughout Galilee and Judaea, Jesus forgave and delivered people from illness and other troubles. This is God-with-us *who is also* God-rescuing-us. How is this possible?

We do not finally need to choose between a God who suffers with us and a God who rescues us from our suffering. Why? Because what we suffer from is ultimately humanity's own attempts to push God away. We do not suffer because of our sin. *Sin is our suffering*. God-with-us is what rescues us. This isn't quite as strange as it may sound, especially if we consider what it is like to suffer from fear. Life's biggest fears are all, at root, the fear of absence and loss. We fear death of the ones we love because we don't want to lose them. We fear our own deaths because we will be estranged from everyone and everything we love. And while we suffer from fears, we also suffer when the things we fear actually come about. We become separated from the things we lost. God's presence with

---

3 Robert W. Jenson, 'On the Ascension' in *Loving God with Our Minds: The Pastor as Theologian*, ed. Michael Welker and Cynthia A. Jarvis (Grand Rapids: Eerdmans, 2004), 331–40.

the world in Christ, as one of us, not only shares in the frailty of human life that makes us vulnerable to fear and suffering. It also intervenes – *as presence* – in order to rescue us from both the worry and reality of absence and loss. Jesus' last words in Matthew are a promise that the Incarnation never ends. 'And remember, I am with you always, to the end of the age' (Matt. 28.20).

Crucifixion and sacrifice

The crucifixion of Jesus Christ is obviously extremely important. But it is not celebrated on its own in isolation from the rest of the story of God. The crucifixion of Jesus is part of the larger story of God's determination to be with us through incarnation and then again in resurrection. This is a story of God giving God's very self to humanity, of humanity's rejection of God, and then rather than us receiving punishment for what we had done, it is a glorious account of God's self-giving again. It is a story about the over-flowing goodness of God to a world that 'knew him not' (see John 1.10). Taken on its own, the crucifixion is definitely humanity's lowest point. It stands there as a sign that we don't fundamentally want to be saved. We destroyed our saviour. If the disciples had been faithful followers of Jesus, he never would have been denied (by Peter), betrayed (by Judas) or abandoned (by everyone else). Instead, the disciples would have followed Jesus to the cross themselves and literally shared in his crucifixion (giving meaning to his command, 'Take up your cross and follow me'). So there is no reason to celebrate the cross when it signifies betrayal, abandonment, suffering and death.

At the same time, Christians do celebrate Jesus' willingness to go to the cross, to not forsake his mission in order to avoid the death that his enemies conspired for him, and to not fight back against his adversaries, instead entrusting himself and his fate to God's justice. None of these things makes the cross 'good'. Yet the judgement of the Church throughout the centuries has been that Jesus acted faithfully and righteously by going to the cross since doing so has been understood to be an act of self-sacrifice.

In this section, we look at these ideas of sacrifice and self-sacrifice as core features of Christian ethics. Still thinking about the crucifixion, we recall that Jesus embraced life but didn't cling to it at all costs. This qualifies any notion of the good that might seek well-being for oneself or others as the highest aim. In truth, crucifixion shows that a good, moral life sometimes might not amount to much. A life's goodness might be involved in its being cut short and of little use to others. There are plenty of reasons to be suspicious of any ethics that roots itself in stories of sacrifice.

At first glance, sacrifice might seem to undermine ethics altogether. When we sacrifice something, we give up something good, not something bad. It isn't a sacrifice to give up eating rubbish; but it is a sacrifice to give up eating chocolate. On the other hand, chocolate isn't *morally* good, and when we give it up, as a Christian might do when observing the season of Lent, we think about what makes it morally good to do so. But there are deeper objections to the concept of sacrifice. It can be a problem because it seems to imply the triumph of scarcity. The fact of there never being enough wins the day. I give up something good for you because we can't both have it. There's not enough to go around.

Self-sacrifice in these cases is a response to a world in which there isn't enough. But is this the whole story? In the Bible, God's very detailed commands to the Israelites to bring him sacrifices can actually be seen as implying the opposite. In many of these sacrifices, an animal or some grain is given as an offering of gratitude for the abundance that God has given. The faithful Israelite gives back only a portion of what God has given. Rather than interpreting this as a condition of scarcity (in which you have to give something up because there isn't enough to go around), we ought to see such sacrifices as joyous thank-yous to God for the fullness of his plenty. I can give up something good because I know that there is no limit to good things.

The most theologically serious sacrifices, however, in some way bring about reconciliation or deal with injury or sin. These are the sacrifices that Israel's priests offered at the Temple. We should ask: what does God really want when he says he wants sacrifice? Is the God of Abraham, Isaac and Jacob so much like the Aztec gods that his wrath must be appeased by the death of an innocent victim?

It is important to understand that this kind of sacrifice is actually closely related to the offerings of thanksgiving. God gets back the first and best portion of his provision. The requirement that an acceptable offering be unblemished ensures that what is given back to God is the best that one has. ('Unblemished' has nothing to do with moral perfection.) The sacrificial animal is not being punished and is not thought of as innocent or guilty. To be sure, God asks for sacrifices by priests on behalf of the people. Yet the Old Testament never understands this as a transfer of punishment to the animal. Instead, it is usually offering something good and valuable in order to show gratitude (the same as putting money in the offering plate at church) or a matter of cleansing by the blood of an animal. Unlike other instances of contact with blood that defile, the blood of an animal that is set apart for God as an offering cleanses, which is a difficult idea for modern people to grasp.

Much of the Old Testament, continuing into the New Testament, is concerned with explaining the *true* meaning of sacrifice. There one encounters some of the strongest language for undoing the idea that they are necessary. Samuel the prophet declares that to obey is better than sacrifice (1 Sam. 15.22); God, in Hosea, says: 'For I desire steadfast love and not sacrifice, the knowledge of God rather than burnt-offerings' (Hos. 6.6). Jesus cites this text from Hosea two times in Matthew (Matt. 9.13; 12.7), urging his listeners to learn what it means. So should we conclude then that God doesn't actually require sacrifice? In a way, yes. God himself sacrifices his requirement for sacrifices.

Still, in our world, offering God our steadfast love and seeking more genuine knowledge of God will come at a cost and may involve suffering. The point is never that God wants us to suffer, however. It is just that God's call is very high and runs counter to key values in our world. What Christians give up by following the way of Jesus are the benefits, pleasures and securities that seem to go along with those other values. Jesus' teaching about enemy-love is a good example: 'But I say to you that listen, Love your enemies, do good to those who hate you, bless those who curse you, pray for those who abuse you' (Luke 6.27–28).

What are Jesus' followers being asked to give up, to sacrifice? They are being asked to sacrifice their normal responses to enemies, to give up what comes naturally when faced with people who hate them and are intent on doing them wrong. The normal response is to punish them and make them pay, or stronger: humiliate them and exact revenge. These things are included in the normal definition of what an enemy is.

Yet God isn't like this, nor is Jesus. God causes the rain to fall (a good thing!) on both the just and the unjust, those who deserve it and those who don't. God sacrifices the normal response to injustice when he blesses them with his indiscriminate goodness. Everyone gets to enjoy the benefits of God's grace. Jesus taught that normal human customs hardly reflect God's will:

> For if you love those who love you, what reward do you have? Do not even the tax-collectors do the same? And if you greet only your brothers and sisters, what more are you doing than others? Do not even the Gentiles do the same? (Matt. 5.46–47)

These rhetorical questions have the answer 'yes!' There are notions of love out there that are perfectly rational and normal – where you love your neighbour but hate your enemy. But God isn't like that and neither should be those who follow him.

It's important to notice what this means for calling the crucifixion 'good'. It wasn't that Jesus' death was good or necessary, but that death was the end (at least for a time) of a life committed to these good teachings. If Jesus had lived by some other teachings (such as hating one's enemies), he might have saved his own life. When Jesus went on to say, 'Be perfect, therefore, as your heavenly Father is perfect' (Matt. 5.48), we mustn't object to the language of perfection, strange as it may sound. 'Perfect' here refers to the moral quality of wholeness or inclusiveness that, when exercised, involves sacrificing the normal requirements of justice against our enemies in favour of loving them.

Jesus demonstrated this perfection himself when he forgave his killers from the cross. And the killers were not only the Romans and the Sanhedrin (the Jewish leadership) in first-century Palestine – the ones who literally conspired to bring about his death. The story of the rejection of the Son of God is a story about all of humanity rejecting God. As John writes, the Son of God came into the world that he had made, 'yet the world did not know him' (John 1.10). What Jesus sacrificed on the cross is not just his life that in a mysterious way turns out to be 'for us'. Rather, in sacrificing his normal and just response to his enemies (to us!), God didn't kill us in return. Paul summarizes that 'in Christ God was reconciling the world to himself, not counting their trespasses against them' (2 Cor. 5.19). While it would have been normal and understandable to count their trespasses against them, God in Christ loves his enemies, blessing and forgiving rather than punishing them in return.

This way of understanding sacrifice is considerably deeper than many common notions, especially those 'Aztec' ideas of sacrifice described above in which God requires sacrifices in order to restrain his wrath or to forgive us for our sin. God is seen to be forgiving sinners for the death of his Son by giving again what was taken – his life. So in a very important sense, God can be said to *sacrifice his Son*. But we need to be very clear about the sense in which this is the case. Just as Jesus taught his followers to love their enemies, God's love of enemies involves sacrificing the divine prerogative for exercising violent wrath against those who have wronged him. But once that is given up, then Jesus is defenceless at the hands of his killers. This is clear when he refuses to fight back, as his disciples did in the Garden of Gethsemane. Here I disagree with some theologies that I think get this wrong. The point is not that Jesus *needed to die*, as some Christians claim. That perspective isn't careful enough, in my view. The point is better made by saying that Jesus is likely to die at the hands of a dangerous world that makes no place for God, especially as he refuses to fight back in the normal ways. *This* is Jesus' sacrifice and it cost him his life.

There are two things to notice. First is that Jesus' teaching and example blend together. As we also saw in the last chapter, Jesus isn't asking his followers to do something that he himself isn't doing. Following Jesus involves more than just following his teachings. It is following *him*, sometimes quite literally, as the disciples found when they did the opposite by fleeing after Jesus' arrest. In Mark 14.51–52, an unidentified disciple continues to follow on a little bit, but then also flees when the authorities come to arrest him. There is a broader ethical point to this. Christian ethics is, at root, nothing different from following Jesus. If one disregards Jesus' teachings, then it is impossible to follow Jesus' example. For all of Christianity's pious words and devotional strivings about being 'Christlike' and 'conformed to his image', when it comes down to it, there is no union with Christ apart from hearing and obeying his commands, as he taught: 'Those who love me will keep my word . . . Whoever does not love me does not keep my words' (John 14.23–24). The reverse is also the case. Following Jesus' example is a moral activity that coincides exactly with his teaching. Jesus never taught anything for his disciples – whether loving enemies, turning the other cheek, giving to beggars, forgiving the wicked or trusting his life to the Father – that he did not undertake himself.

The second thing to notice is that an ethic of sacrifice blends with an ethic of non-violence:

> When the days drew near for [Jesus] to be taken up, he set his face to go to Jerusalem. And he sent messengers ahead of him. On their way they entered a village of the Samaritans to make ready for him; but they did not receive him, because his face was set towards Jerusalem. When his disciples James and John saw it, they said, 'Lord, do you want us to command fire to come down from heaven and consume them?' But he turned and rebuked them. Then they went on to another village.
>
> As they were going along the road, someone said to him, 'I will follow you wherever you go.' And Jesus said to him, 'Foxes have holes, and birds of the air have nests; but the Son of Man has nowhere to lay his head.'
>
> (Luke 9.51–58)

It is interesting that readers aren't actually told *why* Jesus rebukes his disciples. They are only told that he doesn't like the idea of consuming the Samaritan villages. But 'fire from heaven' in the Bible actually has a long history of being associated with sacrifices and the acceptability of sacrifice. If God accepts a sacrifice, he consumes it with fire (for example, in the story of Elijah's confrontation with Baal's prophets). But Jesus is here refusing to allow violence against the enemies of his movement to count as a sacrifice to God. This is the kind of sacrifice that meets its decisive end with Jesus.

Still, what is at the core of the Christian story – *sacrifice* or *the rejection of sacrifice*? According to the influential anthropologist René Girard (1923–2015), it matters how one understands what is happening in sacrifice. Girard described the near ubiquity of one kind of sacrifice in literature and human cultures that he called **the scapegoat mechanism**. Human social life, according to Girard, is characterized by competition over scarce goods. We all want what others want *because they want it*. Desire is 'mimetic', meaning that it generates the same desires in others, who imitate it. Whole societies will form in order to pursue the same desires. But the thing that brings them together also contains the seeds of their destruction since shared desire for scarce goods also promotes violence. What is to be done? The community will single out an individual or group as a scapegoat who bears the brunt of the community's wrath. Collective violence against the 'guilty' scapegoat makes the community feel satisfied for a time, reinforces its sense of innocence and brings about a feeling of unity. The scapegoat is sacrificed for the good of the community; peace is achieved through violence.

According to Girard, this is a 'bad' kind of sacrifice. The reason is that it must be repeated over and over again throughout time. Inevitably, new desires will appear that will lead to new violence, and this in turn will lead to further scapegoating. But there is a deeper reason that this is a bad sacrifice: it is based on a lie. The community deceives itself into believing it is innocent of the crimes for which it blames the scapegoat.

Girard noticed that the story of the Bible very often sides with the scapegoats and against the community: Cain, Joseph, Job. In a story about the wisdom of Solomon (1 Kings 3), two women both claim to be the mother of a child and Solomon is asked to intervene. He offers to split the child in two, to which one of the women responds that she would rather allow the child to go to the other woman than for the child to die. Solomon concluded that she must be the mother, owing to her overriding concern that the child live. For Girard, this story depicts the 'good' kind of sacrifice. The woman gives up (sacrifices) her desire for the child in exchange for the life of the child. The two women wanted the same thing; they were engaged in mimetic desire. The violence that threatened to undo them might potentially be relieved by the child's death. But good sacrifice doesn't require a death at all (although it may make death more *likely*, if not *necessary*).

Most of all, Jesus is the ultimate scapegoat (by human rather than divine design) since in this case 'the community' is the whole of humanity who reject God. And Girard insists that Jesus is involved in a good form of sacrifice – he gives up his desire ('Not my will but yours be done') for justice in the face of being unjustly accused and executed. For whom? For what? For the life of the world. But not because his death was necessary. *We* (humanity) made it necessary because we believe the lie of the scapegoat mechanism. Jesus, in suffering as the innocent scapegoat, exposes the lie for what it is and offers the *real* solution to violence and mimetic desire: forgiveness. Forgiving someone means forgoing the justice to which you have every right. There is no virtue in giving up, for no reason, something that you need. But where I can become reconciled to my adversary by relinquishing my desire for something that is getting in our way, this is a good sacrifice.

Finally, it must be said that sacrifice doesn't always have to do with death. When the Bible refers to a living sacrifice (for example, Rom. 12.1), it is talking about something that may be offered to God through the manner of the life itself: by following the ways of God. This builds on the practice of offering the best from among one's possessions, the material blessings God has given – animals, grain. But it takes this practice to the extreme. You offer yourself fully and freely to God's mission and service. What God wants is a fully obedient life rather than a death. This was the teaching of the prophets: God wants mercy, love and obedience *rather than* sacrifice. But the 'rather than' here is overplayed. In fact, mercy, love and obedience were what was only ever meaningful about sacrifice to begin with.

Even though the living sacrifice has nothing to do with death, someone who lives a fully obedient life may end up dying early as a result of the ire that his or her obedience generates in others, as was the case with Jesus. This is where good sacrifice and bad sacrifice may end up intermingling. The good of a fully obedient life is the sacrifice of one's sinful desires; the bad sacrifice is one where killing such a person is seen to be a virtuous act by the community for the way that it restores order and purges from its midst an irritating presence. What humans consider a (bad) sacrifice is the death; what God considers a (good) sacrifice is the life that provoked it. The pay-off of the notion of sacrifice for Christian ethics comes when the distinction between good and bad sacrifice can be clearly drawn. Christians do not rejoice in the *deaths* of martyrs, but in the *lives* of martyrs – their faithfulness is shown most clearly in the manner of their living as they approach death.

Resurrection and worship

The resurrection of Jesus Christ is the heart of the Christian message. The cross is certainly its most prominent symbol. But Christians declare 'Jesus is risen!' and not 'Jesus was crucified' when they speak the good news. In this section, I focus on the moral significance of resurrection. If the resurrection of Jesus is the good news Christians proclaim, any morality that flows from it is likewise good news. Resurrection is linked with ethics in a general way and it also exhibits a very particular ethic itself. We will look at both of these in turn.

Resurrection explodes our ideas about what is possible. In a universe otherwise governed by laws of cause and effect, the resurrection of Jesus Christ shows that we should not always expect a one-to-one correlation between acts and outcomes. Jesus' way of living got him killed but God raised him from the dead, in effect declaring the human judgement on his life invalid. This is a broad point to make about all ethics: resurrection refuses to be restricted by the usual ways of getting things done.

Because the gospel of Jesus calls for complete and total surrender to God in self-sacrifice, its assurances cannot depend on anything within our control. Resurrection therefore loosens our grip on the accepted methods for making things come out all right. Yes, the resurrection was a good outcome to a story that might otherwise have ended with our rejection of God's offer to us in Christ with nothing more to add. But the Bible is very clear that the resurrection wasn't our doing – we neither performed it nor forced God's hand to bring it about. God raised Jesus from the dead as a sign that God's gift of Christ would not come to an end through human acts. As for Jesus, likewise for us: God may add to any of our acts, especially faithful acts. Such acts may even be done without an eye to consequences at all.

The resurrection therefore sets an asterisk next to whole areas of moral theory. Most obviously it radically qualifies all consequentialist ethics, that is, weighing what to do based solely on the consequences. (We will look at consequentialism in more detail in Chapter 5.) Resurrection means that any good outcomes from anything come from God and are to be celebrated as God's work. This holds true for our best-laid plans and most confidently calculated acts in which we are strongly tempted to take the credit ourselves. It also holds true for our misjudgements and missteps where God closes the gap between what we do and what happens as a result. Finally, it holds true – as it did for Jesus – for those righteous and faithful actions that don't achieve the results we had hoped for. This is good news for those who work for racial or economic justice but see little to show for it.

In a well-known speech in 1965, Martin Luther King drew on the resurrection of Jesus for hope when the Civil Rights movement was experiencing a setback:

> I come to say to you this afternoon, however difficult the moment, however frustrating the hour, it will not be long, because truth crushed to earth will rise again.
> How long? Not long, because no lie can live for ever.
>
> (25 March 1965)

Truth rises in resurrection as a pure gift to those whose struggle for justice is not presently succeeding. Resurrection is therefore much more than that something hard to believe happened in the past. It is a continual hope for all Christian people. Paul understood that Jesus' resurrection was merely the 'first fruits' of the resurrection of many more to come (1 Cor. 15.20). It was unprecedented, but not unique. It was the first of many. Christians can come to understand the nature of this hope when their faithful efforts are failing and when they see the truth 'crushed to earth'. God will mount an eventual victory for all truth, including acts that are too small for those in power to notice or that are easily overlooked amid the constant selfish posturing of so many actions in the world. The resurrection of Jesus means that God notices these things and will be our deliverer, and not only of our lives, but of the projects for justice, righteousness and peace to which we give ourselves in God's service. People are sometimes convinced that their work will 'not be in vain', hoping that there will emerge something to show for it eventually, perhaps added to by the work of others. Something similar can be said with the general Christian conviction of resurrection, with the added element that it is God who will raise up and complete these good things if indeed they are part of the work of the kingdom of God.

What I am calling 'resurrection' in its broadest sense is God's delivery on the deep human hope that our actions will yield something good especially when it looks as though they won't accomplish much on their own. It's important to notice that this is a hope of weak and vulnerable people, or at least the only kind of hope anybody has when they are weak and vulnerable. Powerful people have no need of this hope; indeed they probably do not think very much about resurrection in this sense. If they believe in the resurrection of Jesus, it probably lacks this crucial element, since it is not necessary. They might have said that there is not much difference between a resurrection-world and a world without resurrection. In the same way that the news of the kingdom of God is considered good by those who will be helped by its coming but not by others, the resurrection is especially meaningful for people who lack the clout or privilege or power to see their work succeed in this world.

This is why resurrection is such a decisive break with what comes before. Jesus doesn't rise of his own accord or on the basis of his own power. His death doesn't plant a seed that grows to new life three days later. There are no unseen worldly forces at work. God the Father of Jesus has to intervene in this world to pull Jesus out of the grave. Only God can do this. John Howard Yoder (1927–97), a Mennonite theologian who taught for many years at the University of Notre Dame, understood this very well. He linked the end of the world with the resurrection since nothing in the world rises:

> When tyranny seems to dominate the world, the only way the victim can see the end of tyranny is as the end of the world as it is, and any survival beyond that as a resurrection, with both the end and the beginning demanding divine intervention.[4]

The point isn't just that those who are in no position to bring about a decisive end to tyranny and injustice are the ones whose hope is essentially for resurrection. It is also that ethics begins with this kind of hope. If we have power to bring the kind of change we want, we will act to bring it about and call those acts 'good'. We will think that we have discovered an ethic and will think that we are being moral. The old and dangerous idea that 'might makes right' is really a counterfeit ethic that mistakes power for goodness. The idea nearly discredits all ethics, but resurrection keeps it alive (or rather brings it back to life) by draining all power from hope that we might not experience loss, suffering or death. This is an argument made by British theologian John Milbank who concludes, 'To be ethical therefore is to believe in the Resurrection, and somehow to participate in it.'[5]

Friedrich Nietzsche (1844–1900), the nineteenth-century German philosopher and critic of Christianity, especially objected to language in the New Testament that talks about the righteous receiving a 'reward' in heaven despite persecution in this world. He thought that this reveals Christianity to be just as crude as anything else that appeals to a person's desire to have good things and to secure their own well-being. But it must be said that resurrection radically qualifies any connection between obedience

---

4 John Howard Yoder, 'Armaments and Eschatology', *Studies in Christian Ethics* 1.1 (1988): 43–61 (n. 28).
5 John Milbank, *Being Reconciled: Ontology and Pardon* (London: Routledge, 2003), 148.

and reward. Resurrection is a promise that doesn't come about through cause and effect, but through faith, trusting in God. It is true that the word 'reward' can imply something that is earned, but it should be thought of instead as a gift received. Nietzsche was most interested in exposing Christian hypocrisy by pointing out that it preaches self-sacrifice but then appeals to self-interest. No doubt there are Christians who are in it for a reward, but the approach here is to set forth the resurrection as the central theme that disputes this.

In addition to this general way that resurrection relates to ethics, there is also a particular ethic that flows from resurrection. Despite being rejected by humanity, Jesus gives himself to us again, complete with the possibility of being rejected again. This is an ethic of self-giving and it doesn't allow repudiation to be the last word or to thwart God's generosity. This is a theological theme crucial to reconciliation.

Many of us are by now so familiar with the story of Jesus and his resurrection that we can overlook how the story might have gone very differently. If there is a seriously unjust killing and the victim comes back to life, the normal thing that would happen would be for the victim to seek some kind of justice or vengeance. The killers wouldn't celebrate the victim's return; they would fear for their lives. This doesn't happen with Jesus, of course, but it is important to the *meaning* of the gospel that we allow ourselves to be struck by how abnormally the story plays out. When Peter preaches to the crowds in Acts, he routinely talks about Jesus 'whom you crucified' (Acts 2.23, 36; 4.10) but whom God has raised up. In response, the members of the crowd wonder 'What shall we do?' They didn't automatically hear resurrection to be good news; they needed to learn that God raised Jesus for a non-vindictive, reconciling purpose.

Christians participate in the resurrection of Jesus when they give their lives to others as Jesus did and don't let rejection stop their self-giving. Not stopping demonstrates their belief that the resurrection is true. 'If God raised Jesus from the dead,' the Christian will say, 'then he will raise me too. I can give myself to others and do all of the very dangerous and risky things Jesus talked about because, come what may, my life rests with God.'

What I am calling the *particular* ethic of self-giving and reconciliation isn't the only thing that flows from the resurrection of Jesus. But it is important to see how it is very closely related to the general effect resurrection has on all ethics (its disregard for consequences). One impulse that might lead us to hold ourselves back from fully giving ourselves to others is a protective one. What if I get hurt? What if it costs me my life? The point isn't that God wants people to get hurt any more than God wanted

Jesus to get hurt. It's that God has a way of dealing with the self-protective objections because God has a way of dealing with death. This way (as we said above) literally makes ethics a possibility.

In the account given here, resurrection deprives us of reasons by presenting us with effect that doesn't flow from causes. Ethics become possible when there is only hope rather than actions that might be performed strategically with an end goal in mind. The self-protective reasons we might give in objection to a particular Christian ethic are deprived of their force by the content of the resurrection promise made to those who believe. Resurrection therefore spills over and around the normal course of things. In this way, we can appreciate that the Christian response to belief in the resurrection of Jesus isn't first morality, but *worship*.

There is something about worship that at first seems profoundly at odds with ethics. When we ask about what is right and good to do, we naturally assume we need to offer some explanation for what makes it right and good. But what distinguishes worship from some other activities is that it is never *for a reason*. Christians don't worship God because of something they get out of it. God is to be enjoyed, experienced, loved, feared, obeyed and undergone. Worship, especially in this sense, is meant to be the crucible for all of life. Since the Christian life is to be understood as the very life of the risen Christ (Gal. 2.20), this shouldn't be a surprising place to end up. Resurrection life is unburdened from the need to perform moral calculation in order to be assured that our 'good' is somehow 'good enough' to warrant an outcome or some kind of reward. Then again, Christians learn to pass everything that happens outside worship through the lens of worship in order to understand it rightly. This begins with the unburdening of a worshipful life.

Christians do not worship God in order to be formed morally, even though Christian worship is deeply formative. In this book we will frequently look to worship practices for insight. It is in worship that Christians are given practices for rehearsing the right relationship to one another; we are gathered by God despite our differences. We come to terms with the right approach toward our sinfulness; we confess it to God and receive forgiveness with gratitude and thankful hearts. We learn the right relationship toward money and possessions; we give them back to God since they come from him and belong to him – we are stewards rather than owners. Learning such things comes to us as a gift that exceeds every possible calculation of moral benefit, just like resurrection.

Part 2

WHAT MAKES CHRISTIAN ETHICS *ETHICS*?

4

Classical roots

Up until now, we have been considering a number of Christian themes that are relatively distinctive and that shape what it means to be good Christian people. The story of God includes within it God's providential goal for all of creation as well as God's plan of salvation and healing for broken people and a broken world. Christians are those people who claim this story as their own and seek to locate their own lives within it. Along the way, Christians will seek to grow in goodness by trusting God to enrich their faith, mould their desires, and guide their actions more perfectly to reflect God's will and the life and spirit of Christ.

At the same time, Christians are not only interested in becoming good *Christian* people; they also believe that this overlaps with what it means to be good people generally. God's story isn't only the story of people who are willing or able to find themselves within it. It is also the story of the whole cosmos, including those parts that don't know or acknowledge God. Even the inanimate stones threaten to cry out in praise if the people don't do it, as Jesus said (Luke 19.40). In fact the stones, like absolutely everything else that exists, are already glorifying and praising God by their very existence. No matter how much a creature (that is, anything that exists) is in a state of rebellion, disbelief, apathy or neglect, it cannot fully deny God without opposing the fact that its very nature is God-given and God-directed.

Even though these convictions are Christian ones, they pertain to all things. The same goes for Christian attitudes on moral matters. If there are convictions, actions and practices that please God, that place us more fully within God's story, then they have an importance far beyond a narrow understanding of what it means to be a good Christian. To be a good Christian, Christians believe, is to be a good human being. It is, in fact, to become more fully human since sin makes us less than we should be, less than human, in a significant sense. Christ is the most fully human one among us – he both showed and led the way back to God, which is the same as saying that he brings to us the restoration of our humanity.

Thoughts like these explain why, from the beginning and with few exceptions, Christians have confidently and selectively appropriated what they took to be the best insights from other traditions such as Greek philosophy. This chapter looks at the main classical sources that Christians have drawn on throughout the centuries.

Plato and the good

Before looking into some detail about how Christian ethics has been influenced by classical Greek philosophical ethics, it is worth considering the much more cautious approach. Even while St Augustine confidently (though not uncritically) described Christian use of pagan philosophy using the biblical image of the Hebrews plundering the Egyptians as they escaped Pharaoh's grasp, some theologians have mounted a much more straightforward *resistance* to pagan philosophy.

One of the best-known objections to using pagan philosophy came from Tertullian (*c.*160 – *c.*225) who saw a sharp contrast between uniquely biblical, Jewish and Christian ideas on the one hand and Greek philosophical ideas on the other hand. This disagreement is nothing less than the difference between pagan wisdom and religious faith:

> What indeed has Athens to do with Jerusalem? What concord is there between the Academy and the Church? What between heretics and Christians? Our instruction comes from 'the porch of Solomon,' who had himself taught that 'the Lord should be sought in simplicity of heart.' Away with all attempts to produce a mottled Christianity of Stoic, Platonic, and dialectic composition! We want no curious disputation after possessing Christ Jesus, no inquisition after enjoying the gospel! With our faith, we desire no further belief.[1]

Tertullian objected to the idea that Christian truth could be discerned through a process like dialectic – the back-and-forth disputes of reasoning minds that so characterize Plato's work in the form of Socratic dialogues. Dialectic might work if the truth can be known by merging the best thoughts from the sharpest minds by getting them to hash things out with each other. But the things of God – the forms of knowledge that characterize theology – are much different. These can only be known to us by divine revelation and in response call for faith, not dialogue.

There is a significant difference between Tertullian and Augustine on these matters. Augustine believed that, no matter how much the Greek philosophers might deny it, the one God that they contemplated was actually the God of Israel. Many of this God's attributes could be ascertained by

---

1 Tertullian, *On the Prescription of Heretics*, ch. 7, in *Ante-Nicene Fathers*, vol. 3, ed. Allan Menzies and James Donaldson (New York: Charles Scribner's Sons, 1903), 246.

the light of reason – God's uniqueness, omniscience, transcendence – but there were limits. Philosophy could not tell you God's name (YHWH) or this God's story with a particular people (Abraham and his descendants). Nevertheless, Christians like Augustine had the confidence to appropriate Greek thought for two main reasons.

First was a very strong conviction that the God of Israel has, in Christ, been decisively shown to be a God for Gentiles too. The story of God with Israel must not be taken to imply that God had been ignoring the other nations. When Paul stood up in the marketplace in Athens (Acts 17), he declared that the God of Israel and Jesus, while an 'unknown god' to the Greeks, was also one whom they had already been worshipping. Likewise, we might say, with the noble death that Socrates had earlier suffered for the sake of his monotheism and some moral ideas Christians were later to judge compatible with Christian morality. In being the Christian God for both Jews and Gentiles, this God was understood to be universal and therefore could be found anywhere.

The second reason for this extraordinary Christian confidence in working with philosophical ideas has to do with the manner of doing it. Unlike Tertullian's suspicion about human reason, others like Augustine placed a limited but real trust in reason because of the fact that Christ, in John's Gospel, is described as the *Logos* or reason (or logic or Word): 'In the beginning was the Word, and the Word was with God, and the Word was God' (John 1.1).

The idea of *Logos* was already important in classical Greek thought, identifying the inherent rationality or reasonableness of the world. This quality of things made academic study possible; hence the suffix '-ology', sharing the root *logos*, is used to name many of the different disciplines. Geology (study of earth) and biology (study of life) exist as fields of study because they are believed to be able to be studied by reason. Christians, of course, understood theology to be the study of God (*Theos* = God) and, as different as God is from everything else that people study, even theology is possible because God has made the Logos flesh and to dwell among us (John 1.14). Christ is the inherent logic of theological discourse. But he is also more than this. The claim that Christ is the Logos is also a radical acknowledgement that Christ is the principle that provides things that are available to reason with this astounding quality.

This means that things will be more fully known for what they are by relating them to God and Christ, God's Logos. This chapter will show a number of ways that this admittedly abstract claim gets worked out as Christian thinkers make use of pagan philosophy. The first concerns our study of ethics directly – the meaning of **the good**. Is it more important to *do* good or to *be* good? Many people reasonably assume that ethics is about what you *do* – *doing good*. You may learn what that will involve and then either decide or not decide to do it. If the focus is on doing good, then the decision to act plays an important role. But there is a deeper question: *why* be good? Why, we might ask, is it good to be good? Plato took this question seriously.

Much of the philosophy Plato produced was meant to argue against a group of teachers called the Sophists. Sophists taught what today might be called a radical form of empiricism; that is, they believed that the sum total of reality is that which can be taken in by the senses, whether observed with the eyes or perceived in some other sense-oriented way. The way to know things is to take them in through the senses and not to imagine, believe or discern that there is a deeper reality. Plato strongly held the opposite view and argued his case in many ways. One of the best known has to do with change.[2]

All things change, whether they are objects, institutions, societies or anything at all. They come into being, decay, grow, move, shift, wither or go away altogether. All of these changes are available to the senses. But is there an essence that underlies all of these changes that will allow us to say that, however much change a thing undergoes, it is nevertheless the same thing that it was before? Over time, a football team's players all change, as do its owners and managers, and the design of the uniforms. What then makes this the same team?

The Sophist view was that if everything we can know comes through the perception of our senses, then things are no more stable than they appear to be. If what appears is things changing, that must mean that change is all there is. Plato (and Socrates) disagreed with the Sophists on this and taught instead that there are two realms: one in which things are constantly in flux and another in which things are permanent. What we see empirically with our senses are things that are in various states of change, always short of expressing to us what they truly are. In the realm of forms, however, things are only their essences, meaning that they do not change.

Plato is famous for this metaphysics and it has some important implications. One is that the world that we see and take to be real is not as good as the world of forms. When we see things, we see shadows, not things as they truly are in their essence. We can think about some things that are deeply important, but that are beyond the reach of our senses: love, justice, goodness. For Sophists, these are just words we use to describe various

---

2 Here I follow Harry J. Huebner, *An Introduction to Christian Ethics: History, Movements, People* (Waco, TX: Baylor University Press, 2012), ch. 1.

states and phenomena, but there is nothing that roots them beyond how we see and experience them. If we wanted to know what makes a good human being, we might go around asking people this question and then settle on the conclusion that a good person is like what people think a good person is like. For Plato, on the other hand, all humans are shadows and appearances of the ultimate form of humanness. There doesn't need to be a separate form of goodness, since the forms are all good. A good eye is one that sees well and therefore does what eyes are meant to do. Saying that some eyes don't do this is parallel to admitting that not all people are good.

Gaining knowledge of the forms is the work of philosophy. This turns out to be a risky enterprise since it means that a small number of people, enlightened with this knowledge, will probably offend everybody else with news that reality isn't what it appears to be. Even so, philosophy requires the intellectual courage to seek the truth no matter the cost.

Socrates works out the metaphysics of form and appearance in dialogues found in Plato's *Republic*. Socrates is presented with an argument by the Sophist Thrasymachus who insists that there is no essence to justice, but that justice is only defined by those in power who use justice to their own convenience. Another interlocutor, Glaucon, carries this argument further by claiming that people will only act justly for *instrumental* reasons, that is, because of how it will benefit them. Justice on its own isn't enough to compel people since 'no one is willingly just'.[3] And because *appearing* to act justly brings social benefits, people will claim to value justice even if they don't. 'If a man chooses injustice and at the same time fabricates a contrary reputation for justice, he can expect to live like a god.' This teaching follows the belief that the way things appear is more important than how things really are. The ethic that results is that 'To *appearance*, then, one must turn one's efforts without stint . . . If one wants happiness, this is the way to go.'[4]

To illustrate his own position, Glaucon discusses the legend of the ring of Gyges in which a shepherd finds a ring that makes the wearer invisible. With this power, Gyges commits a number of immoral acts, including murder, and eventually manages to become the king. Glaucon insists that any person will do what benefits him or her if no one is watching. As long as there is no recognition or reward for acting justly, people won't do it. Even if a good person comes into possession of such a ring, the result will be the same. Everyone will do what is evil when there is no one watching – when

---

3 Plato, *The Republic*, trans. Richard W. Sterling and William C. Scott (New York: Norton, 1985), Book II, 360c, p. 56.
4 Plato, *The Republic*, Book II, 365b, pp. 60–1, emphasis added.

one's actions cannot be tied to rewards such as the praise and admiration of others. The invisibility of the wearer is meant to highlight the superficial way in which what we call justice belongs only to a world that values appearance. So people might *do* good (appearance) but won't *be* good (essence).

Socrates disagrees. He argues that a good person desires to do what is good no matter what. The reason he gives is that a virtuous person knows something that a wicked person doesn't: that *being good is its own reward*. There is simply something about being good that is inherently satisfying, that produces happiness. This kind of reward is not external, instrumental or *extrinsic* (such as fame or fortune) but internal or *intrinsic*. The fullest account of the association between goodness and happiness was developed, in a different way, by Plato's pupil Aristotle and will be discussed in the next section. For Plato, things that we affirm as good or just should be understood as participating in the eternal forms of the good and of justice.

These ideas have been very influential in Christian thought. For example, Augustine is indebted to Plato in many ways, but he also departed from Plato's metaphysics at crucial junctures. Instead of talking about things in the world participating in the forms, Augustine identified God as the meaning and source in which things participate. God is goodness itself and not just characterized by goodness. In the same way, God is truth, not just truthful; God is beauty itself, not just beautiful.

By raising the prospect of another, real world, of which this one is only a pale reflection, some have understood Plato to have significantly downgraded the importance of our earthly existence. On the one hand, this made sense to some elements of Christian thinking, where an eternal heaven is contrasted with a temporary earth. When Christians cry 'How long, O Lord?' amid suffering, the permanent, perfect realm is a great comfort. Then again, the Christian belief in the goodness of the created order, as well as the belief that Christ is incarnate (not only in the past but continually), requires a more robust affirmation of life in this world. In this, Augustine managed a metaphysics of participation that also affirms the goodness of creation. In fact, Augustine's teaching about evil derives from his concept of God as goodness.

As we pointed out in the Introduction, Augustine taught the counterintuitive position that evil has no existence. 'For you [God] evil does not exist at all, and not only for you but for your created universe.'[5] His argument for claiming this is that everything that exists is good, as the book of Genesis states. Existence itself derives from God's goodness which means

---

5 Augustine, *Confessions*, trans. Henry Chadwick (Oxford: Oxford University Press, 1991), VII.xiii.

that existence is a good. So long as things exist, then, they must be spoken of as good if for no other reason than that they exist. Evil, on the other hand, if it were completely devoid of goodness, could not exist. The idea here is that what we call evil is not a *thing* (even though we are right to use the word 'evil'). Instead, Augustine taught that evil is an absence, a lack, a *privation* of goodness. It can never be a complete absence, but the sense in which something is less than it was created to be is what we call evil.

We will recognize Plato's distinction between essence and appearance here, even though Augustine's solution differs, especially in how we ought to respond to evil. One doesn't hope to escape this world of appearances and bodily existence in order to reach true essences any more than one must defeat evil or fight against it. If evil is a lack, then there is nothing to fight against. Instead, the thing to do in response to evil is to fill up the gap or lack with goodness. Moreover, rather than maintaining Plato's sharp distinction between appearance and reality which can have the effect of diminishing the importance of material existence, Augustine's vision of reaching God is thoroughly bodily. In this, Augustine is signalling Christian belief in resurrection of the body rather than the ascent of disembodied souls that characterizes Plato's vision.[6]

Finally, Augustine followed Plato in insisting that *knowing* what is good and *wanting* what is good are intimately connected, despite the best efforts of much of philosophy to separate will from knowledge. In everyday experience, it seems as though this distinction is vast. After all, we know that plenty of things are good for us even though our desire and will is for other things. Anyone who has tried to stop smoking or lose weight knows this. But Augustine believed not only that we sin out of a disordered will – wanting the wrong things – but that the true knowledge of the good (which, for him, simply is the knowledge of God) will align our desires with what is good. To know the good is to want the good. The desire to be healthy would always be greater than the desire for cake if we really knew and believed in the goodness of health. And since all truth is God's truth, knowing God will, above all else, produce in people the genuine desire for God.

Aristotle and happiness

In contrast to Plato who took what some consider to be a rather abstract approach to defining the good, Aristotle thought about the good much

---

6 See Janet Martin Soskice, 'Monica's Tears: Augustine on Words and Speech', *New Blackfriars* 83.980 (Oct. 2002): 448–58.

more empirically. He began with the kinds of things that ordinary people mean when they use the word 'good' in everyday conversation. After all, this isn't a word that is only used when talking about morality. So, for example, a chair can be good. What do we mean when we say this? We probably mean that the chair does what chairs are supposed to do – hold you up when you sit in them. (And if it can do this while also being comfortable, sturdy and lovely to look at, so much the better.) If there is a chair that fails to do this, it certainly isn't a very good one. There is a goal to which all chairs aspire: being good at holding you up when you sit in them. This way of speaking about goal, in Greek thought, is called the thing's *telos*. It is the thing's purpose for being what it is.

Even though it sounds as though we are not discussing morality when we talk about what a chair should be, Aristotle taught that we actually are. After all, we started by asking what makes a chair good. Now, what is a good roommate? A good spouse? A good friend? These are fairly empirical questions that we can try to answer for ourselves. Maybe we would answer that a good roommate or spouse or friend is a person with various 'good' characteristics, someone who is patient, trustworthy, understanding, loyal. And if these are things that it is good to be, then we are certainly talking about things that are moral qualities. But notice that they are not first things you *do*, but things you *are*. They are qualities of a person's character. They are what Aristotle called the **virtues**. The virtues have a few key features.

First, Aristotle taught that the virtues travel in herds. If we were to make a list of what makes a good roommate, it would probably be very similar to lists of what makes a good spouse, a good friend, a good employee or a good employer. The virtues that are common to these lists are not just coincidences but are indications that there is such a thing as a good person regardless of the role they play in other people's lives, in the workplace and in the public sphere. The virtues are 'transferable skills', we might say. If someone is a terrible flatmate while unmarried, he or she can't expect all of a sudden to make a good spouse.

Second, virtues aren't the kinds of things a person can aim at directly and hope to achieve. The virtues that really matter must be acquired obliquely. They are the character qualities that a person needs in the course of doing particular activities ('practices') that demand them. The foremost practice is life itself since the explanation for the unity of the virtues is that virtue-engendering activities are simply microcosms of life. Then again, life pure and simple may be lived in many ways, so these microcosms turn out to be better ways to focus on acquiring the virtues.

For example, consider the way that learning to excel at playing a sport includes the virtue of sportsmanship, so much so that we say that however skilled a player may otherwise be, he or she can still be a 'bad sport' if these qualities are lacking. What is sportsmanship? It is a combination of things like the ability to balance seriousness for competition with the light-hearted recognition that it is just a game. If someone is too light-hearted, he or she is not taking the game seriously enough. Likewise, it is unsportsmanlike to allow the desire for winning to overwhelm what is fun about playing. Sportsmanship lies in the middle.

It's important to notice that no one is likely to take up a sport with the explicit idea of gaining these qualities. Doing so might even be counter-productive, since one's focus would be on the virtue rather than excelling at the sport – a rather unsportsmanlike distraction from what is important. On the other hand, there is no other way to become sportsmanlike than to develop the qualities (alongside the others) necessary to become good at the sport. A good carpenter and a good swimmer will both be self-controlled, for example. Qualities like self-control, together with courage, truthfulness and other things, are not specific to only one activity, but are actually part of what makes for a successful, true, moral human life, a life well lived. It's not as though the point of life is to develop the virtues; living must have an overriding, engrossing effect such that growing in the virtues is necessary to achieve it. This effect is happiness.

Happiness is the third feature of the virtues. Happiness in the sense that Aristotle discussed it is a deeply important concept since his claim is that virtuous people are happy people. We can get a sense of what Aristotle means by happiness by asking about the reasons for doing anything at all. For Aristotle, after all the answers to this question have been given, there is really only one left standing: happiness. This happiness, which in Greek is *eudaimonia*, is the ultimate explanation for doing everything. Why get an education? To get a job. Why might a person want a job? To earn money. Why does a person want money? ... Eventually, this series of questions and answers will arrive at an end point. After a while, an answer will be given for which 'Why?' makes no sense. For Aristotle, this answer is happiness. 'Why do you want to be happy?' It turns out that this is a strange question. It doesn't really need an answer. Only someone who doesn't know what happiness is would ask such a thing. Happiness is its own reward. It is thus, as Aristotle taught, the *telos* of human life – the goal that gives meaning to anything you might do. Even bad people do bad things because of happiness (although they may be self-deceived since not everything we think will make us happy actually does so).

Before going on to unpack Aristotle's ethics further, let's pause to point out that these ideas about happiness and the goal of human life are ideas that many Christian thinkers have been able to work with. God desires our happiness and, in Christ, shows us what true happiness is. We must first be disabused of our false ideas about what will make us happy since we are generally not the best judges of this. But when God heals our wounds, forgives our sins and lifts up the fallen, he is trying to make people happy. This restoration of our true and full humanity, once it is recognized, will also be seen not only to be the good and better way to live for having received these good things. It also highlights and clarifies how we ought to *be* these things for others, for ourselves and for God. As the Irish Dominican priest and theologian Herbert McCabe (1926–2001) noted, we study ethics in order to learn 'how to be good at being human'.[7] McCabe is reflecting centuries of Christian thought that appreciated how goodness and happiness go together.

When it comes to the virtues, the fourth trait that Aristotle emphasized is one that many non-specialists know: the golden mean. When considering sportsmanship, we noticed that it may be hard to define what it is with precision. Instead, we resorted to describing it as the balance between two extremes (overly competitive on the one hand and overly light-hearted on the other). Aristotle taught that the virtues can always be thought of as a mean between two extremes. The courageous person, for example, is neither too cautious nor too bold. We will be aware that sportsmanship and courage are both good, desirable qualities, but might struggle to identify just what they mean and how to go about growing in them.

Fifth, the business of identifying and understanding the virtues is related to the golden mean: it is not an exact science. The virtues don't tell us what to do with any precision. It's more like when a person says, 'I sure wish so-and-so were here; he'd know what to do.' Virtue ethics is not so much about finding and settling on a right answer as about looking into what a virtuous person would do. How then do I come to be virtuous myself so that my judgements display virtue? Just asking what a virtuous person would do (like asking 'What would Jesus do?') might give us an answer, but it's not complete if the person asking the question doesn't share in the judgement of the virtuous person. Growing in virtue is not like acquiring knowledge; it is more like learning a skill.

---

7 Herbert McCabe, *The Good Life: Ethics and the Pursuit of Happiness*, ed. Brian Davies (New York: Continuum, 2005), 9.

This insight is actually easy to see in the case of the question 'What would Jesus do?' and why so many Christians have sought to appropriate Aristotle's ethics. When someone asks 'What would Jesus do?', the point isn't so much to get an academic answer (knowledge) that will satisfy one's curiosity, but to become like Jesus himself (gain these 'skills'). Rather than being told what to do, the Christian disciple is given an example to follow: be holy as I am holy. This is why Jesus did not just provide us with answers, but invited people to follow him. 'Follow me', as it happens, is an absolutely, morally serious proposition. Jesus made disciples, not people who would just know the right answers, but people whose sense of judgement is also transformed.

Let's look at a couple more examples of how this works. We might think about what is involved in learning the virtues like we might think about learning to juggle. Juggling is a difficult skill that can't be learned just by reading books about how to do it. No one would claim to 'know' how to juggle just because they could give other people instructions about it. Knowing juggling is quite simply the ability to juggle. This points to a deeper form of knowing than we are often content to have.

To take a different example, think about anger. If the virtues are skills in which a person comes to share in the judgements of virtuous people, we would expect that virtuous people get angry at the right things. Anger may not sound like much of a virtue, but it is, so long as we use the principle of the mean to identify it. Some people clearly get angry too easily or over the wrong things. Other people under-react and should show more anger if the circumstances call for it. It's not enough simply to know that a virtuous person would get angry in a particular situation. Aristotle said:

> [A]nyone can get angry – that's easy – or can give away money or spend it; but to do all this to the right person, to the right extent, at the right time, for the right reason, and in the right way is no longer something easy that anyone can do.[8]

Virtue ethics is not an exact science because, unlike science, its goal is not to give answers and knowledge, but to form people.

Someone will object that it's obvious that this way of talking about the virtues is not an exact science; in fact it's so inexact that it's completely unhelpful. It's as though we give someone some soup and ask how hot he or she would like it, and the person replies, 'Not too hot and not too cold.' That's common sense, perhaps, but doesn't sound particularly helpful.

---

8 Aristotle, *Nicomachean Ethics*, 2nd edn, trans. Terence Irwin (Indianapolis: Hackett, 1999), 1109a25–30.

In a way this objection is absolutely correct. Aristotle doesn't actually tell us what the virtues entail, but only how they differ from the vices. Yet this is deliberate. Virtue ethics is deliberately modest. It's not a system that we can go to for answers, but a way of training us to ask the right questions. The first thing it is meant to have us do is look for role models or moral exemplars. If you want your soup just the right temperature and you don't have a thermometer (a scientific instrument!), you will need to find another bowl of soup that is just right and then aim at that. The same is true for the moral life. To know how much fear is not too much and not too little, you need to find a courageous person and aim at that. This is what we meant by calling Aristotle's approach *empirical* – one actually needs to look around and find people whose lives are worth imitating. These people will be both virtuous and happy; the two go together.

Virtue ethicists will often point out that we make most of our moral choices without even realizing that we are doing so. We usually act out of habit and character, doing what comes naturally instead of stopping to think about it or to weigh our moral options. Most of our lives aren't spent agonizing over choosing the right thing; we usually just choose without even recognizing that we're doing it. When a good person walks past someone at the edge of a cliff overlooking a beautiful vista, it doesn't even occur to him or her that there exists the moral choice between shoving or not shoving the other person off the cliff. This choice will only register *as a choice* for a morally depraved person regardless of how he or she ends up choosing. This is because what counts as a choice for us already reflects a moral stance. The good person has indeed chosen not to shove the person at the cliff, but he or she has chosen, in a sense, *by not choosing* – by not being the kind of person for whom this registers as a choice.

There are matters that are prior to choosing and over which we may have little conscious control. Who we are will often already be enough to signal what registers on our moral radar. But surely this can't count for everything worth saying about morality since everyone, including Aristotle, recognizes that some people will want to become more moral, to be happier, and will be willing to put in the effort to make it happen. If this is so, how do we go about changing who we are? Aristotle's answer was useful to Christian thinkers on this, but didn't tell the whole story. We'll look at specific responses in the section below. This long process of becoming a different sort of person is what we call the **formation** of one's character. For Aristotle, it was an empirical matter of identifying people who display desirable virtues and then imitating them, mindfully responding as they respond, until those responses become natural and ingrained in one's character. As we develop morally, we will probably less and less often have a crisis of conscience. We will experience life as a serene existence in which we act intuitively. The good is more and more a part of who we genuinely are.

Christian virtue

Christian ethics generally followed Greek ethics in its belief that *being good* is more important than *doing good*. It's better to be a good person who does wrong than to be a bad person who does what is right. Dietrich Bonhoeffer wrote that it is worse for a liar to tell the truth than for a lover of truth to lie. A **character** witness might be called on to testify to the overall goodness of the person. This kind of testimony is valuable for looking at the kind of person someone is; individual acts will often make sense once we have a sense of this. For example, we might expect that a liar who all of a sudden tells the truth could have ulterior motives for doing so.

In this section, we will look at the main ways that Christians have worked with, modified and built upon Aristotle's account of happiness and virtues in particular. Augustine and Thomas Aquinas (1225–74), the two most important theologians in Christian history, both worked with these ideas, although only Aquinas used and responded to Aristotle's writings. Both thinkers were at ease using pagan philosophy to help enrich Christian teaching. Unlike others like Tertullian who have been suspicious about appealing to the ideas of the Greeks, urging caution rather than engagement, Augustine and Aquinas believed that truth could be found all around us. The distinctiveness of Christian beliefs doesn't mean that Christians should isolate themselves from the best of non-Christian learning.

These two thinkers agreed with Aristotle that all things have a *telos* – final end or goal – that gives their existence purpose and meaning in answer to the question, 'What is this for?' The most important version of this question asks about the purpose of human life, which Aristotle took to be a life lived virtuously and therefore happily. Since reaching a *telos* involves fully utilizing the capacities that are natural to a thing, the full flourishing of human beings will mean realizing the virtues that go with all of our natural capacities. Like so many philosophers, Aristotle took the faculty of reason to be what makes humans unique among the other animals. Aquinas agreed, relating this to the meaning of the claim made in Genesis that we are created in the image of God. To Aquinas (in which he explicitly follows the Eastern Orthodox theologian John of Damascus), being made in the image of God implies 'an intelligent being endowed with free-will and self-movement'.[9] Where reason itself flourishes most fully in contemplation and the display of intellectual virtue, the human *telos* is realized.

But the Christian appropriation of Aristotle doesn't end here since there is a further goal toward which the human being is directed. This is beatitude and friendship with God. Humans were not only made to contemplate and embody the good. We were made to enjoy and love God, the source of all goodness. We are meant for a communion that transcends our own lives and those of our neighbours. This friendship and enjoyment is not something we are capable of attaining on our own, but comes to us as a gift of grace from the loving God who created us for this.

We have already seen how doing good and being good go together, especially in Aristotle's ethics. In addition to making the move to enlarge the *telos* of human life beyond this life strictly speaking, Christian thought has also insisted on the important fact that our very concept of goodness comes from God. Augustine reflected on how lots of things can be good: food is good when it is tasty and gives health; air is good when it is pleasant and clean; a house is good when it has good symmetry, and is spacious and bright. But what happens when we try to look at what goodness *itself* consists in, apart from all of the various things that we might name as being capable of being good? 'Take away this and that and see good itself if you can,' he wrote in a book on the Trinity. 'In this way you will see God, not good with some other good, but *the good of every good*.'[10] God is the goodness of all good things.

If we try to understand how this works, Augustine asks us to consider the mere fact of the existence of things. Before we can evaluate or describe any of their qualities (shape, colour, size, texture, temperature), we need to appreciate that just by existing, things can be said to be good, as indeed God said upon creating them. By existing, things desire and praise their creator who gives them life and sustains them in all things. But this way of speaking about goodness isn't separate from what we normally mean when we say something is good. In fact, Augustine's point is that the goodness that things (like humans) turn to in order to be good is the same good that gives them their being as a thing in the first place. Again we notice that an indebtedness to Greek philosophy is taken much further in Christian hands.

---

9 Thomas Aquinas, *Summa Theologica*, trans. Fathers of the English Dominican Province (Allen, TX: Christian Classics, 1981), I-II, prologue (hereafter *ST*).

10 Augustine, *The Trinity*, trans. Edmund Hill, OP (New York: New City Press, 1991), Book VIII, ch. 2 (244), emphasis added.

It won't be surprising, then, to learn that Christians didn't name God just as the goodness of things, but as the source of all human happiness. Aquinas wrote, 'Happiness is the attainment of the Perfect Good.'[11] The perfect good here is God, and the attainment of the perfect good is communion or beatitude and friendship with God. Aquinas is certainly aware that people think all kinds of lesser things will make them happy. He lists wealth, honours, fame or glory, power and bodily health as possibilities, although all of them fall short. The reason they fall short isn't that these things are evil, but that there is something beyond them. They are potentially steps on the way to happiness, but we can often be happy without them. When our happiness depends on them, it still lies beyond them. For example, sometimes the desire for wealth can arise from good reasons, such as to meet natural needs such as food and shelter. But Aquinas says that these serve a further purpose, the support of our lives, which must themselves have some further end beyond just remaining alive.

This further purpose is simply beholding God. As Aquinas puts it, 'Final and perfect happiness can consist in nothing else than the vision of the Divine Essence.'[12] It's not enough to use one's mind to contemplate and think about God since, as Aquinas says, this is an act of the intellect alone, which is limited to knowing that God exists. Knowing this, the Christian desire for God will be even stronger, yearning to reach God and to be united with God.

Speaking this way, it might seem that we have moved away from the study of ethics and toward the language of worship and devotion. This is appropriate, though, since approaches to ethics that emphasize these themes have a different focus from those that deal with the good of individual actions. Here the good of the whole human person is in view. Before we can look at specific ethical issues, moral dilemmas or hard choices, our deep awareness of the purpose of all of human existence will orient us from the start.

For one thing, we will be oriented away from discrete acts performed by isolated individuals. For Aristotle and his Christian interpreters, humans can only fully flourish within a well-ordered political community. When Aristotle wrote his work on ethics, he meant it to be a prelude to a separate work devoted to politics. The idea is that since the good is public and collective rather than private and autonomous, the task for forming

---

11 Aquinas, *ST*, I-II.5.1.
12 Aquinas, *ST*, I-II.3.8.

virtuous people must be carried out by what Stanley Hauerwas (b. 1940), an American theologian at Duke University, calls **communities of character.**

Aristotle understood these communities to be political in the most straightforward sense. They were societies modelled on the city-state, served by constitutions and laws, and kept alive by the active participation of citizens. The Christian tendency has been to take the insight about the communal nature of virtue-formation, but reimagine the nature of political community. Because the kingdom of God (intentionally invoking political nomenclature) is inherently a challenge to all human political communities, God can be said to be forming virtuous, righteous and holy people who are first and foremost citizens of heaven. For Christians, the most concrete expression of this new society isn't the nation or the city, but the Church. Especially in the last few decades, a number of Christian virtue ethicists have been working to show in great detail how the community of the Church, especially in its liturgical life, forms virtuous Christians.[13]

In this Christian use of the virtues, the Church provides the faithful with the moral exemplars that we ought to emulate. You may recall that Aristotle taught that someone who wanted to grow in courage ought first to identify a moral example of courage and essentially copy that person. At first it may be necessary to copy that person's actions mechanically, but the goal is eventually to internalize the less tangible aspects of his or her character, such as attitude and judgement, since these are crucial to acting well. A prominent example Aristotle gave is a soldier who shows courage in the face of danger. Since his ethics was meant to prepare the way for his politics, it is no surprise that Aristotle highlights civic virtues that serve the state.

In the eyes of some Christian thinkers, it won't do simply to link moral goodness with worldly citizenship in this way. Aquinas agreed that courage is a genuine human virtue, which means that Christians ought to strive for it as well. But he didn't think soldiers provide the best exemplars and instead instructed readers to look to the Christian martyrs whose courage is displayed in how they stand firm in the face of danger and the threat of death. 'Martyrdom consists essentially in standing firmly to truth and justice against the assaults of persecution.'[14] A martyr's courage surpasses that of the soldier because the calm demeanour he or she displays when

---

13 See, for example, Stanley Hauerwas, *In Good Company: The Church as Polis* (Notre Dame: University of Notre Dame Press, 1995), esp. ch. 10: 'The Liturgical Shape of the Christian Moral Life: Teaching Christian Ethics as Worship'.
14 Aquinas, *ST*, II-II.124.2.

being killed is given by the Holy Spirit and is formed by charity or love. Aquinas even speaks about martyrs as 'warriors' as a way of signalling that there is a higher form of courage. Not only do martyrs suffer rather than inflict violence, but their minds are set beyond 'civic fortitude' and 'human justice', focusing instead on receiving the gift of a strong soul from God for the sake of divine justice.[15]

In addition to modifying Aristotle's ethics with regard to the *telos* of human life, the source of goodness and happiness, the specific moral exemplars we ought to look to and the nature of communities of character, Christians have also been quick to modify the specific virtues themselves that make a life a good one. Since Aristotle's virtues are meant to have civic application and importance, they are very practical and concrete. Virtues like courage, temperance, truthfulness and modesty are all useable to a Christian ethic, as is the way of describing each of them as the mean between two extremes. As we have seen with courage, however, the actual content and display of the virtues will look different from the perspective of seeing the world storied by a loving and gracious creator who is redeeming it to a future beyond itself.

Moreover, the most significant Christian virtues weren't qualities that Aristotle would have been able to recognize. Drawing on 1 Corinthians 13.13, Aquinas spoke of the **theological virtues** of faith, hope and love. These are given or 'infused' by God and are not acquired by imitation and habit-formation the same way that cardinal virtues (like courage) are. Christians may learn courage by imitating martyrs whose acts in the face of persecution instruct their habits and ultimately their attitudes and dispositions. But the real source of a martyr's patience is God, who fills the martyr with deep *faith* to follow Christ even to death, with *hope* of being raised with Christ at the last day, and *love* for fellow believers, the Church and even his or her killers. God both permits and enables the martyrs to die joyfully, blessing those who kill them, refusing to harbour hatred and calling for no revenge. And just as Paul said that the greatest of these theological virtues is love, so also Aquinas held that love is the form of all of the other virtues.

We have been looking at classical ways of doing ethics, especially the most prominent ways coming out of Greek philosophy. And we have seen some ways that Christians have worked with and modified them. But it should be clear that these approaches aren't stuck in the past. In particular, a revival of virtue ethics in the past half-century has mostly been in

---

15 Aquinas, *ST*, II-II.124.2.

response to dissatisfaction with the main modern approaches, which we will look at in detail in the next chapter.

At this point, and to conclude this chapter, we can look ahead to one way that modern options can be dissatisfying. We will be looking more into Immanuel Kant's ethics. Kant (1724–1804) thought that knowing the right thing to do would often be at odds with what we actually want to do. In these cases, moral knowledge needs to overcome our wills. If we *know* what we ought to do, we should do it, even if we don't want to. The most moral person will be one who is able to rise above personal desire and act in accordance with what he or she knows to be true. So there will be a conflict between knowledge and will.

It is easy to see how different this is from a virtue-based approach that doesn't focus just on doing the right thing, but on also being the kind of person who shares the attitudes and judgements (including the desires) of those who act a certain kind of way. Even though he wrote centuries before Kant, Thomas Aquinas exceeded Kant. For Aquinas, as we have seen, there is a higher morality, one in which one's knowledge and will are perfectly aligned. It is not just that it is better to know the good *and* want to do it. Aquinas agreed with Augustine (and Plato, for that matter) that if we truly knew the good, we would of course want to do it. We fail in this because our knowledge is limited and our wills are corrupt.

The more moral we are, according to Kant, the more there will be an internal conflict between what we want to choose and what we know we *should* choose. We will always be struggling and frustrated, constantly confessing our inadequacy and sinfulness. In this, Kant reflects a certain Protestant tendency to accommodate itself to sin. Left out is the possibility of a serene, joyful contentment in which desire and knowledge are in harmony. The person of virtue is one who not only knows what to do, but even more importantly also wants to do it.

5

Modern options

The dominant ways of doing ethics began to change in the early modern period. The Scottish philosopher Alasdair MacIntyre (b. 1929), who taught for many years at the University of Notre Dame, tells the story of ethics in the West by especially focusing on changes that occurred in the early modern period that were connected to the Enlightenment, a European intellectual movement in the seventeenth and eighteenth centuries. The approaches to ethics that are the focus of this chapter display some of the key elements of Enlightenment.

The moral ideas that most characterize the Enlightenment are noteworthy for having a strong focus on the individual as the seat of moral deliberation. In a few different senses, Western ethics moved from being fairly communal-based to being based on the individual. Aristotle's ethics had been meant to be a prelude to his politics, an indicator not only that 'man is a political animal', but also that ethics is lived in and given its coherence by communal life. Related to this, the approaches of the modern options reflect a shift away from practical reason and toward a discourse about legality where law is valuable primarily for its role in safeguarding the rights of individuals. Ethics becomes more like law than formation, focusing more on decisions and less on the person who must decide.

The Enlightenment was mixed in its explicit attitudes toward religion. Yet even though only some wings of the Enlightenment were outright atheist, some have argued that Christian versions of Enlightenment had a damaging long-term effect due to how they tried to make religion optional. Immanuel Kant, for example, was Lutheran, but produced ethics that were meant to be understood by and binding upon all people on the basis of what all people share, namely *reason*. The human faculty of reason comes from God, but Kant didn't think it was necessary to believe in God to see the truth of his ethics. He also wasn't interested in deriving moral guidance from particular Christian sources such as the Bible. In doing this, Kant thought he was doing Christianity a favour, protecting it from rational scrutiny into what is essentially subjective, non-rational piety. Religion is about religious experiences rather than rational claims, and moral teachings that get by most of the time saying that certain things are morally right because God commands them.

For example, Christians claim that God is good. But this is open to the question about what we mean by 'good'. Kant feared that Christianity has a tendency to be turned in on itself, and believers reply by asserting that we know what goodness is by looking at what God is like (which amounts to claiming that God is what God is like). This circular reasoning bothered Kant who looked for ways of identifying goodness outside religion.

This move is a significant departure from how medieval Christians thought. For them, there was nothing 'outside' of religion. At least in principle, everything could be related to God's presence to creation. Now a 'secular' space had been created in which religion did not seem to add anything significant. The world would pretty much be the same whether God exists or not. This new attitude had the advantage of **universality** – a person doesn't need to be a Christian for the ethic to be binding. Ethics arises from the lowest common denominator, *reason*, which all humans have. It is no coincidence that freedom and liberty emerge as the primary political goals during this era of revolutions. The new philosophies of the Enlightenment declared their emancipation from the medieval ways of thinking that they characterized as blind adherence to inherited dogma. The ideal reasoner is one who is detached from all histories and traditions, including his or her own. Ironically, as many contemporary thinkers have pointed out, all of these characteristics of modern ethics make up their own tradition.

Deontology

In Greek, the word *deon* refers to duty or obligation. Deontological ethics therefore highlights those things it is one's duty to perform. It is often characterized as a rule-based approach to ethics and it prizes most of all those rules that are exceptionless. Those who take a deontological approach to ethics will agree that this is the best way of doing ethics, although they may not agree on which rules should guide true morality. It is important to remember that the modern options we will discuss in this chapter – deontology, consequentialism and virtue – name *approaches to ethics* and not content-rich moral schemes. For this reason, they are referred to as **meta-ethics**.

Often the rules in Christianity such as the Ten Commandments are thought of deontologically. Why is it wrong to break the Sabbath or covet one's neighbour's spouse? It might be enough to answer that these things are wrong simply because God declared them to be so. God is free and therefore is able to command or forbid what he wants. If there were some prior logic that lies behind the rules, then God as lawgiver simply repeats and reinforces what we might have come to know by other means. Perhaps we might think that breaking the Sabbath is wrong because of the negative consequences that come with breaking it. Everyone needs a rest from labour, so that rest is not only good for human well-being, but this goodness is what makes keeping the Sabbath *morally* good. This would be a consequentialist rather than deontological way of thinking. It may be saying something true about rest, but on its own it is theologically inadequate since it places God in a subservient role to something else, such as human reason, that is not befitting divine sovereignty.

Then again, it is possible to critique this supposition based on the sheer reality that not everyone agrees on which rules, commands and duties we ought to live by. We can appreciate that the Ten Commandments were *revealed* by God and, while some of them are not very surprising to any human culture, some are. The Ten Commandments prohibit murder, but so does the eighteenth-century BC Babylonian code of laws fashioned by King Hammurabi. Still, the requirement to keep the Sabbath and worship only the God of Abraham is surely not something that human reason alone would generate. Related to this, the revealed nature of these rules – on stone tablets, given to Moses and so on – clashes with the modern deontological tradition, which has relied on reason alone in its pursuit of a universal ethic, rather than something as particular as revelation given to some people and not others.

Moreover, within the sweep of the story the Bible tells, these commands are not given to nor intended to be followed by all people. They are given to Israel in order to highlight its distinctness from the other nations in how its people act toward the poor, toward immigrants, toward their neighbours and toward their God. In fact, the idea seems to be that they are manifestly *not* part of a universal ethic, but an alternative to all other ethics.

Finally, Martin Luther pointed out that commands that prohibit some acts (as most of the Ten Commandments do) should really be understood against the background of positive practices to which they relate.[1] Although these commands seem to stand alone in some respects (do not commit adultery, for example), they actually do not. In fact, they only make sense within a larger framework that is supplied in a much less direct way by the

---

1 Martin Luther, 'Treatise on Good Works' in *The Christian in Society I, Luther's Works, vol. 44*, trans. W. A. Lambert (Philadelphia: Fortress, 1966), 109.

creation of a people who are both produced by and who produce the Bible as their holy text. This means that the narrative portions of the Bible are crucial to the lists of commands and laws. The prohibition against adultery can only be understood within a context where there already exists the practice of faithful marriage, which is something that is given shape in the story the Bible tells. Hence in the *Small Catechism*, Luther presents a wholly positive meaning to the command not to commit adultery: 'What does this [command] mean? We should fear and love God so that we lead a sexually pure and decent life in what we say and do, and husband and wife love and honor each other.' It is only among a people who practise marriage in this way that a prohibition against adultery makes any sense.

Recent linguistic philosophy has made a similar point about the narrative context for understanding rules. The twentieth-century philosopher Ludwig Wittgenstein (1889–1951) explained how phrases like seemingly straightforward commands are actually embedded in social practices. The rule 'You cannot castle while in check' literally makes no sense unless you know the game of chess. Likewise, the tendency or perhaps temptation to isolate rules from their total social and linguistic contexts is something that must be overcome. The danger is that the practices they depend on for being understood will simply be assumed rather than highlighted, giving the *appearance* that these rules belong to a universal ethic, when in fact they are located squarely within cultural and linguistic traditions that are shot through with particular practices. Bioethicist H. Tristram Engelhardt (b. 1941) gives the example of a rule that most of us wouldn't think to question: 'It is immoral to torture or kill the unconsenting innocent for sport.' What makes this true? Apart from locating it within a Christian ethic that values life, especially innocent life, because it witnesses to the goodness of God evident in all of creation, this kind of rule might still be something most people in our cultures will agree to, but they will agree to it simply out of convention.[2] We might be able to get by for a period of time with this level of agreement, but every morality will eventually be tested to its depths to see if it stands. Indeed, Western sensitivities toward torture have in recent years been shown to be remarkably up for debate. A deontologist might claim that much of the richness that originally gave shape to the prohibition against torture has disappeared, although we only come to notice that this has happened when called on to support it in the

---

2 H. Tristram Engelhardt, *The Foundations of Bioethics*, 2nd edn (Oxford: Oxford University Press, 1996), 37.

face of strong consequentialist arguments (that is, arguments that point to projected good outcomes).

From this example and others we might think up, it should be clear that deontologists sometimes find themselves in the position of defending themselves against the charge that sticking with a certain rule might sometimes cause more harm than good. In fact, being put in this position can often clarify for a person whether the rule he or she is defending is meant to be *absolute* (never to be broken, no matter what), or whether it is meant to function with less weight than this. Some rules might simply be **rules of thumb**; they should be followed in general, most of the time. Wisdom from elders sometimes takes this form, such as when a child is told, 'Don't talk to strangers.' It is easy to think of times when a child *should* talk to a stranger, which tells us that this rule is only a rule of thumb rather than absolute. A rule is said to be *prima facie* when it is absolute except in cases where other absolute rules come into play and they cannot all be upheld at the same time. If one tries to hold to the principles of protecting innocent life and not lying, there may come a time when they come into conflict. A situation in which protecting the innocent seems to require lying to a murderer would seem to require prioritizing one of the principles over another.

It should be clear that even if one decides that deontological ethics is the best approach overall, this only solves *some* problems. The problems that are still left to be resolved are the ones I've been recounting here. Which rules, principles and duties should count the most? What is their weight relative to others? Roman Catholic teaching, for example, holds the prohibition against killing to be *prima facie* while prohibitions against lying, adultery, abortion and homosexual acts are absolute. In fact, Pope John II's 1993 encyclical *Veritatis Splendor* ('The Splendor of Truth') introduced the term 'intrinsically evil acts' to underline the exceptionless quality of the Church's prohibition against this latter group, in addition to theft, euthanasia, blasphemy and contraception. These can never be justified by the circumstance or the agent's intention, nor can they take a back seat to other acts in a *prima facie* fashion.

Once one has the right rules and has settled on how they are to be weighted, there are still always going to be questions about the *meaning* of every rule. We see this in the debates Jesus had with Pharisees over the meaning of the command to observe the Sabbath. In Mark 3, Jesus heals a man with a withered hand on the Sabbath and gets into trouble with the Pharisees as a result. The issue was that keeping the Sabbath by not doing any work on that day had required scholars to elaborate on the question of what exactly constitutes working. The Pharisees took the weight of the command to be absolute. They also considered Jesus' act of healing to be work, and thus a violation of the command. Jesus' reply – 'Is it lawful to do good or to do harm on the sabbath, to save life or to kill?' – silences them. They clearly hadn't been considering whether Jesus had done good, but only whether he had done work. In replying this way, Jesus wasn't declaring that it's all right to break Sabbath observance. Instead, he was enlivening and even reissuing the original meaning of the command to keep the Sabbath by drawing attention to its true significance. As he had announced earlier, 'The sabbath was made for humankind, and not humankind for the sabbath' (Mark 2.27).

We have been looking at specifically Christian forms of deontology. However, deontology emerged within secular ethics in the modern period as a way of underwriting principles of Christian morality using reason alone. The philosopher Immanuel Kant stands out. The Western world had, in an earlier age, been held together by common religious ties that included morality, custom and faith. Following the Protestant Reformation in the sixteenth century, however, a variety of disunities began to characterize these cultures, eventually leading to figures like Kant who sought a way of doing ethics that is available to all people regardless of who they are. Rather than depending on those things that are not shared by all people – language, ethnicity, religion, and so on – Kant's ethic based in reason alone was in principle something shared by all since it appeals only to a faculty we all have just by being human.

Kant's most famous formulation of ethics is known as the **categorical imperative**. 'Imperative' refers to something you must do. 'Categorical' means that the imperative stands regardless of what you hope to achieve by acting. He was well aware of the fact that much of what we do intends to bring certain things about. If I want to pass a test, for example, I must study for it. He is not against such things, but the imperative 'I must study for it' is not categorical; it is hypothetical. This is because it might change depending on what I hope to achieve – whatever imperatives arise from *hypothetical* scenarios are always going to be moving targets, since it is possible to find a different scenario that prescribes a different action since it aims at a different outcome.

An example Kant gives of a categorical imperative is the need for keeping promises. Because keeping a promise is tied in with what a promise is, it would be irrational to make a promise but not keep it. This will stand regardless of what might be achieved by either keeping or breaking the promise. In the past, imperatives like promise-keeping might have been given a different justification, such as Jesus' teaching in the Sermon on the Mount about oath-taking and letting one's yes be yes (Matt. 5.34–37). Kant was maintaining the traditional Christian morality but giving it a different justification, one based wholly in reason alone.

In doing this, Kant was motivated by a desire to find peace among differing moral traditions and communities. Elsewhere he wrote powerfully about the need for an international organization that could appeal to a universal ethic.[3] The creation of the League of Nations in 1920 and the United Nations (UN) in 1945 can be thought of as the fruit of Kant's vision, complete with the UN's Universal Declaration of Human Rights. These rights are meant to be true and apply across the world and therefore across all cultures, regardless of their vastly diverse moral histories, customs and traditions. The intellectual spirit of Kant's age was the Enlightenment, characterized by its reaction against authority and tradition, both associated with the medieval world that must now be surpassed. Kant's own formulation of Enlightenment as 'emancipation from self-incurred tutelage' points to the liberating function of reason that boldly breaks with the past.

Many now consider Kant's project to have failed and his vision to have been naive. According to Engelhardt's usage of some important vocabulary, 'The term *Enlightenment project* (and related terms) is used to identify the endeavor to establish a canonical, content-full morality in secular terms justifiable to persons generally. Postmodernity is the recognition that this project is in vain.'[4] One argument along these lines is that Kant was not forthcoming, or perhaps genuinely was not aware, about how particular his ethic really was. He mistook his ethic as arising purely from reason alone whereas it actually owed quite a lot to his own place in the world and in history. What Kant himself took to be moral generally aligns with centuries of Christian thinking in the West and, more particularly, also reflects the prevailing attitudes and customs of the Lutheran world of northern Europe in the eighteenth century. His single-minded intention to only use reason, in other words, disguised the many ways that other factors were at work.

Explorers like Captain James Cook were paving the way for modern anthropology at this same time. Cook's expeditions to remote islands in the Pacific led him to encounters with cultures that were extremely different from what he and his crew were used to. The Hawaiians enjoyed 'free liberty in Love, without being troubled or disturbed by its consequences', and women ate their meals separately from the men. Both of these customs

---

3 Immanuel Kant, *Zum ewigen Frieden: ein philosophischer Entwurf* (1795).
4 Engelhardt, *Foundations of Bioethics*, 23.

shocked the Europeans, especially since the Hawaiians offered no moral justifications for them except to say that such things were right and good to do. It is likely that Kant was able to get by thinking that his morality was universal because it was purely rational so long as it was not confronted with quite different cultures with strange morals. In fact, the history of European conquest of new peoples generally accounts for these differences by describing the *irrationality* of natives rather than their *immorality*. And since rationality defines humans as humans, strong moral disagreement can confirm suspicions that natives are subhuman and therefore must be ruled over.

We have looked at two versions of deontology. One is upfront about being Christian and biblical; the other tries to offer a secular account of Christian and biblical morals based in human reason alone. But the Enlightenment project of finding a shared, universal morality based only in reason actually produced a variety of other approaches, another of which is consequentialism, which we will look at next. This has led some thinkers such as MacIntyre to conclude, not only that the project has failed, but that it provided an imposing intellectual framework for what was only ever going to be a collection of somewhat arbitrary particular moral viewpoints that were nevertheless asserted as universal. Exposing the violence encoded in this project has been one of the features of our postmodern moment.

Consequentialism

If we go back to basics again and ask what it is good to do, a second modern option – consequentialism – answers it by looking at the *outcomes* of the action. A good action is one that is judged to bring about a desirable state of affairs. Should I tell a white lie about my friend's new ugly haircut? If the desirable outcome is my friend's happiness, and the truth would hurt her feelings, I might try to justify the lie on consequentialist grounds. But maybe this way of thinking is too simplistic. If I consider my friend's happiness on a deeper level, I might decide that her own development of moral courage is something I want to encourage so that she would rather hear the truth than be lied to. Are there good reasons to tell the truth – good outcomes it may bring about – beyond another person's feelings? Will the truth serve my friend or our friendship in other ways? If so, I would justify telling him or her the truth, *also* on consequentialist grounds. This example points to the fact that there are always lots of consequences one can choose to take into account while still staying within a consequentialist framework.

Plato argued on consequentialist grounds that it is just for doctors to lie to patients in order to get them to take their medicine. This alone doesn't suffice to make him a consequentialist and may instead show that rigidly adhering to a single method in ethics is something few people do, even philosophers. In truth, consequentialism as we will discuss it here is a modern phenomenon.

Modern consequentialism began with the English Enlightenment philosophers Jeremy Bentham (1748–1832) and John Stuart Mill (1806–73). Both argued for a particular version of consequentialism called **utilitarianism**, which seeks to determine whether an act will produce a net overall benefit in the world. It is, by definition, other-focused (as opposed to **ethical egoism** which seeks only to maximize benefit for oneself, an eminently unchristian view). Utilitarianism focuses on the consequences that an act will have in the world for the benefit of the greatest number of people rather than on anything intrinsic within acts themselves. Some have worried that this approach will too easily justify sacrificing a small number of people for the sake of a large number. But if the small number who will be hurt by an act will be hurt quite badly, then there is not likely to be a net increase in goodness overall. Even so, this critique continues to resonate for other reasons, which we shall look at below.

There have been many forms of utilitarianism since Mill published a book by that title in 1863. One called **rule utilitarianism** shifts the focus away from individual acts toward rules. It asks which rule ought to be applied that will lead to maximum benefits. Whereas deontology shows a preference for rules that apply regardless of whether the outcome is good or bad, rules function here as available options to be used only when the outcome is desirable. One problem is discovering what counts as a rule. How general does a rule need to be in order for it to make sense calling it a rule in the first place? After all, if it is only right to apply some rules in some cases but not in others, do they really provide much moral guidance? Wouldn't it be more important to pay attention to whatever it is that commends a rule's application, namely, the principle of utility itself?

Still, other candidates (such as the principle of love) have been proposed. Joseph Fletcher (1905–91), an Episcopal priest and ethicist, proposed a consequentialist Christian ethic based on love rather than the pleasure principle of classic utilitarianism. To Fletcher, there are no absolute moral rules apart from always acting in the most loving way. Love is always good and when it looks as though we must choose between what is good and what is loving, it is a false choice since they are really the same thing. What is considered loving will vary according to the situation, though, which is why Fletcher's profoundly influential book was called *Situation Ethics*.

If 'good' is what is most loving, something similar is applied to 'true', as Fletcher says when discussing truth-telling: 'we are to tell the truth for love's sake, not for its own sake. If love vetoes truth, so be it.'[5] Fletcher wants to steer clear of legalistic formulations that become universally applied (such as 'Never lie') as well as the assumption that the more rigid a rule, the more morally serious it must be. Instead, 'If a lie is told unlovingly it is wrong, evil; if it is told in love it is good, right.'[6] The examples of situations Fletcher discusses in which what we usually think of as wrong can actually be the most loving choice are extreme. In one example of 'sacrificial adultery', a German woman who was captured by the Russians in the Second World War became aware that she would only be released and be able to be reunited with her family if she was pregnant. She asked a guard to impregnate her and, when her pregnancy was verified, she was moved to Berlin and welcomed by her family. They supported her choice and loved the child together.[7]

Some of the most important criticisms of Fletcher's situation ethics are similar to criticisms of other forms of consequentialism. For one thing, it is almost always very difficult to predict the outcomes of our actions. So long as choosing the loving thing means choosing the option with the most loving *outcome*, it is crucial to recognize that a myriad of other factors are always at work. Might it sometimes make sense to talk about a loving choice that has a disastrous outcome, at least when viewed one way? Christian martyrs who took their children with them to be burned at the stake did so out of love. Where one stands will determine whether one considers the outcome to be a good or bad one. It may be telling that Fletcher was an advocate for euthanasia and the right to die.

Moreover, Fletcher's situation ethics is typical of other consequentialist approaches in that it restricts ethics to a sphere of difficult choices. One problem with this is that it excludes so much of everyday life. Everybody knows that what makes difficult decisions hard is that there are no purely good options. But once ethics is thought mainly to be about these kinds of cases, then entertaining the thought of doing something wrong for a good or loving outcome envelops the whole enterprise. In addition, appealing to extreme situations only works as long as the rule that it seems wise to

---

5 Joseph Fletcher, *Situation Ethics: The New Morality* (Philadelphia: Westminster, 1975), 65.
6 Fletcher, *Situation Ethics*, 65.
7 Fletcher, *Situation Ethics*, 164–5.

violate in the name of love is usually in place. How should we decide on what *those* rules are? (This problem is shared with rule utilitarianism.) Put differently, by neglecting the whole of the moral life and focusing only on difficult situations, it is not obvious what counts as a situation within which a decision needs to be made.[8]

Finally, many Christians will detect something troublingly atheistic at the heart of consequentialism. The morality of actions is reduced to their effects. Things *mean* only as much as what they *do* and no more. It could be that Fletcher himself realized this since he later renounced his Christian faith and began identifying himself as a humanist. When representatives of today's New Atheist movement address moral questions, they tend to do so as consequentialists. An example is Sam Harris (b. 1967) who argues in *The Moral Landscape* that moral questions have objectively right and wrong answers based on whether or not they increase happiness or suffering, both of which can be measured scientifically.[9]

Other critics note the way that consequentialism leads to a view of life in which every action we perform must bear such a burden of moral weight that it leaves no room for spontaneity and enjoyment. Christian ethicist Gilbert Meilaender (b. 1946) of Valparaiso University argues along these lines.[10] Why should I take the time to play with my children or plant a garden when my time might be spent in ways that generate more good for more people? In fact, isn't it true that life is most valuable when it is made up of moments, connections and activities that are difficult to account for in consequential, instrumental terms? For example, what becomes of friendship if it is called on to demonstrate its moral worth in terms of its consequences? Aren't friends precisely those people whose value to us surpasses whatever we might say about what good they do for us and others?

The force of this critique isn't just that there is no real pleasure in a life spent maximizing good consequences. It is that those things that are left out are also goods themselves. We should probably be suspicious of a moral code that includes one kind of goods and leaves out another. The ones that are left out here point to the fact that there is something particularly inhuman, perhaps, in asking people to forsake the unique and specific bonds and loves that we have in favour of the more general well-being of all.

---

8 Stanley Hauerwas makes this critique in *Vision and Virtue: Essays in Christian Ethical Reflection* (Notre Dame: University of Notre Dame Press, 1981), ch. 1.

9 Sam Harris, *The Moral Landscape: How Science Can Determine Moral Values* (London: Free Press, 2010).

10 Gilbert Meilaender, *Faith and Faithfulness: Basic Themes in Christian Ethics* (Notre Dame: University of Notre Dame Press, 1991), 89–113.

Meilaender agrees that there is something atheistic about consequentialism. The reason he gives is that it places on us the complete burden of achieving the well-being of the world. As a consequence, we are robbed of the freedom to do at least some things that do not contribute to the overall good. The spontaneous expressions of rapture and joy that are so much a part of Christian worship and Christian lives spent delighting in God's world are made to give an instrumental account of themselves, which of course they cannot.

> An obligation to love separated from the freedom to trust in God's providential care makes life a heavy burden indeed, for then we constantly bear the godlike responsibility of providing in our every action for the general well-being. The consequentialist must be a stern moralist; each action must be weighed and calculated to determine whether it really fosters the greatest good. To play with one's child, walk with one's love, read a book, write a friend, work in a garden, devote long hours to a work of art or craftsmanship, spend one's talent in a small and narrow circle – all such possibilities given in the particular time and place that is ours will (on this theory) require justification from the impersonal standpoint of universal well-being. And even if we think such justification possible, a task taken up for that reason can never be the same.[11]

The pleasurable activities Meilaender talks about (to play with one's child, and so on) don't usually have a place in a discussion of ethics. But the reason Meilaender thinks we need to include them is that they are expressions of a person's freedom from needing to think of every element of life in a strongly moralistic way. If they are also expressions of trust, as Meilaender insists they are for Christians, then we can see that they are not really outside of ethics, but perfectly at home within a richer account than we may be used to. God is the one responsible for making things come out right, for steering history in the right direction. If God is not around or is incapable of saving the world, then this responsibility will no doubt be one that the most moral among us will insist is one we ought to take upon ourselves. In the next chapter, we will have more to say about the way that, while this looks very much like ethics, it cannot be Christian. Indeed, Meilaender follows Karl Barth in insisting that if we were to develop ethics solely along the lines of being responsible for good outcomes, we would be giving in to the same temptation the serpent presented to Adam and Eve: not to trust, to love without limit and to be like God.[12]

---

11 Meilaender, *Faith and Faithfulness*, 99–100.
12 Meilaender, *Faith and Faithfulness*, 90.

However, the alternative to taking this responsibility is not to be irresponsible. The point is not that people can just do as they please since of course caring about the good of others is part of the Christian responsibility. The point is simply that sharing one's food with a hungry person can be a genuine expression of joy at the overflow of God's blessing, an indication that God's garden is a place of abundant provision, that this meal of love may include a stranger in one's own company, which is ever expanded to include unlikely and surprising guests in recognition that God sets this table and hosts the meal. Yes, such a meal might be part of a campaign to end homelessness or fight world hunger, but this is almost beside the point. A Christian ethic will have its own reasons for sharing food that are not driven by purely instrumental factors such as the need to fix a problem.

It might be argued that because God takes responsibility for the meaning and direction of history, God should be thought of as a consequentialist. God takes upon himself the outcomes of all actions, not by way of a straight, linear progression to consequences, but by way of saving us from them. God does not commit us to the fate that our acts make for ourselves, but forgives, restores and redeems people to another destiny. Such a destiny isn't contained within the simple calculus of cause and effect; the effect exceeds every natural cause. So if God is a consequentialist, we do not have to be.

Nevertheless, Meilaender even goes beyond this. To Meilaender the desire to have a universal standpoint at the neglect of our loves is a kind of 'playing God'. Ironically, though, even God's love is not 'universal' in this sense; rather, it is irreducibly particular. If we are free to do things without constantly weighing cause and effect and making calculations about outcomes, this is not because we can count on God to be a cosmic bean-counter in our place. It is because these expressions of human joy and freedom actually participate in God's own joy and freedom – and ultimately love. After all, love isn't really love if it is so austere that it must check itself to be sure it is calibrated toward achieving the greatest good. Or, finally and paradoxically, perhaps it is the case that the greatest good can only finally be countenanced by this kind of love.

Natural law

Natural law is a style of moral reasoning that attempts to derive at least some moral ideas from nature itself. Since God created the world, natural law thinkers expect that acting with, rather than against, what is natural ought to be moral. There are non-Christian and quasi-secular versions of natural law, but we will be most concerned with Christian versions, such as Thomas Aquinas's. Even so, because natural law appeals to something more widely shared than religion – to nature itself – it looks for a more widely shared set of convictions and values than those arguments that are more strongly doctrinal or tied to specific Christian practices. The idea is that some things are prohibited because they are wrong; it is not that they are wrong because they are prohibited. Much of the wisdom of Proverbs has this form, speaking truths about the reality of human life that are meant to hold without offering additional rationale. When Proverbs claims that 'Pride goes before destruction, and a haughty spirit before a fall' (Prov. 16.18), everyone can nod in agreement as though this is simply an observation about the nature of things. No one needs to be told, in addition, that pride and a haughty spirit are to be avoided.

This feature of natural law means that Christians shouldn't be surprised to find that people from other religions and moral traditions share some of the same moral convictions. Natural law thinking isn't disturbed by the fact that various cultures and religions condemn murder just as the Ten Commandments do. In fact, natural law thinking positively expects to discover many such commonalities.

Thomas Aquinas is certainly the most important Christian natural law thinker. He took the basic principle of natural law to be something that is universal – that we ought to pursue what is good and avoid what is evil. How we know the difference between good and evil partly has to do with our nature, the kinds of beings that we are. Working with Latin translations of Aristotle's writings, Aquinas agreed that all things have a nature that specifies what something is, as well as the trajectory it should pursue in order to fulfil its nature. The animal nature of humans means that we share with the other animals certain drives such as seeking reproduction and pleasure. But we are unlike the rest of the animals in other respects and Aquinas followed Aristotle in identifying what distinguishes us: reason. Using reason to reflect upon what is given to us by nature is itself part of humanity's nature, and is therefore included in discovering the natural law.

Some outcomes of natural law reflection are more straightforward than others. Those that can be lifted from 'the way the world is' sometimes focus on biology. If a healthy diet is 'good' (as in 'Eat broccoli because it is good for you'), then there is a kind of ethic that can be discerned from observing the ways that different foods affect the body. Valuing health more generally, however, isn't something that can be discerned through observation. And this is where the more significant moral questions lie. Is it good to value and pursue health? Our animal instincts furnish us with the drive to try to remain alive as well as induce strong revulsions to things that indicate poison or other contamination. Acting on instinct, however, isn't moral on its own.

Sometimes it is a faithful Christian act to violate what comes to us naturally. For example, the act of sacrificing one's life for another or for a good cause surely involves opposing the strong natural drives that in normal circumstances lead us to seek safety and comfort. At best, these normal drives establish a baseline that might provide moral guidance even though they will need to be open to revision from other sources. A good example of this is the current debate centred on the role of disgust. Scholars appear to be split over what kind of role, if any, the human feeling of revulsion to various ideas and realities ought to play in ethics. Can disgust function as a moral guide?

Those who say yes, disgust can be a moral guide, follow the reasoning of Leon Kass, chair of the President's Council on Bioethics (a US advisory group) from 2001 to 2005, who acknowledged the feeling of repugnance at the cloning of Dolly the sheep and the prospect of cloning human beings.[13] He thought this reaction was morally significant. While 'disgust is not an argument', wrote Kass, nevertheless 'repugnance is the emotional expression of deep wisdom, beyond reason's power to articulate it'.[14] But is it? Not everybody agrees.

Martha Nussbaum argues the opposite of Kass.[15] She is open to attaching wisdom to human emotions, but claims that disgust is a particularly unreliable guide. One reason is that disgust tends to follow social norms. Societies that associate disgust and pollution with the female body and insist that men and women eat separately, for example, express nothing like a 'deep wisdom' about the reality of female bodies. Likewise, if some feel disgusted by interracial marriage, the more moral course no doubt will involve attempts to *overcome* this feeling rather than yield to it.

Nussbaum insists that we need to distinguish between the mere feeling of disgust and those things that genuinely put us in danger. We should understand disgust, she thinks, as arising from impatience with our mortality and vulnerability. Because so much of what causes disgust has to do with bodies, she detects a lurking dissatisfaction with the fact that we are beings that break down and decay. Overcoming disgust, then, will actually

---

13 Researchers at the University of Edinburgh produced Dolly who was born a clone in 1996.

14 Leon R. Kass, 'The Wisdom of Repugnance', *New Republic* (2 June 1997): 17–26 (20).

15 Martha C. Nussbaum, *Hiding from Humanity: Disgust, Shame, and the Law* (Princeton: Princeton University Press, 2004).

mean embracing these bodily qualities that are simply facts of the nature of humans, which is a natural law argument. But as a natural law argument, it is important to notice that it runs in the opposite direction from Kass, who also appeals to something like natural law by understanding feelings of disgust to be morally significant. This is an indicator that in order to work, natural law arguments require something beyond observation.

Not even Thomas Aquinas believed that reflection on natural law would provide Christians with everything they need to be moral. In addition, we need positive divine law (from the Bible). Both natural law and divine law will reflect eternal law, which is God's plan and will in governing all things, but may each do so partially. Our reflection requires consideration of both. (Aquinas also wrote about positive human law, although this will only contribute toward making moral people if it also reflects eternal law, and there is no guarantee that it will. History makes this plain enough.)

According to Aquinas and other natural law thinkers, we need to pay attention to those things to which we are naturally inclined, such as the preservation of our own lives. In his argument against suicide ('Whether it is lawful to kill oneself'[16]), Aquinas brings this observation about our natural inclination to stay alive alongside several other sources. Together, they combine to give a more complete moral picture of why suicide isn't considered moral in Christian ethics. He first quotes one of the Ten Commandments – 'Thou shalt not kill' – and cites Augustine's argument that it doesn't only apply as a prohibition against killing others, but also prohibits killing oneself. Next, he cites the natural law that 'everything naturally keeps itself in being, and resists corruptions so far as it can'. His implication is that this isn't simply an interesting observation about the way things happen to be, but it is a clue that acting this way is in line with God's will for created things. Aquinas concludes by citing Aristotle who says that suicide injures the community and by making the general point that life is a gift from God which ought to be preserved. As is typical, the natural law argument is found alongside other kinds of moral arguments.

Yet, again, it is worth considering that neither Aquinas nor any other Christian thinker would argue that a person must cling to his or her own life at all costs. Jesus' call to costly discipleship and his own death for the sake of not abandoning his movement show that the desire to remain alive cannot overrule obedience to God. In this case, then, what can be known from nature is not only set alongside other considerations (such as obedience), but is qualified by them.

---

16 Aquinas, *ST*, II–II.64.5.

Some Christians draw conclusions from natural law that are controversial. This alone is an indicator of the partial nature of appeals of this sort. Those that touch on sexual ethics are some of the best known in our own time. For example, the fact that homoerotic acts are not procreative is cited as an argument showing that they are against nature and therefore immoral. Although he was incorrect about this, Aquinas thought that homosexual acts aren't found among other animals and drew a natural conclusion from it. Critics insist that this shows that what we call 'natural' is often just an imposing way of expressing moral views that we hold for other reasons. After all, we have already seen that Aquinas believes humans are *unlike* other animals when it comes to reason. Perhaps we are *like* other animals when it comes to sex, but perhaps we aren't. Deciding that would seem to be prior to appeals to natural law itself.

Moreover, some critics will point out that there is a problem with assuming that all sex acts must be inherently procreative. Aquinas argued that non-procreative sex acts (not only homosexual ones) are unnatural and lustful.[17] It is clear that procreation is very important and (at least in humans and many other species) what Aquinas called the 'natural manner of copulation' is necessary for it to happen naturally (as opposed to artificially). But the requirement that all sex acts be inherently procreative isn't as clear and it cannot be established by natural law.

The debate about sex and procreation is worth thinking about more. What is the significance of the fact that one group of people think they find something obviously moral that flows from nature's design whereas it is not obvious to others? What are trees doing when they are raising their branches? Are they doing what they need to do in order to 'keep themselves in being' by maximizing photosynthesis? This is how things look to the eyes of science that see only naturalistic explanations for things. Are the trees lifting their limbs in praise of God their creator? This is not obvious if we look at things naturalistically, but what if it is the most significant thing we can say about trees? Christians will want to develop eyes to see every tree as a worshipper of God. It is just not clear that this can come from most formulations of natural law.

In addition to these attempts to read morality off the page of the observable, natural world, the use of reason as a source for discovery of natural law is also debated. Theologians have long argued over the extent to which the Fall affects the reliability of faculties like reason and the will, or desire. Anglican theologian Richard Hooker (1554–1600) noted that human

---

17 Aquinas, *ST*, II-II.154.11.

sinfulness means that we are in a situation in which our reason desires God but cannot find God.[18] Martin Luther was more sceptical, insisting that we should distrust reason and our innate judgements. When arguing that God arbitrarily offers salvation to some and not others, Luther was aware that such an idea seems unjust. But he insisted that because God is 'incomprehensible and inaccessible to man's understanding', so too is God's justice.[19] One day, says Luther, God's justice and righteousness will be shown to be what they are. In the meantime, our task is to learn to distrust our moral instincts as they apply to God.

This points to some of the key dynamics we have been rehearsing in this section. How much should we pay attention to moral instincts? Do they convey 'deep wisdom' to us? Are they sometimes inadequate? Can they even lead us astray on occasion? Returning to Jesus' teaching about loving one's enemies, for example, we appreciate that it is so radical that the teaching itself comes with the acknowledgement that it goes against our 'natural' moral instincts:

> You have heard that it was said, 'You shall love your neighbour and hate your enemy.' But I say to you, Love your enemies and pray for those who persecute you, so that you may be children of your Father in heaven; for he makes his sun rise on the evil and on the good, and sends rain on the righteous and on the unrighteous. For if you love those who love you, what reward do you have? Do not even the tax-collectors do the same? And if you greet only your brothers and sisters, what more are you doing than others? Do not even the Gentiles do the same? (Matt. 5.43–47)

There is something perfectly rational-sounding about only loving those who love us back. But this doesn't mean that it is actually rational since it is out of harmony with our nature as God's creatures who have been created in the divine image to love with the indiscriminate love of the Father. Jesus' followers are given an ethic that surpasses the ethics of the Gentiles. As a result, what we thought we knew about what it means for something to be in conformity with reason is vastly enriched and expanded. What is at issue isn't the proper working of reason itself, but correctly identifying and understanding our nature. It takes Jesus commanding us to do something that doesn't come naturally, let alone seem natural or rational, in order to arrive at a genuine Christian ethic. Then again, notice that we actually come more fully to understand our nature through Jesus' neighbour-love

---

18 Samuel Wells and Ben Quash, *Introducing Christian Ethics* (Oxford: Blackwell, 2010), 119.

19 Martin Luther, *On the Bondage of the Will* (1525), xix. Cited in *Martin Luther: Selections from His Writing*, ed. John Dillenberger (New York: Anchor Books, 1962), 200.

teaching rather than arriving at a neighbour-love ethic independent of Jesus. This kind of observation leads some to distrust talk of natural law altogether in favour of appeals to divine commands and revelation. This is not because God is against reason, but that we are prone to rationalize and dignify sinful desires using the language of morality.

It should be clear that appealing to what is 'natural' is not very straightforward. Natural law is usually thought to belong to what theology calls the 'order of creation' rather than the 'order of redemption'. It constructs an ethic on the basis of how things were created and what they were intended to be and to be for. The idea that the nature of things includes their purpose, end or *telos* is something for which Thomas Aquinas is very much in Aristotle's debt. But Aquinas also knew that Christians will conceive of ends differently from how a pagan philosopher will. Christians don't just discern the purpose of something on the basis of how and why it was created; they come to see what things are truly for in how God is redeeming the world. And the story of redemption isn't just a return to origins and original designs. God redeems things precisely by 'repurposing' them. Yes, in the process of being repurposed, we come to find out what the original purpose was after all. Creation and redemption aren't opposed to each other. But this is a discovery that only comes about as things are being redeemed and not before. This is why Jesus Christ, our Redeemer, is more decisive for any genuine Christian ethic than is, say, the book of Genesis. Better still is reading the story of origins and purpose with new eyes, seeing made possible by the one who makes all things new. Indeed, this was the ancient Christian practice.

6

Contemporary challenges

Christian ethics is never done in a vacuum. It is always done alongside and in conversation with other disciplines like theology, philosophy, history and many others. And like all disciplines, it reflects and responds to characteristics of its time and place, including the reigning convictions of the cultures in which it is produced. In our day, the contexts of Christian ethics in the West can be described in many ways. One context is the past several hundred years of modern moral theory that seem to have produced a limited range of options for doing any ethics whatsoever.

Several urgent challenges have arisen in reaction. This chapter tells a story through what readers will see are some relatively complex philosophical and abstract arguments. A different approach would achieve less depth but cover more ground. The approach I have taken here goes as deep as we need to in order to detect how many of these challenges are interrelated.

We can trace three significant moves for Christian ethics in the wake of modern moral theory. All three express different kinds of exasperation with the ethical options in modernity. The first involves voices like Søren Kierkegaard and Dietrich Bonhoeffer who throw the very idea of ethics into question by seeing it as an alternative to genuine living faith. If ethics is abandoned, however, are all choices simply relative to all others? Alasdair MacIntyre represents a different critique of modern moral theory that also can appear relativistic as long as the modern options are thought to be the only options. His solution, however, differs from Kierkegaard and Bonhoeffer, emphasizing communal traditions rather than individual faith. It is against this that the third move is made from postcolonial theorists whose critique of using tradition in this way is meant to show that traditions don't tend to represent themselves honestly. Instead, traditions (like the abstractness of the modern theories) neglect and overpower elements that, in practice, produce untold political and military victims. This final challenge relates to the way that the story of Christian ethics in the West is told, not walled off from the rest of the world.

Christian critiques of ethics in general

Some serious Christian critiques of the whole project of doing ethics in the first place have arisen in response to the modern ways of doing ethics outlined in the previous chapter. One of the most important comes from the nineteenth-century Danish philosopher Søren Kierkegaard (1813–55). In his book *Either/Or*, Kierkegaard distinguishes between two ways of life, which he calls *aesthetic* and *ethical* existence. Living aesthetically means reacting pre-reflectively to situations involving pleasure and pain. He argues that a person may move past the aesthetic to the ethical in which the will is engaged in making choices that may decisively alter one's existence. The ethical person will come to terms with his or her own exercise of free choice, including the fact that there are unknown possibilities that might have been realized by choosing differently. The ethical is, for Kierkegaard, a more mature way to live, but is also one that may only be recognized as more mature when viewed from the ethical side. From the aesthetic side, the ethical appears laden and burdened, even obsessed with the thought that every moment in life calls for conscious decision-making between good and evil, right and wrong.

On these grounds, Kierkegaard makes clear his preference for a third, even higher, option: the *religious*, which he treats at length in his book *Fear and Trembling*. There Kierkegaard reflects on the story from Genesis 22 in which Abraham is commanded by God to sacrifice his son Isaac. In particular, Kierkegaard notes that Abraham is asked to do something that is manifestly unethical (kill his son). No respectable ethic includes this kind of act within it. On the other hand, the Bible clearly commends Abraham for his willingness to do it. Both the Old Testament and the New Testament applaud Abraham's faith. To make sense of this, Kierkegaard argues that the story displays two different ways of acting that differ sharply: the *ethical* and the *religious*.

As before, the ethical searches for ways of acting that are universal, that make sense to everyone. When a person acts this way, he or she is understood and admired by other people. So according to the ethical, Abraham is a murderer (or would be if he had actually carried out the sacrifice of Isaac). In talking about ethics this way, Kierkegaard was responding to the strong influence of the German philosopher Georg Wilhelm Friedrich Hegel (1770–1831) who sought a comprehensive account of ethics. Kierkegaard wanted instead to argue for the provisional nature of morality in which we should finally abandon ethics (as Hegel understood it) in favour of the *religious*. After all, the story doesn't condemn Abraham but praises him because it is aware of a deeper but also deeply troubling way of acting and being. The religious person must take a leap of faith in full awareness that no one will understand him. Rather than following universal guidance, Abraham needed to follow the particular command of God – to Kierkegaard, this is too bad for the universal. Because it cannot (and probably should not) be generalized beyond the concrete instance, the particular is a way of behaving that can never be codified or recommended to others. No one suspects the Bible of wanting to commend human sacrifice generally. But Abraham was confronted by God in a crucial moment that called for a decision based on sheer faith, without reference to the codes of ethics or custom.

Kierkegaard refers to Abraham's religious-inspired decision to sacrifice Isaac as the 'teleological suspension of the ethical'. Abraham *suspends* but doesn't *reject* the judgement that would make him a murderer. He does what the religious requires in this particular circumstance but which cannot be understood by theory. The limitations of the ethical approach are clearly shown, particularly the idea that ethics is universal and general. In the same way, the Abraham story is not being used to show that the ethical is invalidated generally; it is just put in its place and surpassed by the religious. This, it will be obvious, is a problem for anyone wanting an ethic that is also Christian.

The thing to notice is how Kierkegaard is raising a Christian objection to the very idea of ethics. Why would we even need ethics in the first place? Because we have abandoned the religious, because we lack faith or because we are looking for ways of assuring ourselves of our own goodness apart from the crucial moment of obedience to God's command. When God commands, a person must obey without consulting the rule book or first checking this concrete circumstance against ethical theories. Rules are given ahead of this encounter and we must puzzle over whether a given situation calls for the application of a rule, whether another rule applies, or face the prospect that perhaps we lack a rule for a time such as this. And this goes for both deontological and consequentialist approaches. But in the time of God's command – the *now* of God's confrontation with the person who is before only God – the truly religious response is what is called for, even though it defies ultimate explanation and no one will understand the one who acts solely on faith.

Kierkegaard has sometimes been blamed for inventing modern, moral relativism with the idea of criterionless choice. If there is no theory (such as deontology, consequentialism or natural law) that can justify choosing one way rather than another, then what can we say is the *reason* for ever choosing one thing over another? Does our choosing simply come down to personal preference and taste, like a person's choice of chocolate over vanilla ice cream? In the absence of more fundamental criteria for choosing, Kierkegaard's idea of the religious approach is accused of being alone, free-standing and detached from all moral deliberation. Thus the charge that he has left our choosing to be only arbitrary and therefore simply relative to the various tastes of individuals. (This is Alasdair MacIntyre's claim in his seminal work *After Virtue*. See the next section in this chapter.)

What Kierkegaard calls the religious is beyond ethics, beyond the calm situations in which one may patiently weigh pros and cons, rights and wrongs, good and evil. We spoke this way when offering a Christian critique of consequentialism. Faith lies beyond knowledge; hope can never be nailed down with certainty; love defies instrumentality. But if these are key Christian responses to God, then, whatever else needs to be said, the way of living that Christianity promotes must nevertheless include these. Acting on faith means acting in spite of or in ignorance of consequences, but acting anyway, even in the face of great trials. Here Christian ethics is at its most deontological, not for trying to follow rules legalistically, but for relying solely on faith. This is why Christian ethics is less like a formula or calculation and more like the pattern of cross and resurrection. Christ himself obeys even unto death and, in this, throws himself, his future, and the meaning and outcome of his faithfulness at God's feet. God redeems his life through raising him up and promising that those whose faithfulness is cross-like will likewise be raised with Christ in the end. This is surely beyond all modern ethics.

Notice that, in this, Kierkegaard is not making the argument that there is no such thing as ethics or that ethics is impossible. He is saying that religion – Christianity specifically – is in the difficult position of undoing itself (losing its faith) if it places too much stock in ethics. The German Lutheran theologian Dietrich Bonhoeffer wrote similarly. According to Bonhoeffer, there is no moral certainty in the world even though ethics names the discipline of trying to achieve it.

Like Kierkegaard, Bonhoeffer believes that all actions must be delivered up to God for judgement. We can't know with certainty ahead of time whether what we are choosing is the right course, but we will be tempted to try this with the help of ethics. Bonhoeffer is resolute:

We cannot ... even set foot in the field of Christian ethics until we have first of all recognized how extremely questionable a course we are pursuing if we take the 'ethical' and the 'Christian' as a theme for our consideration or discussion or even as a subject for scientific exposition.[1]

We are always in the middle of things and therefore not in a position to see things from an objective point of view. Every choice, decision and act is carried out from this middle place. It is a risky step into the unknown. Each of us is a living, mortal, finite creature and 'not essentially or exclusively a student of ethics'.[2] Every situation is unique and concrete and not distinctly 'ethical' in any larger sense. We may want to classify this situation that we are facing as the classic dilemma of whether to lie in order to save a life, which is something philosophers have thought and written about for hundreds of years. So we might consult their wisdom and help to formulate a response.

Nevertheless, Bonhoeffer worries that in doing so, we would be simplifying and reducing the actual details of this specific and concrete situation in order to classify in this way. We will be tempted to take comfort in ethics, in other words. We will be drawn to making what seem to be tough decisions before we find ourselves in them, before we are actually faced with the concreteness and historical specificity of real-world situations, all of which are impossibly complex, with hosts of factors that we couldn't have known ahead of time, and which certainly can't be reduced to tidy schemata that we might look up in books. Nevertheless, as long as ethics exists, we will appeal to its shortcuts and abstractions until, in the situation itself, we discover that what we might have thought of as exceptions are actually the most crucial elements to consider.

For instance, in his book *Ethics*, Bonhoeffer discusses the matter of telling the truth. He gives the example of a schoolboy whose teacher asks him, in front of the class, whether his father comes home drunk. It is true that the boy's father does this, but the boy denies it. He recognizes that what he is being asked is inappropriate in this public setting; the family has its own problems that the teacher has no desire to understand. The teacher wants only to simplify the situation into a simple yes or no question. Bonhoeffer calls the boy's denial a lie, but blames the teacher for his lie. Beyond the privacy of the boy's family situation, his youth is also a moral factor in this case: the boy is being asked to deal with matters above what his maturity is able to handle. Because the teacher neglects this as well, Bonhoeffer believes the teacher is to blame for the boy's lie. The problem is that the teacher did not create the conditions in which the boy could tell the truth

---

1 Dietrich Bonhoeffer, *Ethics*, trans. Neville Horton Smith (New York: Touchstone, 1995), 259.
2 Bonhoeffer, *Ethics*, 260.

in a fully truthful way. The boy couldn't respond in a way that respects the seriousness of the truth about his father and of the concrete way he was being invited to address that truth in that setting.

More generally, Bonhoeffer described the limits of ethics (or the subordination of ethics to faith), using the biblical story of Adam and Eve. He noted that they were tempted to gain the knowledge of good and evil and therefore to be 'like God'. Being like God is sometimes considered a good thing, but not always. Bonhoeffer pointed out that the Garden of Eden is a situation in which it is not necessary to know good and evil, that is, to be able to think through the internal logic of what distinguishes them. Instead, it is enough simply to obey God. Gaining the knowledge of good and evil renders God unnecessary since now one may rely on one's own moral knowledge rather than the command of God. 'The knowledge of good and evil is therefore separation from God.'[3] In fact, Adam and Eve are expelled from both God and the garden. They now have a knowledge that is necessary only if God is no longer present with the original immediacy to humans. Bonhoeffer was teaching that we study ethics because we don't want to trust in God.

As with Kierkegaard, Bonhoeffer is offering a Christian critique of ethics by explaining why humans seem to want ethics in the first place:

> The knowledge of good and evil seems to be the aim of all ethical reflection. The first task of Christian ethics is to invalidate this knowledge. In launching this attack on the underlying assumptions of all other ethics, Christian ethics stands so completely alone that it becomes questionable whether there is any purpose in speaking of Christian ethics at all. But if one does so not withstanding, that can only mean that Christian ethics claims to discuss the origin of the whole problem of ethics, and thus professes to be a critique of all ethics simply as ethics.[4]

Kierkegaard and Bonhoeffer offer similar critiques of all ethics, including Christian ethics. Either God or ethics is necessary for human goodness, but not both. If one has God, notions like good and evil are redundant since obeying God is all one needs. On the other hand, with ethics comes the ability to distinguish good from evil, as well as the likelihood that one will puzzle about God as Socrates did, asking questions like whether God is God because he is good, or whether goodness is good because God commands it. Questions like these can seem absurd for reasons that Kierkegaard and Bonhoeffer understood.

---

3 Bonhoeffer, *Ethics*, 22.
4 Bonhoeffer, *Ethics*, 21.

How shall we respond to these challenges, especially given the tasks of books like this one? One valuable lesson I believe we ought to take from them is that Christian ethics ought to be provisional. If there is a danger that Christian ethics becomes an idol, taking the place of God, it is when its ideas, principles and convictions become too self-assured and self-confident, replacing or avoiding faith in specific, lived, moral questions by appealing to theory. When Christians respond this way, they may be accused of giving in to the opposite of theory-heavy ethics. They may be accused of relativism, but there are better alternatives. We will look at this in detail in the next section.

A more positive response to these challenges lies in not only acknowledging but also celebrating the fact that most of life is simply to be lived and enjoyed in freedom before God rather than be subjected to what Bonhoeffer describes as 'constant criticism, fault-finding, admonition, correction and general interference'.[5] These consequences arise when it is assumed that every aspect of life must fit within the general principles of the ethical – they threaten to overburden life. Instead, God commands what is good for us, what will bring deep joy and set us free. God's command 'does not only forbid and command; it also permits'.[6] In fact, domains of life like friendship and play that might strike us as most free of moralizing belong at the centre of a Christian ethic, but only if it rejects 'all the frowns of "ethical" existences'. These domains are most notably free of necessity. They point to and express a better way of living – one, ironically perhaps, that is better than what Kierkegaard called the ethical existence! Bonhoeffer saw this: 'Perhaps, then, what Kierkegaard calls the "aesthetic existence," far from being excluded from the domain of the Church, should be given a new foundation within the Church. I really think so.'[7] This absence of ethics may turn out to be the greatest Christian contribution to ethics. 'Who ... in our time can still with an easy mind cultivate music or friendship, play games and enjoy himself? Certainly not the "ethical" man, but only the Christian.'[8]

Moral relativism and the new Aristotelianism

Problems of moral relativism are prompted by increased awareness of other cultures and attempts to reason across them. Moral disagreement across

5 Bonhoeffer, *Ethics*, 261.
6 Bonhoeffer, *Ethics*, 272.
7 Bonhoeffer, *Ethics*, 283, n. 2, from a letter from prison dated 23 January 1944.
8 Bonhoeffer, *Ethics*, 283, n. 2.

traditions and cultures is simply a fact that can be described empirically. There is the additional question of whether or not moral judgements are absolute or simply relative to the person, group or tradition making them. If our moral judgements represent a basic commitment to the choice of one moral framework over another, can any justification be given for making this choice in the first place? These are *meta-ethical* questions because they hover *above* actual ethics and ask what we should make of the fact that there are so many. One answer to this fact of moral diversity is given by political liberalism in its value for toleration of the differences.

Liberal toleration is only a partial response, however. Ethics traditionally is a **practical rationality**, a way of reasoning that eventually issues in action. It tries to answer questions about what we should do. In the face of differing and even competing moral frameworks, the *doing* that toleration commends is fairly modest; it offers an ethic of deliberation and conversation that tries to hold the differing conceptions of the good together and long enough to be heard by all. What it is not equipped to do on its own is move the debate along toward a resolution. This may not be a weakness of toleration (after all, it grew out of meta-ethics, not ethics), but it points to its procedural character. On its own, toleration of rival viewpoints isn't trying to be a content-full ethic.

On the other hand, every attempt to be tolerant actually does include limits as to what it will tolerate. In order for constructive, open dialogue to flourish between moral communities, those who have other goals or who are determined to make irrelevant contributions need to be kept from doing so. This means that toleration is not completely devoid of having its own ethical content. If there are forms of moral relativism that go further than making observations about the fact of cultures with differing moral frameworks – that is, they go on to offer a normative ethics of toleration in response to that fact – then it is only honest to regard this ethic as one among many rivals. To claim that it is above (*meta-*) all others or that it is being offered from a neutral vantage point undercuts its original reason for being, which was that it was made necessary by the fact that all ethics are relative to those who hold them.

Recognizing this apparent paradox, some recent ethicists have insisted that *liberalism is itself a tradition*, and not just a procedure for mediating between competing traditions.[9] If so, then no matter how one faces rival moral traditions, we are back to square one in which we only ever do so

---

9 For example, Jeffrey Stout, *Democracy and Tradition* (Princeton: Princeton University Press, 2004).

from within the moral frameworks we are working with. This may not be a reason to despair, however. It is true that Enlightenment liberalism arose by opposing itself to tradition and celebrated courageous free choice based on reason alone. Even so, as long as liberalism can admit that it too is a tradition, it might lead to constructive conversation among people and groups who share enough in common that they will agree to adopt it as a procedure. The thing that hasn't been discovered, though, is a normative ethic that exists above the failure of all other ethics to be objective.

We have already encountered the contemporary philosopher Alasdair MacIntyre, who has made the above argument most prominently. MacIntyre is a well-known critic of what he calls the 'Enlightenment project' which sought ways of reasoning morally that are open to all people. Kant was a figure we have looked at in depth in this regard. MacIntyre's main contention is that in modernity the moral debates have not only become tiring for opposing sides that seem to get nowhere with each other. The situation is worse than this: the debates are in principle irresolvable. They are likely to go on for ever because of the fact that the moral language in which modern moral debates are waged is disconnected from the traditions that gave rise to them in the first place. In this book, I have grouped deontology, consequentialism and natural law together because these are the kinds of modern moral frameworks that MacIntyre believes are often employed in disagreement apart from richer traditions.

In response to an awareness of competing traditions of moral discourse, the modern approaches tried to cut across all of them. But because their particular traditions were now a liability, ties to them needed to be severed or downplayed. The title of MacIntyre's book *After Virtue* (1981) is a reference to our situation now, which comes after traditions that in former times made sense of things like the virtues. We are left with moral fragments of abandoned traditions. When they come into conflict, however, the result is not anything as robust, useful or interesting as the attempt to find the better tradition. Instead, moral language terms (like 'rights', for example) are used in debates as stand-ins for the speaker's emotions, even though they may give the appearance of intellectual sophistication.

MacIntyre's critics dispute the *inherent* interminability of moral debates in modernity. Perhaps these debates simply take a long time, as with the debates in Britain and the United States over slavery. Even though these debates took longer than they should have (especially in the United States), they nevertheless still reached a conclusion. MacIntyre's critics fault him for being undemocratic, of not having faith in democratic procedures and institutions, which themselves sometimes claim only to be in the modest position of brokering rival viewpoints. Unfortunately, nineteenth-century debates over abolition of slavery were very often debates *within* a single (albeit fractured) Christian tradition over the meaning and interpretation of the Bible. In the United States, even though many rational arguments were offered in this debate, even appeals made within a content-full tradition among those who share the same text were not able to resolve the question of slavery; it was decided through the shedding of blood. According to historian Mark Noll, one outcome of this crisis was a shift *away* from using appeals to the Bible in public debate, perhaps out of despair upon discovering that Christianity was failing to function as a morally coherent tradition.[10]

Then again, as Noll observes, disagreement about slavery among American Christians was highest among Protestants who had the greatest respect for the individual's freedom of conscience. Catholic observers at the time contrasted this with their own church hierarchy and mediating institutions of teaching the Bible and doctrine, which much more consistently opposed slavery. Not only are there many different Christian traditions, but many different attitudes toward tradition itself within Christianity. Since writing *After Virtue*, MacIntyre has become a Roman Catholic and a celebrator of Thomas Aquinas's ethics of virtue.

The more general point that MacIntyre has been arguing for decades is that moral relativism only *appears* to be a response to all moral thinking when it is really just a response to the modern options. These options, such as deontology, left their content-full, community-dependent moral traditions behind. In the case of modern deontology, once the idea that God issues commands was left behind by the Enlightenment, all that remained was the idea that there are moral rules that must be obeyed. Thinned out, ideas like this are easily dismissed, which the nineteenth-century German philosopher Friedrich Nietzsche did with great style. But, again, MacIntyre's argument is that this dismissal is historically rooted and specifically only applies to critiques of 'the Enlightenment project' that offered competing universals and sought an independent moral standpoint that doesn't exist. The alternative, MacIntyre insists, isn't relativism, but a return to pre-modern moralities (such as Aristotle's in *After Virtue*, and Aquinas's in subsequent works) that the Enlightenment rejected.

Stanley Hauerwas has been strongly influenced by MacIntyre's critique of liberalism and modern moral theory. Unlike the philosopher MacIntyre,

---

10 Mark A. Noll, *The Civil War as a Theological Crisis* (Chapel Hill: The University of North Carolina Press, 2006).

however, Hauerwas is a Christian ethicist and in his early work can be thought of as responding to Joseph Fletcher's consequentialist proposal of 'situation ethics', which we encountered in the previous chapter. Recall that Fletcher rejected ethics that focus on inflexible rules and principles, instead calling for moral agents to consider every concrete situation, asking what is the loving thing to do.

Hauerwas agrees with Fletcher that universal ethics ought to be rejected, whether it is Kant's sort, or natural law. But Hauerwas thinks Fletcher puts too much emphasis on the moment of decision or choice (also prized by Kierkegaard) on the assumption that the facts of a situation are straightforward and all that is called for is to respond to the difficult task of knowing what to value. Instead, Hauerwas argues that we have moral vision, that what we see is already the result of who we have become by way of other actions we have taken in our lives. So 'moral behavior is an affair not primarily of choice but of vision'.[11] *Seeing* a situation one way as opposed to another is not a simple matter of opening our eyes, but comes about as interpretations and descriptions that are based on our characters. Our characters, though, are in turn shaped by other actions we have taken. This means that we encounter ethics earlier than the moment of an existential choice or decision; we can only act in the world we can see.[12]

Hauerwas claims to take embodied context more seriously than Fletcher does, since the person of the agent embodies a character that influences how he or she 'sees' (interprets and describes) situations. If we witness one army killing another, have we witnessed murder, a slaughter or a war? The vocabulary is already a moral description. Pro-life and pro-choice descriptions of abortion that range from 'murder' to 'termination of pregnancy' are likewise already descriptions that are morally laden in very different ways. This means that the moral life is not able to be reduced to a string of moral decisions and choices. Instead, the 'moral life is a struggle and training in how to see'.[13]

There is an additional element to Hauerwas's approach that he adapts from MacIntyre. This moral training in how to see is not an achievement of individuals but comes about in the context of a community that lives together a particular way. The trick is to be part of what Hauerwas calls 'a community of character', a society or subculture that in its common life

11 Stanley Hauerwas, *Vision and Virtue: Essays in Christian Ethical Reflection* (Notre Dame: University of Notre Dame Press, 1981), 34.
12 Iris Murdoch, 'The Idea of Perfection' in *The Sovereignty of Good* (New York: Routledge, 2002), 36.
13 Hauerwas, *Vision and Virtue*, 20.

develops certain kinds of individuals to be people that they could not have become on their own. This social context comes close to what is sometimes called the spirit of a place or group, or in the world of business is referred to as corporate culture. When they rejected tradition, Enlightenment thinkers like Kant dismissed the crucial role that moral communities play in the life of an ethic.

For Hauerwas, much more than for MacIntyre, the primary community he has in mind is the Church. Yet in Hauerwas's work, the Church is very often contrasted with other communities, such as the political communities of the United States and other nations, with attention to the kinds of people these communities produce. Since these communities tend to be held together by thin procedural bonds like liberal toleration, they aren't likely to be communities of character. The spectre of relativism only arises at this point if political communities are taken to be the only ones. Hence by pointing to the Church as a genuine community of character, Hauerwas is essentially identifying the alternative to relativism that MacIntyre also sought to identify by looking to the moral traditions of Aristotle and Thomas Aquinas, both of whom took ethics to be community-dependent.

Earlier we saw how Kierkegaard wanted to separate the religious from contact with ethics in general in view of the need to have a distinct preserve for the exercise of the will apart from the kinds of universal moral knowledges he identified in the work of Hegel and his followers. If it is to be genuinely Christian, Christian ethics must go it alone and be prepared not to be understood by all other human codes. Bonhoeffer, likewise, thought that a key role for Christian ethics is to give an account for what he calls the 'problem of ethics' – the fact that we ask moral questions to begin with, and devote our thinking to answering them. Only a fall from union with God explains why ethics becomes a human problem.

John Howard Yoder, the twentieth-century Mennonite theologian we have discussed earlier, also offered a critique of all modern ethics. But Yoder aimed his critique more precisely at the implication that our goal is to get the theory right. Yoder was suspicious of tidy systems of thought. In an essay called 'Walk and Word: The Alternatives to Methodologism', Yoder, like Bonhoeffer, appeals to the language of discipleship – the active language of moving, walking, following – to attack moral theories that tend to be static, fixed and unchanging. He asks how modernity has given us several sophisticated ethical theories, all of which present themselves as completely rational and universal.

Life isn't a theory and we encounter situations through a variety of means and in diverse moods and states of mind. What seems fully rational may not even become a factor. This may be for aesthetic reasons (as Kierkegaard presented them) or for the simple reason that our wills immediately dismiss them as options that deserve serious consideration. Still, Yoder is more concerned about the moral life of Christians than about the academic discipline of ethics. He writes that 'The worst form of idolatry is not carving an image; it is the presumption that one has – or that a society has, or a culture has – the right to set the terms under which God can be recognized.'[14] Like anyone else, though, Christians are vulnerable to taking shortcuts by which we might bypass more difficult matters by appealing to general formulas. Instead of actually looking for God and being open to the possibility that God will speak in new or surprising ways, Christians will often rely on moral resources that render the present-tense existence of God and the Christian community redundant.

Yoder presented an account of Christian existence that resists boiling the fullness of the Christian story – including the Bible's story – down to a formula, to some maxims, or to a select number of rules or principles:

> Form must follow function in the sense that *if* the function in question is the continuing accountable common life of a people, whose members call one another to renewed faithfulness to the call of the God who has entered human affairs to save, *then* the forms of that community's discourse must be no narrower than the story itself.[15]

Christians are people who claim the story of God as their own story and seek to live within it and extend it by their living. Just as Kierkegaard and Bonhoeffer also saw, Christian ethics threatens to stamp out the vitality and spirit of actual Christian existence if it transfers the meaning of goodness and faithfulness on to some kind of scheme that may aid in difficulties being decided ahead of time, but at the cost of a more adventurous and authentic form of discipleship.

Postcolonial critiques

So far, much of the language of this chapter has been abstract. But it has also been drawing attention to various critiques of ethics, and especially those modern options that separated the real lives of actual moral communities from their moral philosophies. Postcolonial critiques of ethics

---

14 John Howard Yoder, 'Walk and Word: The Alternatives to Methodologism' in *Theology Without Foundations: Religious Practice and the Future of Theological Truth*, ed. Stanley Hauerwas, Nancey Murphy and Mark Nation (Nashville: Abingdon, 1994), 89.

15 Yoder, 'Walk and Word', 90.

extend this insight by highlighting the violence embedded especially in those ethics that seek to be most universal and abstract. Inevitably left out are the local practices and historical factors that make life what it is in particular settings. These critiques recognize power imbalances between North and South since the colonial period, continuing in several forms today, including the realities of economic globalization.

We have seen that in the history of the West, liberal political communities took the place of more robust moral communities, and in displacing them were left with only thinned-out moral languages. This was MacIntyre's critique of the Enlightenment moral project. We shouldn't miss the fact that this process happened in the early modern period, the age of Western exploration, expansion, colonialism and imperialism. This isn't a coincidence, but is actually a case of ethics functioning to aid this process. An ethic that understands itself to be universal may be applied in any time or place, whether in France and Britain or in the New World. The fact that indigenous people met by Europeans shared nothing of their traditions means nothing since universal ethics are in theory portable from place to place. Violators of such ethics are quickly labelled barbaric and in need of being civilized.

The challenges to Christian ethics posed by postcolonial critiques arise more generally from **postcolonial theory**. Postcolonial theory is concerned with the dynamics of power and the production of knowledge. Who exerts control over the meanings of things? Who is left out when this happens? If meanings are related to practices, as we have been discussing, then whose practices are highlighted and whose are dismissed or ignored? Even worse than ignoring the lives of some people (often poor women and children) are the ways that thinking and knowing are constructed to ensure that they are silent and cannot participate in how power is exercised. For example, the just war tradition (see Chapter 9) has a long and complicated history in the West, but its most notable thinkers have never been the victims of conquest; they have always been on the side of conquerors. Augustine was a powerful bishop close to powerful Christian rulers. He theorized about the just use of violence in the context of employing the Church's coercive powers against heretics. Thomas Aquinas wrote during the Crusades about those cases in which Christians may justifiably fight battles. There are other dominant voices in the just war tradition, but it is telling that the theory has tended to track with military and political power. Postcolonial theory highlights these kinds of relationships.

As sometimes happens, however, attempts to get out from under one situation end up being ensnarled in versions of it in the process. A lot of postcolonial theory is equally abstract and tends to share with opponents the belief that power is exercised in a top-down fashion, even while trying to work from the bottom up. Susan Abraham, a contemporary postcolonial theologian, worries that as much as postcolonial studies are involved in critiquing the violence encoded in universalizing ethics, the result doesn't often move beyond theory.[16] It even hangs on to what another scholar calls the 'politics of the theoretical statement'.[17]

It is common to explain the dangers of overly theoretical accounts by showing how they flatten out both time and space. Real history and local practices give way to timeless, universal truths. In reality, conquerors wield theory that is just as time-bound and spatial as everything else. The difference is that their conquering strength partly comes from disguising these things. In an important recent work, Yale theologian Willie James Jennings (b. 1961) has argued that when colonists displaced native people, they reflected the loss of the theological importance of place. Once people were no longer identified by their place, they were identified by their race.[18] But because Western Christianity had also lost its sense that it was a church of Gentiles, it thought wrongly about race as well. Jennings argues that Western Christians went into the colonial period with theological ideas about their election as God's people, but having forgotten that Gentiles are included in God's salvation through the election of Israel. Retaining this idea of election, however, this Christianity latched on to race. Chosenness was readable through flesh. Those categorized as white were elect while those categorized as black could be enslaved and Christianized. But the Christianity white colonists introduced to blacks wasn't enough to change their relationship. It was a partial and selective gospel useful for this purpose.

Jennings builds his argument around four obscure historical figures, mostly European-trained historians, theologians and church leaders who worked, described and interpreted at the intersection between colonial powers and colonized people and land. The fact that these aren't household names in the history of theology illustrates a deep point he is trying to make. The best-known names are the ones who produced universal theologies and ethics that readers are not used to thinking about in the light of their historical contexts.

---

16 Susan Abraham, 'What Does Mumbai Have to Do with Rome? Postcolonial Perspectives on Globalization and Theology', *Theological Studies* 69 (2008): 376–93 (380).

17 Cited in Abraham, 'What Does Mumbai Have to Do with Rome?', 380.

18 Willie James Jennings, *The Christian Imagination: Theology and the Origins of Race* (New Haven: Yale University Press, 2010).

In much the same way that Susan Abraham is critical of postcolonial theorists who stick to theory, Jennings is also critical of how MacIntyre goes about criticizing universal ethics. There is always a gap – often a big one – between example and theory. This is normal, but there is a tendency to highlight a tradition's triumphs (such as its ideas) rather than its failures. This doesn't just apply to the gap between what a tradition thinks it is and what it actually is (or what it sets out to do and what it actually accomplishes). There are also the ways a tradition will probably fail to lament how the people the tradition has produced are far less triumphant than its ideas. A tradition's wounds are therefore its failures to live up to its own promises and stated ideals.[19]

MacIntyre approves of the Augustinian–Thomist tradition, especially in its creative and selective use of Greek sources, especially Aristotle in the case of Aquinas. Moral exemplars are deeply important to Aristotle since they embody and display dispositions of character, the virtues. In MacIntyre's estimation, this moral tradition of the virtues is superior to its modern rivals. But in how he argues for this superiority, has MacIntyre done anything other than talk about one theoretical account compared to another? What about the people that this tradition produces? Given the theory with its supposed dependence on moral exemplars, shouldn't we look to them to determine whether we're dealing with a superior tradition after all?

Jennings discusses José de Acosta Porres, a sixteenth-century Spanish Jesuit. Acosta was trained in the best that the Thomistic theological tradition had to offer in his day. He was formed in the tradition of Augustine and Thomas Aquinas, learned classical rhetoric and languages, and was formed in the life of the Church. 'By everyone's account,' writes Jennings, 'this young man was exactly what the new emerging order, . . . the Society of Jesus, hoped for – a supremely trained, profoundly devout agent of ecclesial renewal who would foster in those he taught a learned piety.'[20] MacIntyre should be impressed with Acosta's moral formation:

> [Acosta's] deepest theological sensibility was that of a Thomist, with a clear, precise doctrinal understanding and articulation joined to a conceptually clear vision of how the world is and ought to be ordered. As a Thomist, Acosta understood what the joining of Augustinian and Aristotelian logics

---

19 See Jonathan Tran, 'The Wound of Tradition' in *The Hermeneutics of Tradition: Explorations and Examinations*, ed. Craig Hovey and Cyrus P. Olsen (Eugene, OR: Cascade, 2014), 226–52.
20 Jennings, *The Christian Imagination*, 65.

meant for the rational articulation of Christian faith. His teachers understood that in Acosta they had one of the very best, very brightest students.[21]

Acosta became a missionary to Peru and quickly became caught up in the
European conquest of Latin America:

> He stepped onto the shores of Lima a theologian of the first rank, ready to
> do ministry. Not simply a Catholic theologian in the New World, he was one
> of the most important, if not the most important, bearer of theological trad-
> ition of Christianity to set foot in the New World in his time and arguably
> for at least one hundred years after his arrival. *Indeed Acosta was the embodi-
> ment of theological tradition.* He was a traditioned Christian intellectual of
> the highest order who precisely, powerfully, and unrelentingly performed
> that tradition in the New World.[22]

> When Acosta looked out onto the New World, the Christian habitus in
> which he had been shaped became the expression of a colonialist logic.[23]

How could this happen? It cannot be that Acosta was an aberration – he
wasn't. In fact, he was all too typical. According to Jennings, 'Acosta marks
[what MacIntyre terms] an epistemological crisis in the history of Christian
theology.'[24] His presence there is too difficult to explain according to the
terms we're used to using. But this was not something that Acosta himself was aware of. Nor have church historians or theologians thought that
Acosta represents a crisis to the conceptual integrity of his theological tradition. Instead, this is something that Jennings aims to argue in his book.

At stake is the danger of having overconfidence in one's own tradition.
What is the source of the overconfidence? It may be that overconfidence
is especially a problem for teleologically oriented traditions. A vision of
the *telos* might be critically and carefully held in awareness that it is, for
now, seen only through a dark glass. Or, more commonly perhaps, it will
be held with certainty and be allowed to legitimate our present causes and
pursuits. This needn't be a reason to abandon teleological reasoning, of
course. But having a handle on the *telos* can lead to neglect of other factors.
For Acosta, history was made to bend to eternity, and with his help.

It's one thing for a tradition to emerge self-consciously from a crisis or
challenge to its integrity, demonstrating its superiority as a tradition. This
is what MacIntyre's own work claims for the successes of Thomas Aquinas.

---

21 Jennings, *The Christian Imagination*, 68.
22 Jennings, *The Christian Imagination*, 68.
23 Jennings, *The Christian Imagination*, 104.
24 Jennings, *The Christian Imagination*, 70.

But Jennings raises a neglected element. It is possible to look back on earlier stages of a tradition and identify crises that were unacknowledged at the time. The fact that some Christians can come to identify Acosta, despite himself, at a kind of crossroads, may at some level demonstrate that sooner or later the tradition has succeeded by producing people who can do so. The trouble is that this gives too much credit to the tradition. After all, Acosta is never mentioned as part of the theological history of the West. Isn't it more important to ask about the flaws in the tradition he was taught and why they tend to still be with us? What kept Acosta from discerning that the crisis that Jennings calls 'traditioned imperialist modernity' was something right in his midst?

We are always 'in the middle' of something that we are unable to identify or describe. The political scientist Romand Coles points out the consistent tendency to hold others – especially earlier epochs of our own traditions – at arm's length by saying that they are 'pre-' to us. We are 'post-' to them. This tendency causes us to neglect the reality that what we are in the *middle* of, and cannot see, is much more important than what we are *after*.

I have taken the time to lay out some details in Jennings' argument because it presents such a clear challenge to some of the solutions others have proposed in the course of trying to meet *other* contemporary challenges. MacIntyre would have us respond to modern moral theory by returning to community-dependent moral traditions exemplified by local virtue. For Hauerwas, this means the Church. But Jennings warns that tradition can function badly. It can be self-congratulatory by drawing attention to its successes and turning a blind eye to its failures. Furthermore, the Church isn't innocent in the history that produced and benefited from colonial, imperialist theologies and ethics. It is part of Jennings' argument that Acosta himself embodies the start of this project, one that arose from and was expressed within the Aristotelian–Thomist tradition.[25]

Nevertheless, the colonial mindset that Acosta and those like him so easily accommodated alongside (or even because of) their ecclesial and theological formation poses questions that, Jennings argues, are still largely 'untheorized within Western Christian theology'.[26] Why is this? Could it be that there is more going on than MacIntyre's suggestion that a tradition shows what it is made of by facing challenges to its own conceptual integrity? That, in fact, the challenges it fails to notice are themselves the most significant ones precisely because it fails to notice them? Or most harmful

---

25 Jennings, *The Christian Imagination*, 71.
26 Jennings, *The Christian Imagination*, 115.

of all: could it be that failing to identify a crisis *as a crisis* is one of the ways a tradition permits itself to keep singing its own praises?

This last question matters the most for Christian ethicists who make use of the concept of tradition. One of the key postcolonial challenges is to be aware of how tradition can make us blind to people who work with and live out the tradition in ways that are not anticipated by the tradition itself.[27] All traditions are at risk of writing such people out of the tradition's history, in which case we will have a more purified account of the tradition, but at the expense of the individual.

Responsible Christian ethics will resist supporting imperialism and will instead take the time to assess how it affects vulnerable populations. In our day, this means being open to unexpected interpretations of events, ideas and texts from people whose relationship with power is quite different from our own. We must set aside all assumptions that automatically link power with truth, an assumption that may be most powerful in how we read and understand history. The lure of empire is related to a distortion caused by more or less accepting that history is basically about who is in charge. Popular history books and television documentaries are often guilty of this. Based on them, one may ask 'What exactly is history?' and conclude that history is basically two things: rulers and wars. This way of doing history tells us that the most significant people in this world are the ones with the most political power and the most firepower. What they do with all that power is what we allow to count as history itself. That's the way of kings and kingdoms from this world. An aspect of the postcolonial challenge is to bring non-imperial history to consciousness. The smallness of other communities may go unnoticed if we are only looking at empires and nation-states.

However, communities of character can be found in many places. In his book *Lest Innocent Blood Be Shed*, Philip Hallie tells the story of the French mountain community of Le Chambon. Under the leadership of their Protestant pastor André Trocmé, the people of the village hid Jews during the Holocaust, saving many lives. Hauerwas thinks of Le Chambon as a community of character. What kind of ethic did the villagers live by in order to play this risky hospitable role for these Jews? To Hallie, who encountered the story of Le Chambon in the midst of researching the Second World War, their kindness stood out to him as unusual. It didn't fit with the normal political and military language we use to describe wars.

---

27 See, for example, Kwok Pui-lan, Don H. Compier and Joerg Rieger, eds, *Empire and the Christian Tradition: New Readings of Classical Theologians* (Minneapolis: Fortress, 2007).

But Hallie was determined to bring Le Chambon back into a history dominated by large contestations of military forces:

> From the point of view of the history of nations, something very small happened here. The story of Le Chambon lacked the glamour, the wing-spread of other wartime events . . . The struggle in Le Chambon began and ended in the privacy of people's homes . . . In Le Chambon only the lives of a few thousand people were changed, compared to the scores of millions of human lives directly affected by the larger events of World War II . . . But the people of Le Chambon whom Pastor André Trocmé led into a quiet struggle against Vichy and the Nazis were not fighting for the liberation of their country or village . . . Under the guidance of a spiritual leader they were trying to act in accord with their consciences in the very middle of a bloody, hate-filled war.[28]

Not all stories and communities left out of the grand imperial narratives of history are as small as Le Chambon, but noticing them will sometimes require the same virtues. These may not be the triumphant virtues that any tradition will tout as its greatest accomplishments. Like the histories they seek to notice against the grain, they may also be under-celebrated and undervalued. In Christian ethics, the practices of listening to the weak and ignoring the powerful even at great cost are not always highlighted and cultivated, but they should be. One task is to point to the fact that they are part of the Christian tradition. The harder task is to account for why they don't always play the role that they should.

---

28 Philip Hallie, *Lest Innocent Blood Be Shed* (New York: Harper & Row, 1979), 9–10.

Part 3

THE STUFF OF CHRISTIAN ETHICS

7

Baptism and identity

One of the most basic and essential questions for any ethic is 'Who is this ethic for?' At one level, of course Christian ethics is for everybody. This is the sense in which God is calling all of creation to worship, salvation and fellowship. Describing the nature of that fellowship sociologically (as descriptions of actual congregations and communities, for example) includes some people and excludes others. But describing it as God's goal for all things gives content for a Christian ethic that is non-exclusive. Christian ethics may, in this sense, be for all people, but it arises from Christian beliefs and practices. Not everyone is interested in being a follower of Jesus Christ and aligning his or her way of living with God's will. Those who are will serve as the narrower and more immediately useful answer to our question about who this ethic is for.

This chapter's themes are political in the strict sense of having to do with how Christian people conceive of themselves and order their life together. The decisions that we make, as well as the things we do without ever thinking we have made a choice, find themselves within the communal, social and political ways that we are formed. I say they 'find themselves' there because they may or may not always 'fit'. Indeed, we may act or live in ways that are occasionally or for the long term deeply at odds with Christian common life. But noticing that we aren't fitting is actually quite an accomplishment on its own, and it indicates that what we're doing is still 'finding itself' where it is at odds.

A person's identity as a Christian begins with the corporate practice of baptism. This is not just a way that one becomes a Christian; it is the rite for becoming part of a new people, the Church. The ancient Jewish practice of naming a (male) child at circumcision on the eighth day (see Luke 1.59) was partially adopted by at least some Christians in the first few centuries; Christians from a very early point replaced circumcision with baptism while retaining the naming aspect of the ceremony. The Christian's new identity is as one who is now 'in Christ', having been 'baptized into Christ' (Gal. 3.27) and being made a child of God along with fellow believers.

We set baptism up front in this third part of the book before turning to some of the more concrete matters of ethics as a reminder that Christians aren't first individuals. As Pope Paul VI wrote in *Lumen Gentium* in 1964 (ch. 2), 'God does not make men holy and save them merely as individuals, without bond or link between one another. Rather has it pleased Him to bring men together as one people . . .' Baptism creates the Church, a body I am describing as *political* in order to invoke the concept of *polis*, the Greek word for city, which has itself served Christians for hundreds of years. In addition to other political terms like 'kingdom', 'city' provides us with a corporate image of Christian existence that implies a coherence that a collection of individuals simply as individuals doesn't have.

Identities, then, are political when they are referred to the common life of the group. By focusing on baptism here, the group we have in mind is the Church, not the nation in which a person may be a citizen. Of course Christians are also members of other groups. But Christian ethics is first for those who share a common baptism and allegiance to Christ. Baptism creates the Church and the Church grows through baptism.

Not like the other nations

The best place to begin looking at the concrete issues and questions Christian ethics faces is with the identities of the question-askers. Who are the ones who want to know what the good thing to do is? What is this 'people'? What is it about who they are that leads them to ask about the good in the first place? As we saw in Chapter 1, this is also where the Bible begins to deal in concrete matters of how to live. God had set out to rescue the Hebrews from the Egyptians in order that they would be God's own people and worship him (see Exod. 7.16). Only after it is clear that Israel owes its very existence as a nation to God does he give it the law. We see this at work in the start of the Ten Commandments: 'I am the LORD your God, who brought you out of the land of Egypt, out of the house of slavery' (Exod. 20.2). The Ten Commandments follow this sentence. It is important to notice that the Israelites are being reminded of why they ought to obey this God. This is a God who has a history with Israel. God instructed Moses to tell Pharaoh that *God's own identity* is bound up with his people: 'The LORD, the God of the Hebrews, sent me to you.' Israel is meant to live, then, in a manner consistent with who it has become through God's own doing. Because Israel's God is not the god of the other nations, Israel will live differently from its neighbours. This entails at least two things: (1) that God is Israel's king and lawgiver; and (2) that Israel's way of life will be distinctive.

1 God as Israel's king and lawgiver. Now that God has created a people to be his very own, it will not be like the other nations. The chief way it will differ is by not having a human king of its own. God is to be its *only* king (see, for example, Isaiah 44.6 in which God is called king of Israel). God's defeat of Pharaoh should be read as competition not only between two gods, but between two kings. As the story of the Bible goes on, however, the people of Israel grow weary of the idea. They demand a king of their own, which prompts Samuel to remind them that God was to be their only king and that they are rejecting God (1 Sam. 8). Samuel warns the Israelites that a human king will confiscate their lands, draft their sons for war and demand taxes. Still the Israelites demand a king anyway. Some modern readers mistake the teaching here, as though Samuel is appealing to the people's desire to be independent from 'the state'. However, the fact that a king will take these things from the people is primarily an act against God who demands, indeed already owns, the best from Israel.

2 Israel's distinctive ethic. If God was meant to be Israel's only king and lawgiver, it is natural to expect that the laws governing Israel's life together would be distinctive. The claim to *distinctiveness* does not mean that every one of Israel's laws is unshared by any other nation. After all, many of the Ten Commandments are nearly universal legislation: not murdering and not stealing, for example. Rather, distinctiveness draws attention to idiosyncratic laws that most assuredly – if actually practised – would set Israel apart. Consider this law about holding collateral for repayment of a loan:

> If you take your neighbour's cloak in pawn [as collateral], you shall restore it before the sun goes down; for it may be your neighbour's only clothing to use as cover; in what else shall that person sleep? And if your neighbour cries out to me, I will listen, for I am compassionate.　　　(Exod. 22.26–27)

It is worth noting how counter-intuitive and even anti-establishment this commandment is. Regardless of whether or not someone has repaid a loan, his or her cloak, which has been given as collateral, is to be returned. Why? Because the person might get cold without it. This is certainly no way to run a bank! Notice also that commands such as these are not simply metaphors meant to make the point that God is compassionate or to reveal that God cares about the poor. They really are commands meant to be obeyed so that the people of Israel would resemble their God's own compassion through the ways that they live. God is clearly not interested in running a successful banking system that demands the repayment of loans.

God would rather see that the physical needs of vulnerable people are met. What does this say about this God? And what does this say about who the people are who are asking such questions?

The idea I have been describing here is **election** – God has chosen a people to be his own. The point for ethics is that God has not generically delivered a body of wisdom or commands to the whole world all at once. Instead, God created a people to live in a distinctive fashion among the other people of the world in order to fix what is broken.

The New Testament radically expands entry into the people of God. God's children are those who love Jesus Christ and obey his teaching (John 14.23). Now Gentiles (members of the 'other nations' outside Israel) are potentially brought within this people through being grafted into Israel for those who are 'in Christ'. It is important to emphasize that the Church doesn't replace Israel – the dangerous idea of supersessionism we discussed earlier – but represents the expansion of God's promises to Israel to now include all people through Israel. After all, God had promised Abraham that he and his descendants would be a blessing to the nations. Israel was elected by God to bring righteousness and justice to the nations beyond itself. As John the Baptist warned Pharisees and Sadducees, 'Do not presume to say to yourselves, "We have Abraham as our ancestor"; for I tell you, God is able from these stones to raise up children to Abraham' (Matt. 3.9). Inclusion is not on the basis of being children of Abraham only, but of God making people into his people, adopting them as his own children. Christians, whether Jewish or Gentile, are those who are being brought within God's family through God's Son – that is, 'in Christ'.

What exactly does it mean to be in Christ? As far as the New Testament is concerned, this language – 'in Christ' – is not just pious language, but is a technical term referring to baptism. Those who have been baptized have been baptized 'in Christ' or 'into Christ':

> Do you not know that all of us who have been baptized into Christ Jesus were baptized into his death? Therefore we have been buried with him by baptism into death, so that, just as Christ was raised from the dead by the glory of the Father, so we too might walk in newness of life.   (Rom. 6.3–4)

The reason baptism works this way in Christianity is similar to the reason that the exodus event created the people of Israel. In fact, Paul associates the waters of baptism with the waters of the Red Sea (1 Cor. 10.1–2). He even describes the rock that Moses struck and from which the children of Israel drank by saying 'the rock was Christ' (v. 4)! Like the Red Sea, baptism creates a new people who did not exist before. The name for this new people is the Church.

This is the crucial point about Christian identity – baptism creates a new people comprising both Jews and Gentiles. It was neither obvious nor straightforward for the first Christians, who were Jews themselves, to understand how this could be. It was in fact the most debated topic in the apostolic period, as is clear from the books of Galatians and Acts (especially in chapter 15 which tells of a key council on the topic in Jerusalem). Paul was the main advocate for this theology of Gentile-inclusion even though the whole New Testament teaches it throughout. Notice in this text from 1 Peter how language previously used of Israel is now being used of the Church:

> [Y]ou [the Church] are a chosen race, a royal priesthood, a holy nation, God's own people, in order that you may proclaim the mighty acts of him who called you out of darkness into his marvellous light. Once you were not a people, but now you are God's people. (1 Pet. 2.9–10)

These key words – race, priesthood, nation, God's own people – are all the markers of Israel's identity. Yet they are now being used of a new nation, the Church. Early Christian writers such as Clement of Alexandria and Tertullian describe the Christians as a 'third race' in addition to Jews and Greeks (that is, Gentiles). What is distinctive about this third race is that it is made up of members of the other two, whom God has called out to be part of a new people. However, this new race is not *in addition* to the other races. It actually undoes the very idea of race altogether. God's purposes will be found among a people who bear none of the marks of identity that were formerly thought decisive: land of origin, nationality, gender, ethnicity.

The traditional Christian practices of baptism draw attention in a very dramatic fashion to the fact that a new identity is being created. Those preparing to be baptized entered a period of study, prayer and discernment called the **catechumenate**. In some cases, this was a period of three years. Because partaking of Holy Communion is typically reserved for those who have been baptized, traditional practice is for catechumens to leave the worship service after the preaching of the word and before the Eucharist. Then on Easter eve, the whole church gathers for a vigil in which those who have completed the catechumenate are baptized and welcomed into the Church for the first time as full members who may now receive the Eucharist.

Specific baptismal rites vary. But a common practice is to face to the west and renounce the devil and sin. This is also a renunciation of all the old identities, the things you were before. As an ancient baptismal formula puts it, 'There is no longer Jew or Greek, there is no longer slave or free, there is no longer male and female; for all of you are one in Christ Jesus' (Gal. 3.28). All of these former identities are about to be drowned and killed in the waters of baptism. And after renouncing them, the catechumen turns to face east – the direction of the rising sun, the symbolic direction for awaiting Jesus Christ's return. Here he or she declares her belief in and loyalty to Christ right before being baptized.

If all the old loyalties and identities are drowned and washed away in the waters of baptism, then the person who emerges out of the water is one who has been made new. This born-again person now lives the resurrected life of Jesus. He or she belongs to the Church which the New Testament describes as the body of Christ. One feature of this new, resurrected life is a fearlessness of death. After all, if baptism is a drowning of the old self – with all of its allegiances, loyalties, attachments and identities – then there is nothing left to worry about in being killed. Likewise, if the new life is the resurrected life of Christ, then it cannot finally be destroyed. Death has been conquered by Christ.

This dramatic fearlessness in the face of death can be seen in what seems like a strange instruction found in *The Apostolic Tradition* of Hippolytus of Rome from around AD 215:

> If any catechumens [those who are not yet baptized] are apprehended because of the Name of the Lord, let them not be double-hearted because of martyrdom. If they may suffer violence and be executed with their sins not removed, they will be justified, for they have received baptism in their own blood.

The strange suggestion that one might be baptized in one's own blood if killed for the faith only really works if baptism is thought of as itself a death. This thought is reaffirmed by Thomas Aquinas in the thirteenth century. Aquinas wrote that 'the shedding of one's own blood for Christ's sake takes the place of Baptism'.[1] Thinking of baptism this way is especially poignant in places and times where Christians are being persecuted. Since baptism essentially declares that Jesus is Lord and Caesar is not, it is a deeply dangerous act. Yet Christians are permitted to face death without fear out of confidence that in baptism they have already died.

---

1 Thomas Aquinas, *Summa Theologica*, II-II.124.2.

What are we to make of the idea of Israel's distinctiveness if, in Christ, the Church will be composed of both Jews and Gentiles? What had formerly been said of Israel, including its distinctive way of living, is now said of the Church, in terms of both kingship and its distinctive ethic.

The faithful in Israel had been awaiting a king of their own who would rule the nation in righteousness and justice. David had been the key figure for this kind of rule and was not just a concession to the wishes of the people as Saul had been. And even though God had promised David that a descendant of his would be on Israel's throne for ever, the reality did not last very long. Indeed, ever since the exile, Israel had been under foreign rule of one kind or another. Closest to the time of Jesus, the Jewish Hasmonean dynasty ruled in Israel between the Greeks and the Romans (about 140–63 BC), but this was non-Davidic. Jesus was hailed as Son of David, a theme of hope especially prominent in Matthew's Gospel. Among the Christians, this hope was seen to be fulfilled in Jesus of Nazareth whom they proclaimed as Messiah or king. Yet King Jesus is not only anointed chief over the Church; he is Lord of all. Jesus is lawgiver and judge.

The distinctive ethic that was supposed to set Israel apart from the other nations is now meant to characterize the Church in its common life. Gentiles have been grafted into Israel and God's promises to Israel. But this distinctiveness, as with Israel's, does not mean uniqueness in every respect. In fact, early Christian writings like the *Epistle to Diognetus* emphasize that the Christians are actually similar to their pagan neighbours in a lot of ways. They marry and have children like everyone else. They do not go out of their way to dress differently or to break the laws of the land. But they also live in some ways that demonstrate that their loyalty and true citizenship lies with God and not with nation or custom:

> They dwell in their own countries, but simply as sojourners [or resident aliens]. As citizens, they share in all things with others, and yet endure all things as if foreigners. Every foreign land is to them as their native country, and every land of their birth as a land of strangers.[2]

Diognetus is clear that not everything is distinctive about the lives of Christians. At the same time, the text doesn't try to argue that what sets them apart is so reasonable that any thinking person would do the same. The Christian ethic is not obviously rational. It is a way of living that might cost a person his or her life as it cost Jesus his. There is nothing reasonable about loving one's enemies even when they are in the act of killing. But if

---

2 *Epistle to Diognetus*, ch. 5: 'The Manners of the Christians'.

the example of Jesus is to be followed and imitated, as Christianity teaches, then the Church lives by an ethic that is not available for the wider world to discover on its own.

This means that the distinctive ethic of the Christians is not an ethic for every person. It is true that Christians believe that a life lived in obedience to God is always superior to the alternatives. But the obedience Christians strive for is only really possible *as a people God has made*. The ethic is inherently social and communal. It has to do with how people live together. How will they live in peace even when they disagree with each other? Will they forgive when wronged? How will they suppress the urge to seek revenge? How far will their love extend – to strangers and even to enemies? And more mundane, perhaps: how will they make and spend their money? How will they treat their employers and their workers?

Just as Israel was God's experiment for what a nation might be with God as its king, so also is the Church a kind of demonstration plot for the kingdom of God. Here members of the Church are 'citizens of heaven' (see Phil. 3.20) and are enjoined and permitted to live accordingly. There is no need to prop up nations, economies, industries or institutions. There is no prerequisite demand that Christian ethics justify itself as the most responsible path. Christians are set free to take risks that, if God were *not* king, would be utterly foolish and irresponsible.

Going public

The New Testament speaks about the Christian Church as a new people. Besides 'kingdom', of which we have already had plenty to say, there are a number of other *political* terms that are routinely used to describe the transformation of God's creation into a new creation.

One of these is **city**. Jerusalem prefigures the New Jerusalem which itself stands for the society that worships God alone. The final vision the Bible shows is of God dwelling unmediated with the world he created: a city with no Temple, but God simply in our midst, perhaps echoing the way that God originally walked with humanity in the evening breeze (Gen. 3.8). The common tendency to read the book of Revelation, which speaks about this new city, as depicting some entirely future scene is not the best way to read this text. As a text that belongs to the genre of **apocalypse** – a fairly common genre in the first century – its main purpose is to unveil, uncover and disclose the reality of the *present* world. What would the present suffering of the Christians under persecution (since this is the context in which Revelation was written) look like if the veil were pulled back and things were exposed for what they really are?

We would see things as a cosmic battle in which God battles for the good of the persecuted saints, ultimately defeating and subduing evil. The martyrs are celebrated before God for their unyielding steadfastness and commitment to the faith. In the end, violence ends and peace reigns. The city of God is a gathered humanity in which evil has no sway because God is all in all.

Jesus' title **Lord** is also a political title. Just as theology has traditionally seen Jesus fulfilling the three roles of prophet, priest and king, the language of Lord identifies Jesus as sovereign. Christ is not just one sovereign among many, but the one that surpasses them all, serving as their archetype and possibly their source. The title 'Lord of Lords' captures this and is used of God in the Old Testament (e.g. Deut. 10.17) and of Jesus Christ in the New Testament (e.g. 1 Tim. 6.15; Rev. 17.14). The threat that Jesus at the time posed to the Roman Empire was surely small. The Roman fear of Jewish insurrection had merit, and when this happened after Jesus' time under the leadership of others, Rome responded with tremendous strength. Nevertheless, from the beginning, it was the tendency of the Jesus movement to subvert the absolute claims of the emperor that made the Romans most nervous.

In our day, it is more common to miss the inherently political way that this language and these concepts struck ancient audiences. A key reason for this is the modern tendency to separate religion and politics into different spheres. According to William Cavanaugh, a theologian at DePaul University, the story of salvation that Christianity tells is a rival to the stories that justify and explain modern politics in the West. Beginning with Thomas Hobbes (1588–1679) and John Locke (1632–1704), political philosophies of the Enlightenment that gave birth to modern nation-states as we know them told a story of humanity's original state of competition and violence that politics ultimately solves. Hobbes's 'state of nature' description of humanity is the most stark since it begins by depicting humans as isolated individuals who all have equal rights to everything else. But when people desire the same things, they become enemies. This gives rise to violence and it is the job of the state to bring order and peace by safeguarding the interests and rights of individuals – a kind of salvation.

A much more ancient account also points to violence as the original state of humanity. The *Enuma Elish* was the creation myth of the ancient Babylonians, discovered in the nineteenth century in Nineveh. In it, before the creation of the heavens and the earth, the gods Tiamat and Kingu lead a rebellion against the other gods. Another god named Marduk wages battle against Tiamat and defeats her by shooting an arrow through her belly and strangling her. Marduk splits her body in half and creates the heavens from one half and the earth from the other. When he kills Kingu, Marduk creates human beings out of his blood for the purpose of serving the gods as slaves. Marduk thus is shown to be the highest god.

Many scholars believe that the opening chapters of Genesis took their final form partly in response to this Babylonian account of creation. In stark contrast, the Bible shows creation out of nothing (not blood, not dead bodies of gods). This is good news since God is not responding to prior violence and creativity doesn't depend on bloodshed. God also declares creation to be good and very good, and humans especially are given an exalted role to play (not as slaves). Rest, freedom and companionship are also built into God's good creation in the story the Bible tells.

Yes, there is a fall very early in this same story, but Cavanaugh argues that it is crucial that this is a fall *from something*. Creation was in a state of original togetherness and peace, not violence. When humans fall, they fall away from each other and God. The movement is one of scattering. But enmity is not original to creation; it is instead an indicator that disorder and sin have entered the world. Adam and Eve are separated from paradise; enmity is inserted between man and woman, humans and the rest of creation. Cain flees from home and family after the first murder, and the people who build the tower of Babel are scattered throughout the earth. Cavanaugh quotes the French Jesuit theologian Henri de Lubac who reflects on Origen of Alexandria's claim 'Where there is sin, there is multiplicity':

> True to Origen's criterion, Maximus the Confessor, for example, considers original sin as a separation, a breaking up, an individualization it might be called, in the depreciatory sense of the word. Whereas God is working continually in the world to the effect that all should come together into unity, by this sin which is the work of man, 'the one nature was shattered into a thousand pieces' and humanity which ought to constitute a harmonious whole, in which 'mine' and 'thine' would be no contradiction, is turned into a multitude of individuals, as numerous as the sands of the seashore, all of whom show violently discordant inclinations.[3]

The Bible's story of salvation begins with Abraham, and the movement now reverses to become one of gathering. God's covenant is to save not

---

3 William Cavanaugh, 'Discerning: Politics and Reconciliation' in *The Blackwell Companion to Christian Ethics*, ed. Stanley Hauerwas and Samuel Wells (Oxford: Blackwell, 2004), 201.

only Abraham and his descendants, but all nations through him. Jesus too speaks about gathering and, as an agent of salvation, he is depicted as the reconciler of the whole world. As incarnate divinity, Jesus Christ unites all of humanity into God. So the mission of Jesus to save fulfils the gathering energy begun with Abraham for overcoming the scattering of sin. This is not just a religious theme, but enacts a very distinctive politics. Modern liberal politics tries to safeguard an original autonomy, bringing people together only so far as individual interests can be served, but no further. Christian politics of salvation brings people together in Christ for the restoration of our complete humanity according to the original purposes of creation.

To truly call the biblical and Christian story of salvation a politics, however, we need to be able to point to practices that people will carry out. The pivotal ones are liturgical. A communion prayer in the *Didache* reads: 'As this bread was dispersed over the mountains, and has been gathered into one, so may your church be gathered from the ends of the earth in your kingdom.' The Church's political life is modelled on the Eucharist feast, a celebration to which all people are invited as a foretaste of the kingdom restoration of the original unity of creation. This gathering fulfils the deep yearning of humanity and is seen particularly in Israel's understanding of the exile in Babylon. This was its own scattering and the people of Israel longed to be gathered together again, using the language of salvation.

> Save us, O Lord our God,
>   and gather us from among the nations,
>   that we may give thanks to your holy name
>   and glory in your praise.
>
> (Ps. 106.47)

Jesus himself takes on the role of gatherer: 'Whoever is not with me is against me, and whoever does not gather with me scatters' (Matt. 12.30). As Jesus teaches, the wolf scatters but the shepherd gathers in (John 10.12). As the New Testament further develops this idea theologically, Christ is portrayed as the site in which the gathering takes place – the gathering is both *in* and *as* (it has the identity of) his very body (1 Cor. 12.13). Ancient Israel struggled to see how God was at work beyond its borders; this is dramatized in the book of Jonah who is reluctant to preach repentance among the Ninevites. When the New Testament addresses this theme, the other nations are not shown to be streaming to a place (such as Jerusalem or the Temple) but instead to a person. This is dramatized in the gathering at Pentecost – yes, it is a gathering in Jerusalem, but it is turned into a different kind of gathering by the Holy Spirit, at once reversing the Babel story and turning the scattering of the nations into a providential occasion for the gospel mission to spread. The mixed nature of the Church – Jews and Gentiles now grafted into Israel – is a permanent demonstration that both are together now 'a chosen race, a royal priesthood, a holy nation, God's own people' (1 Pet. 2.9). The book of 1 Peter, written 'To the exiles of the Dispersion', entirely reframes *exile* and *dispersion*. As a separate nation, the Church is never really in exile; it is always already gathered no matter where it is scattered.

In some ways, then, the Church has its understanding of itself as nation. This clearly makes it a rival to the state. It has a different account of human togetherness and salvation. It also offers a different mechanism for gathering people, not only bringing them together, but achieving reconciliation between them. Theologically, the description offered here of the political nature of the Church is much grander than that of the state. Its ambitions are much wider and more universal. Nations may speak about themselves in grandiose terms, but they are always smaller than the world. They police their physical boundaries and make appeal to some segments of the human population (such as ethnic groups) rather than all people. At the same time, focus on the Church's liturgy can seem rather parochial and bounded within church walls. Have we just given an account that is only for Christians? How do the practices of the Church relate to the rest of society and, indeed, to humanity as a whole?

The modern options for relating church and state are limited. The Church might see itself as operating alongside other gatherings that function like interest groups within a public space that is essentially geared toward influencing the state. Alternatively, the Church might seek a purer religious life and withdraw from playing this kind of role, instead focusing on more strictly spiritual things like the care of souls. The German theologian Ernst Troeltsch (1865–1923) famously categorized these two tendencies within Christianity as the Church-type and the sect-type. Even though it's possible to identify Christian groups that historically seem to fit one or the other, critics of Troeltsch's classification argue that he has presented us with a false choice.

Surely no concept of church should frame its relationship with culture or the state in all-or-nothing terms. When early Christians adopted the Greek term *ekklesia* (translated as 'assembly' or 'church') for their common life together, they were taking over a secular political term. The *ekklesia* was the place in the city where free, male citizens would gather to deliberate on political affairs. Their free speech exercised for this purpose was guaranteed by the *ekklesia*. By taking over this term, Christians were claiming that they are the true public body and that the gospel demands the exercise of its own free speech (that is, proclamation of the good news) outside the ordinary institutions of political sovereignty. Also, because the Christian *ekklesia* includes male and female, citizens and non-citizens, free and slave, black and white, it is more inclusive and universal than any earthly *polis*. The city of God reflects the kingdom of God in its composition and its politics of reconciliation. Before the end of all things, in which God will be all in all, the Church sojourns among the nations – within all but at home in none. Its different politics explains why.

There is a question about how such a church ought to speak to the wider world, and especially to a secular state. The question accepts an idea put forward by the German Enlightenment philosopher Gotthold Lessing (1729–81) which says that there can be no crossing between historical truths and eternal truths. The no man's land between these two has come to be known as 'Lessing's Ditch'. Typical of Enlightenment thinkers, Lessing believed that reason led the way to necessary truths whereas faith deals with history and revelation. As long as the idea of Lessing's Ditch is accepted, anything historic about Christianity is a liability – the specifics of a first-century Jew, born in a particular place and time, who taught and did things. Attitudes about how the Church ought to speak to the wider world sometimes fall on one side or the other of the ditch.

In our day, **communitarians** emphasize the internal integrity of Christian language and practices, refusing Lessing's logic. They believe that what makes Christianity most interesting, if not also most true, are the very historic claims that embarrassed Lessing. But then the question remains of how well these can be translated into cultures of unbelief. We saw this emphasis expressed in Chapter 6 when we looked at how contemporary Christian ethics responds to moral relativism. The concern here is a little different since now a question is being raised about the Church's witness. As John Howard Yoder characterizes the communitarians, 'They will not risk the challenge of telling the world that servanthood, enemy love, and forgiveness would be a better way to run a university, a town, or a factory.'[4] They believe that only a deep involvement in the life of the Church and the story of God will make Christian witness understandable to any audience.

Yet clearly most of the world can be thought of as outside the Church to varying degrees. Communitarians respond with a message of 'Come and see'. Spend time with this strange people, unlearning the corrupt and

---

4 John Howard Yoder, *For the Nations: Essays Public and Evangelical* (Grand Rapids: Eerdmans, 1997), 49.

empty ways of the world, and begin to adopt the speaking and acting habits of this alternative culture. Scholars in this school appeal to Aristotle on practices and Thomas Aquinas on habits. In addition, many appeal to more recent linguistic philosophy when it comes to this talk about language, especially the work of Ludwig Wittgenstein.

Public theologians offer a different answer to the question of witness. Public theology looks for ways of influencing the state and the wider society with the leaven of the gospel and are usually content to present a thinner gospel than communitarians would like. Its advocates hope to present a persuasive witness that doesn't have the hang-ups (as Lessing would think of them) that are too particular and esoteric to bear the force of necessary, eternal truth. Yoder says:

> By dropping the particular baggage of normative servanthood, enemy love, and forgiveness, they think they might make it easy to get across Lessing's ditch and to talk their neighbors' language, but they do so at the cost of having nothing to say that the neighbors do not already know.[5]

Public theologians recognize that not everyone in any society is a Christian. They therefore try to make connections between Christian belief and widely shared belief found in the surrounding culture, 'translating' Christian belief into non-Christian language and moral categories. With this strategy, there will always be the question of what is lost.

Yoder himself argues that Christians shouldn't feel the need to choose between these two. Sometimes one or the other strategy will be most appropriate. The real danger is in assuming that this question needs to be solved at the level of method ahead of actually trying to communicate something of substance. Public theology can relax since Lessing represents discredited philosophy which his ditch reflects. Communitarians need a less rigid distinction between church and world as cultures that speak differently. As Yoder points out, 'Real people in linguistically divided cultures do in fact communicate good and bad news, imperfectly but adequately, all the time.'[6] When the Church allows all members to have the floor because the Holy Spirit may speak through anyone regardless of age, gender, wealth, status or education, this is a witness to a better way of being a society. It may not be immediately understood in depth by an outsider, but it will probably not require translation either. When Christians eat together, all receiving the same regardless of rank or contribution to the Church because God creates

5 Yoder, *For the Nations*, 49.
6 Yoder, *For the Nations*, 25, n. 23.

a new body by means of his, this is a witness to inviting outsiders, to biblical social justice and to God's intention that there 'be no one in need among you' (Deut. 15.4). This practice was already a public witness for the early Christians in the Jerusalem church (Acts 2, 4). Again, a deep understanding of it requires cultural–linguistic skills that church practice develops in people over time, but any onlooker would see that people can provide for one another out of a generosity fostered by their common life.

Civil disobedience

We needed to look at Christian witness to the wider world before discussing civil disobedience since Christian disobedience to the state must always be understood to be an extension of its witness. Christians should never set out with the primary intention of disobeying authorities. Unless those in political power forbid the exercise of Christianity or proclamation of the gospel, Christians are generally expected to live honourably in society, return good for evil and 'For the Lord's sake accept the authority of every human institution, whether of the emperor as supreme, or of governors, as sent by him to punish those who do wrong and to praise those who do right' (1 Pet. 2.13–14).

What Christians are *for* should always determine what we are *against*. There is plenty to oppose and resist: sin, death, suffering, injustice, nationalism, imperialism, pride, abuse of power. Indeed, the cross, the central Christian image, is doubly relevant here. Jesus was crucified for resisting both Roman and Jewish powers. And the fact that early Christians soon after adopted the cross as their symbol powerfully demonstrates their impulse to resist the dominant, imperial account of Jesus' death. That death was really about life; the cross doesn't signal an end, but a new beginning.

One of the Bible's most memorable examples of civil disobedience is set during the exile in Babylon. The two similar stories of Shadrach, Meshach and Abednego (Dan. 3) and Daniel in the lions' den (Dan. 6) both illustrate the determination of faithful Israelites to continue to worship God while in captivity. The details of the stories differ, but acts of worship and prayer to the God of Israel constitute disobedience against Nebuchadnezzar, king of Babylon, and later Darius the Mede, carrying a death sentence. God's miraculous intervention vindicates these faithful acts by showing that God is on the side of his steadfast servants and will reward them.

Jewish disobedience toward political tyranny was a major theme during the period between the Old and New Testaments. A megalomaniac leader named Antiochus Epiphanes ruled for 12 years in the middle of the second century BC. His very name 'Epiphanes' illustrates what a megalomaniac he was. Epiphany, like the season churches celebrate between Christmas and Lent, means 'appearance of God'. But this emperor thought of *himself* as the appearance of the gods. He wanted to unify the Empire, so he outlawed the reading and teaching of the Torah, the Jewish law. If women had their sons circumcised (a practice of the Jewish law and a sign of God's covenant with Abraham), they were executed. Keeping the Sabbath was outlawed. Most heinous of all, Antiochus Epiphanes defiled the Temple in Jerusalem when he erected a statue of the Greek god Zeus there and sacrificed pigs on the altar (which were unquestionably unclean according to Jewish law). Any Jews who refused to eat pork or to give up their religion were killed.

Jews responded with the violent Maccabean revolt, which is recounted in the books of the Maccabees. In 164 BC, the Temple is cleansed and rededicated to the proper worship of the God of Israel, a deeply meaningful event marked by Hanukkah. The eight-day celebration commemorates a miracle in which a single day's supply of oil continued to keep the candles burning in the Temple for a full eight days. Like the stories in Daniel, this miracle showed that God is on the side of the Jewish revolutionaries and against imperial despotism and idolatry.

These events of civil disobedience help to explain the revolutionary tone that sometimes accompanied the Jesus movement during his ministry. Some Jews from the faction known as Zealots took Jesus to be the next revolutionary leader who would lead Israel in revolt against Rome as the Maccabees had done against the Greeks. A great deal of Christian thought has tried to understand Jesus' ministry, crucifixion and resurrection as revolutionary in a deeper sense. Violently replacing one regime with another still obeys the same logic of violence, which only repeats the means with which groups gain and maintain a certain kind of power. A deeper revolution cannot only address specific institutions, but needs to oppose the ways that they keep themselves going. Christian resistance cannot be content with merely gaining control by unseating the control of others. The Zealots were ultimately disappointed with Jesus for this reason, and some scholars think this may have led Judas Iscariot to betray him out of disillusionment.

Then, as now, it seems to have been difficult to discern the difference between a failed political project and a cosmic revolution of all politics. Noticing and expanding on the difference between these two is central to the book of Revelation. Revelation was written near the end of the reign of the Roman emperor Domitian (AD 81–96), whose persecution of Christians for their refusal to participate in the state religion is the book's immediate context (cf. 1.9). The wider context of the Empire's evils occasions a more general critique of absolutizing political, military and economic power against a contrasting backdrop of God's glory.

Domitian was the first Roman emperor to enforce worship of himself as divine, reportedly requiring that his sovereign status be acknowledged using the two words *Kurios Kaisaros* ('Caesar is Lord'), to which the Christians had an equally concise counterpart with 'Jesus is Lord' (Rom. 10.9; 1 Cor. 12.3).[7] The vision of all nations in worship of God enabled those who would resist Rome to see their actions vindicated. To resist attributing ultimacy to the Empire through non-participation in and refusal to profit from its successes required a perspective of transcendence which exposed Rome for the idol it had become.

A letter from Pliny, a governor during the time of Emperor Trajan (who reigned from AD 98 to 117), shows how difficult matters were for Christians:

> In the meanwhile the method I have observed towards those who have been denounced to me as Christians is this: I interrogated them whether they were Christians; if they confessed it, I repeated the question twice again adding the threat of capital punishment; if they still persevered, I ordered them to be executed ... Those who denied they were, or had ever been Christians, who repeated after me an invocation to the Gods, and offered adoration with wine and frankincense to your image, which I ordered to be brought for that purpose, together with those of the Gods, and who finally cursed Christ – none of which acts, it is said, those who are really Christians can be forced into performing – these I thought it proper to discharge.[8]

These examples all provide us with powerful accounts of resistance. They are also extremely clear cases of good versus evil in which readers cannot miss the obvious, stark choices being faced: choose God or choose against God. Much more difficult are those cases, as we have discussed and will continue to discuss in many versions, in which choosing the good creates victims beyond those who choose. For example, in Shusaku Endo's novel *Silence*, which recounts persecution of Japanese Christians, a priest is told to renounce his faith in order to end the torture of his fellow Christians. He is told to trample on an image of the face of Christ, which in the end he does. And he imagines Christ urging him on:

---

7 Brian K. Blount, 'Reading Revelation Today: Witness as Active Resistance' in *Resistance and Theological Ethics*, ed. Ronald H. Stone and Robert L. Stivers (Oxford: Rowman & Littlefield, 2004), 160.
8 Cited in Blount, 'Reading Revelation Today', 161.

Trample! Trample! I more than anyone know of the pain in your foot. Trample! It was to be trampled on by men that I was born into this world. It was to share men's pain that I carried my cross.[9]

For Endo, even choices that seem clear may not be so clear when they are viewed differently.

Just as difficult are cases where the choices themselves seem less clear. Historically recent and prominent examples of Christian civil disobedience such as demonstrations for human rights and against war are theologically weighty, but they are also not exclusively theological. People of other faiths and no faith often take part in them, sometimes with apparently sincere Christians taking up opposing positions. In these cases, the resistance cannot really be said to take the form of Christians against 'the world'. Instead, some Christians are choosing a prophetic role that is partially designed to provoke the conscience of fellow believers to act in accordance with justice. Two strategies stand out.

The first sometimes involves the creative use of language and actions we looked at above when discussing communitarians and public theologians. When the Christian task is prophetic and not simply disobedient, the idea is sometimes to get those on the other side to recognize something about themselves that they don't want to acknowledge. Some claim that Gandhi's movement in India succeeded against the British because he was forcing the British to confront a brutality normally covered up by civility. If so, Martin Luther King's appeal to language in the United States founding documents about the equality of all people exemplifies something similar. For King, this was a strategy for being heard. By citing the Declaration of Independence ('all men are created equal . . . they are endowed by their Creator with certain unalienable Rights . . .'), King appealed to the highest professed ideals of a nation that, in denying basic civil rights to African Americans, was not living up to them.

The second strategy doesn't just confront the opponent with an uncomfortable truth. It goes further by performing a counter-logic to the only tools the oppressor has available. This is less tactical and more sweeping and requires an appreciation of what we're up against. The New Testament uses the terms **principalities** and **powers** to describe much more than what we have been saying about the state. These words indicate an idolatrous spiritual dimension, not only to authorities, but to ideas and many other things as well. Paul recognizes the human tendency for many things to be

---

9 Shusaku Endo, *Silence: A Novel*, trans. William Johnston (New York: Picador, 1969, 2016), 183.

elevated higher than they ought to be, either being asked to play a role that takes God's rightful place in some way, or else doing so through their own assertion. Nailing down just what the Bible means by principalities and powers can be difficult. The lay theologian William Stringfellow (1928–85) offers a fairly comprehensive definition. According to Stringfellow, the principalities and powers include

all institutions, all ideologies, all images, all movements, all causes, all corporations, all bureaucracies, all traditions, all methods and routines, all conglomerates, all races, all nations, all idols. Thus, the Pentagon or the Ford Motor Company or Harvard University or the Hudson Institute or Consolidated Edison or the Diners Club or the Olympics or the Methodist Church or the Teamsters Union are all principalities. So are capitalism, Maoism, humanism, Mormonism, astrology, the Puritan work ethic, science and scientism, white supremacy, patriotism plus many, many more – sports, sex, any profession or discipline, technology, money, the family – beyond any prospect of full enumeration. The principalities and powers are legion.[10]

All of these things, and many more, are competitors to God's Lordship over all aspects of our world and lives. The Bible's attitude toward them seems to be that they are fallen and in rebellion against God, but also that God uses them providentially to help order our lives. Christ has defeated them by exposing their pretence on the cross (Col. 2.15). These concepts require some unpacking to understand. We will first look at the fact that the powers have been defeated and then consider the strange idea that they are still used by God.

We saw above that the Bible is working with its own decisive stories of God's people rebelling against idolatrous powers. The fate of Jesus' particular rebellion works to subvert the normal ways that political change is achieved – by violent force. Instead, Paul says that Jesus 'disarmed' the powers, making a public example of them, and nevertheless 'triumphed' over them.[11] Obviously unarmed himself, Jesus also instructed his disciples not to use weapons. He further explained to Pilate, the Roman governor, that the non-violence of his movement indicates a different order compared to worldly powers:

Then Pilate entered the headquarters again, summoned Jesus, and asked him, 'Are you the King of the Jews?' Jesus answered, 'Do you ask this on your

---

10 William Stringfellow, *An Ethic for Christians and Other Aliens in a Strange Land* (reprint, Eugene, OR: Wipf & Stock, 2004), 78.

11 See René Girard, 'The Triumph of the Cross' in *I See Satan Fall like Lightning*, trans. James G. Williams (Maryknoll: Orbis, 2001).

own, or did others tell you about me?' Pilate replied, 'I am not a Jew, am I? Your own nation and the chief priests have handed you over to me. What have you done?' Jesus answered, 'My kingdom is not from this world. If my kingdom were from this world, my followers would be fighting to keep me from being handed over to the Jews. But as it is, my kingdom is not from here.'   (John 18.33–36)

What Jesus said here to Pilate is what is later demonstrated on the cross. The way of violence is the way of the world, of revolutions and counter-revolutions, of armies that defend the status quo and armed hordes that attempt to replace it. On the surface, the cross is a continuation of this pattern. A powerful empire uses violence to put down a potential uprising from the people. But this mechanism is also, at a deeper level, shown to be exhausting itself, doing its worst, which is the most it can do. Theologically, the tool being used is not just violence but death. This is important lest it look as though Jesus is only a non-violent revolutionary. He is. But the Christian version of non-violence most at work in the event of the cross isn't just a refusal to use force. It is a refusal to consider that death has the final word ('Where, O death, is your victory? Where, O death, is your sting?', 1 Cor. 15.55). This conviction not only holds as an article of personal piety in which a person faces death unafraid. It also holds for the profound myths that prop up the meanings and directions of all social orders:

> By assuming the status of innocent victim, Jesus destroyed the credibility of the persecuting majority's self-serving account, according to which the primal murder, at the foundation of all social order, was somehow just. The words of Caiaphas ['You do not understand that it is better for you to have one man die for the people than to have the whole nation destroyed' (John 11.50)] can be taken straight. Jesus is revelatory in that he obliges violence to tip his hand, to reveal the fictitiousness of its self-justification.[12]

Death and violence are simultaneously shown to be the inner logic of the powers. Their defeat is dramatized when the way they function socially is exposed for everybody to see. Their failure is concretized in resurrection when a new kingdom that knows no death at all prevails for good.

Still, as we have also said, God still continues to use the defeated powers providentially. Paul taught something like this in Romans 13, a text that has probably received more attention than it should, since it is sometimes made to bear the full weight of providing an entire political theology. Paul's claim is that political authority comes from God and therefore

---

12 John Howard Yoder, review of *The Scapegoat* by René Girard in *Religion and Literature* 19.3 (Fall 1986): 89–92 (90).

everyone ought to be subject to it. At the same time, Paul wrote several of his letters from prison in Rome (Philippians, Colossians, Philemon, and Ephesians if Pauline) and, with Silas, had been condemned by a city magistrate and spent time in a jail cell (Acts 16). Being subject to authorities may sometimes just mean accepting their punishments for disobedience. Paul willingly endured his punishments even though he did not always obey.

Karl Barth returned to Jesus' conversations with Pilate in order to understand what Paul meant. Jesus acknowledged that Pilate's power comes 'from above' whether used for good or evil. Yet even Pilate's evil choice to crucify Jesus was not something beyond God's sovereign use.[13] No human act is.

---

13 Karl Barth, 'Church and State' in *Community, State, and Church*, trans. G. Ronald Howe (Eugene, OR: Wipf & Stock, 2004), 109–10.

8

Mercy and peace

Ephesians characterizes Jesus' mission this way: 'He came and proclaimed peace to you who were far off and peace to those who were near' (Eph. 2.17). The argument is that God in Christ has created a new, single humanity from one that had been divided. The end of this division is peace in the Hebrew sense of *shalom* which means wholeness, coherence and togetherness. God's forgiveness and reconciliation are directed not only at individual sinners, but at different groups that have different identities. These either fall away or are reframed (as is the Jew–Gentile relation, for example), indicating that God's work generates a new people, as we have just been studying in the previous chapter. Now the focus is on the prospects, processes, hang-ups and roadblocks to this happening in our world. The fact is that people sometimes divide in order to *achieve* peace. But this isn't the peace of God, which has little to do with keeping a safe distance or agreeing to disagree. In this chapter, we will look at some of the specific questions and meanings involved with these claims.

How much has God's intention of reconciling the whole world to himself (2 Cor. 5.19) been realized already? Was this work that was only begun but not completed? Should we mostly live according to a more 'realistic' ethic for now? Should God's reconciling mercy instead be understood *for us* to be mostly a future hope? Moreover, how should we understand the relationship between Jesus' non-violence and the work of forgiving and reconciling? How should Christians approach the hard work of loving enemies, which Jesus taught? Some of the questions we will consider are simultaneously theological and practical, such as whether forgiveness and punishment can go together, or whether we need to choose between them. Other questions will take us to the extremity of moralities of forgiveness that we are probably used to admiring, such as when we ask what it means to think of a person or act as 'unforgivable'.

The approach taken here is to identify biblical and theological aids in thinking about the fact that mercy and peace aren't just good things Christians hope to receive, but are included in the possibilities given to disciples to live.

God's vision of the human future

The story the Bible tells was the subject of Chapter 1. But this story is not just about the past; it is also about the future. The Bible frequently talks about 'the days to come', 'the day of the Lord', the return of Christ, a future judgement, and a new heaven and new earth. When the Bible discusses these things, however, there is always more going on than foretelling future events. Readers are given a glimpse into the final *purpose* of all things. One of the points at which differing viewpoints within Christian ethics diverge sharply is the question of the relationship between this vision of the human future and how people ought to live now. The peaceable vision from Isaiah in which wolf and lamb live together, for example, is clearly not a present reality – creation seems characterized more by the opposite: violence and destruction of life. Is Isaiah's vision only meant to give us something to hope for in the future while we live now by a different ethic? Or is this future promise meant to shape the present?

Jesus proclaimed the fulfilment of the kingdom of God and drew heavily on these prophetic visions of the future found in the Old Testament. Those who see this vision as normative for Christian living now will point to the fact that Jesus declared it to be no longer an entirely future hope, but at least partially the present reality for his followers. This is why Jesus can ask his disciples to live in the radical ways he does. They are able to turn the other cheek, love their enemies, forgive without limit and go the extra mile because the old ethic in which we love our friends and hate our enemies reflects an old world – not quite a world that has gone away (since it's very much still with us), but a world that is certainly going away. It's this certainty that allows Jesus to speak about the future as now. Scholars use the word 'proleptic' to describe this way of speaking in which a certain future reality gets spoken of in the present tense. On its own, however, this proleptic way of speaking doesn't settle the question about whether the ethic of Jesus is normative for Christians. Some have agreed: yes, it will all be very different from how it is now; but it would be irresponsible to actually live that way today. Let's look at the different responses to Jesus' proleptic way of teaching by considering the ethics of peace some more.

Reinhold Niebuhr (1892–1971), a towering twentieth-century Protestant Christian ethicist, agreed that Jesus' ethic is in line with the vision we get from the prophets in the Old Testament such as Isaiah. According to Niebuhr, Jesus had a 'pure love' ethic. But in a sinful world, the fact that Christians must also seek justice means that they will often find love and justice to be at odds. Niebuhr's career flourished between the two world wars and he was particularly troubled by the fact that many liberal American Christians were reluctant to enter the Second World War. These mostly Protestant liberals 'adopted the simple expedient of denying, in effect, the reality of evil in order to maintain [their] hope in the triumph of the ideal of love in the world'.[1] With the Nazis, it is worse than naive to ignore evil. To Niebuhr, defeating the Nazis was a clear matter of justice, and one he knew was not easily squared with an ethic that says to turn the other cheek.

Niebuhr's approach might strike some as unusual. It's important to see that his strategy wasn't to deny that Jesus taught a radical ethic of non-resistance. In a short book he wrote called *Why the Christian Church Is Not Pacifist*, he argues that it is a waste of time ('futile and pathetic', in fact) to try to make the case that Jesus wasn't himself a pacifist who taught pacifism:

> It is very foolish to deny that the ethic of Jesus is an absolute and uncom-promising ethic . . . The injunctions 'resist not evil,' 'love your enemies,' . . . 'be not anxious for your life,' 'be ye therefore perfect even as your Father in heaven is perfect,' are all of one piece, and they are all uncompromising and absolute.[2]

The question, for Niebuhr, was not what Jesus taught, but whether he expected his followers to obey it in all circumstances. To Niebuhr, the paci-fist ethic often isn't appropriate for today, given evil in the world. When we discuss war in Chapter 9, we will see this more in a distinction that Niebuhr makes between Jesus teaching a private ethic for people to use in interper-sonal relationships and a public ethic that needs to draw on sources other than just the pure love ethic if it is also to be of use for achieving limited justice in a fallen world. He understood Jesus to be teaching individuals how to live *as individuals,* but insisted that this needs to be understood separately from the 'political problem' (society-wide and world-wide ques-tions of justice).

We should notice that Niebuhr's approach is one that allows Christians to fight in wars and also believe that they should 'resist not an evildoer' (as Jesus taught in the Sermon on the Mount; see Matt. 5.39) and not con-tradict themselves. The difference is between a public and private ethic. Niebuhr may have allowed that one day the whole of creation will be as God

---

1 Reinhold Niebuhr, *An Interpretation of Christian Ethics* (New York: Harper & Row, 1935), 153.

2 Reinhold Niebuhr, *Why the Christian Church Is Not Pacifist* (London: Student Christian Movement, 1940), 16.

intended – the wolf will live with the lamb – at which time the public ethic will also be the pure love ethic. But until then, Christians must look somewhere other than to Jesus to guide how they should live as public people.

Many Christians, it must be said, simply find themselves supporting war but are not able to give a detailed explanation of why they are able to do so without disobeying Jesus. Niebuhr offers a very bold, even risky, take on our question about when Jesus' difficult teachings about peace are normative for Christians. But it at least has the advantage of being clear about the fact that Christians may well be contradicting Jesus sometimes – he just has an account to explain how this would still be moral to do.

A variation on Niebuhr's position is offered by Paul Ramsey (1913–88), a twentieth-century Methodist Christian ethicist who taught at Princeton University. Ramsey wrote about the so-called 'strenuous sayings' of Jesus which included his teaching about non-resistance. Ramsey argues that Jesus had an **apocalyptic expectation** of the coming of the kingdom, by which he meant that Jesus expected that the kingdom was coming very soon. Some biblical scholars had been making this same point since the late nineteenth century. During times when the spirit of the culture has been optimistic, this viewpoint has waned; but when it has been pessimistic (such as during the First World War), apocalypse has tended to be more heavily emphasized. Apocalypse breaks into history decisively and abruptly. If people believe that history is progressing relatively well, they will think apocalypse is unnecessary. But when this kind of expectation is present, and when intense enough, it naturally leads to some fairly radical ethics, especially those that aren't concerned with long-term planning and building. 'Jesus' expectation of the immediate end of the kingdoms of this world qualifies almost all his teachings.'[3] We might cite that Jesus taught us to give wealth away rather than save for retirement, and not to worry about tomorrow; and he seemed to ignore responsible questions that leaders in a society might ask such as how to run a government with justice:

> In face of the inbreaking kingdom, moral decision was stripped of all prudential considerations, all calculation of what is right in terms of consequences which in this present age normally follow certain lines of action. Not only all prudential calculation of consequences likely to fall upon the agent himself, but likewise all sober regard for the future performance of his responsibility for family or friends, duties to oneself and fixed duties to others, both alike were jettisoned from view.[4]

---

3 Paul Ramsey, *Basic Christian Ethics* (Louisville: Westminster John Knox, 1950), 37.
4 Ramsey, *Basic Christian Ethics*, 39.

Ramsey believed that it would be irresponsible for modern Christians to hold this same kind of ethic since clearly Jesus was mistaken about the imminent arrival of the kingdom. For this reason, Ramsey taught that modern people are right *not* to share this expectation with Jesus, nor the ethic that comes along with it. Like Niebuhr, Ramsey therefore identifies something irresponsible in Jesus' ethic. If followed, it must be without 'prudential calculation of consequences'. Not only may the one who follows it suffer loss or be killed as a result; this may also happen to the disciple's loved ones. For Ramsey, this is a feature of the apocalyptic expectation that Jesus and the early Christians had. It seems obvious to Ramsey that Jesus and the early Christians were wrong to have this expectation, hence their ethic was incomplete (at the least) or even misguided.

John Howard Yoder is one of the best-known twentieth-century critics of Reinhold Niebuhr. Yoder's Mennonite Christianity belongs to a group called the Historic Peace Churches – groups that emphasize that the peace ethic of Jesus is for Christians to live now, and not only in private. Yoder's book *The Politics of Jesus* argues (as the title indicates) that Jesus was in fact teaching a 'political' message when he taught non-resistance. This is the opposite of Niebuhr who held that these teachings were for private individuals only.

At a fundamental level, Yoder understands the normativity of Jesus' ethic differently from Niebuhr. Yoder takes Jesus' ministry to be primarily about the gathering of a collective people and giving them a new way to live together. It's not that Jesus bore a message for individuals to appropriate as individuals, but rather to appropriate it into their shared life as a community of faith – Yoder simply called this community 'church'. The Church is itself a political entity, according to Yoder, and Jesus' ethic of non-resistance that otherwise looks impossible or irresponsible for individuals is something Jesus meant to be taken on by the community as a whole. '[Jesus] did not say . . . "you can have your politics and I shall do something else more important"; he said "your definition of polis, of the social, of the wholeness of being human socially is perverted."'[5]

Yoder was suspicious of the tendency he saw in Niebuhr to prefer a 'responsible' ethic that takes charge of history and tries to make it come out all right. This is God's job, not ours, Yoder taught. God is working to bring down the mighty from their thrones and exalt the humble and weak (as Mary prays). But because taking this on as a human project for justice

---

5 John Howard Yoder, *The Politics of Jesus: Vicit Agnus Noster*, 2nd edn (Grand Rapids: Eerdmans, 2002), 107.

will inevitably mean using violence, Yoder rejects it. He wrote that, in the face of evil structures and powers, the Christian is providentially freed from 'needing to smash them since they are about to crumble anyway'.[6]

Notice, then, that Niebuhr and Yoder both have a future dimension, although they are very different. For Niebuhr, the future will bring a time when Jesus' pure love ethic simply is the only ethic that there is and it will perfectly correspond with justice. Achieving justice won't require violence. For Yoder, on the other hand, the future will bring the certain end to injustice that Christians must not use violence now to bring about. He thought that Niebuhr was wrong to take the image of the powerful leader as the highest example of what it means to be political.

Yoder's response to apocalyptic expectations is similar. Recall how the popularity of this expectation comes and goes as Christians feel optimistic or pessimistic in varying degrees. To Yoder, this demonstrates how quickly Christians are willing to abandon God's promise to transform the world when it looks as though their own efforts to do so are succeeding. But seeing the world this way is reassuring to those in power who have an interest in believing that the way things are is the way they should stay. Apocalyptic, Yoder argues, is not primarily about the temporal end of the world, but about showing that a different world is possible beyond the self-evident one. Apocalyptic texts and the apocalyptic spirit generally are meant to give hope and energy to people on the margins of society; they are not for those who rule or who make up a comfortable majority. The oppressed need to be assured that the current state of affairs is not static nor inevitable; it can and will be transformed. Seeing apocalyptically is not primarily a matter of being able to describe the end of the world, but of describing the present world transformed. '[Apocalyptic] redefines the cosmos in a way prerequisite to the moral independence which it takes to speak truth to power and to persevere in living against the stream when no reward is in sight.'[7] It is a great challenge to live 'against the stream' when it doesn't look like doing so will ever be rewarded. For this is needed resurrection, the belief and the reality that God will make good on the risks people make based on barely a glimpse of what is possible beyond what seems inevitable.

God's vision of the human future is more than a prediction. It is a message meant especially for those who are not now beneficiaries of the alignment of power, wealth, fame and honour in our world. It is therefore a vision of justice, of things set right. The point of seeing it is to inspire hope

---

6 Yoder, *Politics of Jesus*, 187.

7 John Howard Yoder, 'Armaments and Eschatology', *Studies in Christian Ethics* 1.1 (1988): 53.

in areas where it would quickly disappear if it weren't constantly renewed. In this way, we can better understand the ethics that go with it. It is not surprising that the 'strenuous sayings' of Jesus are the ones some scholars are most prepared to explain away. These are the kinds of teachings that actually most call for the vision of the future that apocalyptic brings. In truth, many Christians probably ignore these teachings most of the time, meaning that they do not need to be told that the oppositions they will face by obeying them will come to an end and that the world is not a closed system of cause and effect. People for whom the effects generally work will not be interested in seeing it change. But if following the way of Jesus is more difficult and costly than this, the apocalyptic promise of resurrection could not be more relevant.

We have asked the question before: 'Who is the Bible for?' This discussion is meant to show that the Bible isn't primarily for those in charge of things. It is for those who are victims of the status quo. Apocalypse both promises that the status quo won't last for ever and shows what a more just state of affairs looks like beyond it. So rather than writing off Jesus' hardest teachings, a more responsible way of reading is to imagine the kinds of promises most appropriate for those who would actually dare to follow them.

Forgiveness

If the Bible is primarily for victims rather than the engineers and beneficiaries of the status quo, it should not be surprising that forgiveness is at the heart of the Christian message, strongly linked with Christian practice and duty. There is a lot for victims to forgive. The Lord's Prayer organically associates receiving forgiveness from God and forgiveness we are to give to others. Paul writes in a similar vein, 'Bear with one another and, if anyone has a complaint against another, forgive each other; just as the Lord has forgiven you, so you also must forgive' (Col. 3.13). What is involved in forgiving someone for some wrong that he or she has committed? Do we expect the other person to do anything to merit our forgiveness? Do we need to see remorse or hear an apology first? We will look at the Bible and some theology before considering concrete practices of reconciliation in the next section.

Genesis gives at least two profound examples of forgiveness between brothers. Much of the drama of the book can be thought of as sibling rivalry, often breaking down and occasionally being healed. Cain and Abel, the first brothers, engage in a rivalry that leads to the first murder, as well as a recognition that, while this merits death as punishment, God will step in to preserve the life of the murderous Cain. It is an account of forgiveness at its most basic – forgoing a deserved punishment. But it is also quite a bit short of reconciliation, which two other stories demonstrate. In these cases, forgiveness and reconciliation are passed between brothers.

In the first, twin brothers Jacob and Esau are rivals from the moment they are born. In the context of both their culture and the story of God's covenant with Abraham their grandfather, birth order was not only about inheritance of wealth and property, but about the line through which God's promises would be fulfilled. By deceiving both his father Isaac and his brother, Jacob manages to have the birthright transferred to himself. Esau resolves to kill his brother in revenge, prompting Jacob to flee, not returning to the area for many years. When they are about to meet again, Jacob, aware that he is still in Esau's debt, offers gifts ahead of their encounter. Meanwhile, Jacob wrestles with God at Peniel ('face of God') and insists on receiving a blessing even while suffering injury to his hip. Jacob's name is changed to Israel ('struggles with God') in this encounter. When Jacob and Esau meet, Esau initially dismisses his brother's offerings, but Jacob insists: "'No, please; if I find favour with you, then accept my present from my hand; for truly to see your face is like seeing the face of God – since you have received me with such favour'" (Gen. 33.10).

This story is especially complex. There is fraternal rivalry with the threat of murder (as with Cain and Abel), yet ending with forgiveness and reconciliation instead. There is the element of the birthright tied to Abraham's covenant, which itself fuels the rivalry. There are the two different references to seeing the face of God. And Jacob's wrestling and name change are also deeply significant. For Jacob, seeing God face to face is a mixed kind of blessing. It is more dynamic than static and comes at some cost. It is also woven together with receiving forgiveness from his brother. It is not just that Esau no longer wants to kill him, but instead, in language that sounds like the father's response to the Prodigal Son in Jesus' parable, 'Esau ran to meet him, and embraced him, and fell on his neck and kissed him, and they wept' (Gen. 33.4). Esau's overflowing demonstration of love reminded Jacob of God. Furthermore, Jacob being named Israel is clearly important for Jewish identity, throughout history but particularly during and after the Holocaust when Jews have had to wrestle with the idea that being Jewish means struggling and being wounded (by God, no less), while also being blessed. The blessing is also a burden. We will return to the question of how suffering is being framed in this story below.

The second story of brotherly forgiveness involves Jacob's sons, Joseph and his brothers. Due to repeated expressions of favouritism for Joseph from their father, Joseph's brothers seethe with resentment toward him. They sell him into slavery, which takes him to Egypt where he ends up impressing the Pharaoh and ascends influential ranks. This story of scapegoating backfires with Joseph's success, which his brothers must confront when famine drives them to seek help in Egypt and Joseph is the one who will decide whether to help them. The brothers beg Joseph's forgiveness for the wrong they have done to him. Genesis ends with Joseph not only declaring his forgiveness, but demonstrating it and offering a short theological rationale for it. The demonstration of his forgiveness comes in the form of a promise to provide for his brothers and their children (thus setting the stage for the next phase of the story in which generations of Hebrews come to live in Egypt). The rationale he offers comes in response to the brothers' declaration that 'We are here as your slaves', making plain the role-reversal (Gen. 50.18). Joseph announces that he is in no position to punish them (or withhold forgiveness, which amounts to the same thing) since he is not in the position of God. Instead, 'Even though you intended to do harm to me, God intended it for good, in order to preserve a numerous people, as he is doing today' (Gen. 50.20). A tit-for-tat approach to being wronged is too narrow to account for a universe in which God is sovereign and good can be brought from harm.

Both of these stories raise some difficult issues. When forgiveness is offered, it is not only good because it restores things to their prior state. For serious wrongs especially, there is no going back to the way things were. The wrong will always carry forward into the future, even when forgiveness is offered and received. These stories imply that the future that forgiveness creates might actually be a *better future* than would have existed had the wrong never been committed. In her important book *Moral Repair*, Marquette University philosopher Margaret Urban Walker (b. 1948) discusses an account of forgiveness given by philosopher Hannah Arendt (1906–75). Forgiveness is necessary, Arendt thought, in order to release us from the 'irreversibility' of human action. Without forgiveness, we are forever bound to the past. Walker agrees, but thinks that Arendt doesn't quite appreciate how much forgiveness itself should *also* be thought of as creating new instances of irreversibility. This happens because forgiveness opens up a future that is incalculable and uncontrollable; it has effects that we can't know or predict. 'This is one reason why an account of forgiveness needs to capture that part of forgiving that looks ahead hopefully to an uncertain future and not only the part that looks to settle something in the past.'[8]

---

8 Margaret Urban Walker, *Moral Repair: Reconstructing Moral Relations after Wrongdoing* (Cambridge: Cambridge University Press, 2006), 151–2.

Given that we began this chapter with God's vision of the human future, it might be immediately obvious that Walker (who is not a theologian) is articulating something very close to the Christian hope. The future of all things isn't just a return to the way things were, but a reality that knows that it has undergone redemption. Then again, this is where the difficulty comes in since putting things this way can come close to calling evil good. It comes close to saying that a world in which people are wronged but learn to offer and receive forgiveness is better than a world in which there are no wrongs (and hence no need for forgiveness). Where the wrongs are especially horrifying, such as with abuse or genocide, there seems very little to gain by making this kind of case.

What is the continuing significance of the wrong suffered even when one offers forgiveness? Does the saying 'Forgive and forget' capture what should happen (forgetting) when we forgive? But what about Jacob's limp that remains after God blesses him? And does it matter that Esau eventually agreed to receive Jacob's gifts? Walker argues that what lingers can serve a positive role, even when it doesn't fuel resentment. Following a political settlement in which victims of oppression agree to transition into a new state of affairs in order to live alongside their former persecutors, what lingers can invigorate a more just future by haunting it with memories of the past. 'A live edge of pointed just anger or continuing sorrow for things and people lost may accompany their honest agreement to go on in civility and cooperation without demanding that further accounts be settled, prices paid, or apologies tendered.'[9]

We might say it was big of Joseph to forgive his brothers and let go of what they had done to him. But is this 'letting go' simply a matter of heroically exerting a will not to let the wrongs of the past come to mind? The Croatian-American theologian Miroslav Volf (b. 1956) has argued that the hope of the gospel is that in the end (eschatologically), victims of trauma, suffering and injustice will not only not be troubled by their memories of these wrongs, but the wrongs themselves will fail to come to mind.[10] Some are troubled by any suggestion that anyone should forget wrongs suffered. After all, Jesus Christ still relates to us as the Crucified One and will eternally bear scars as the slain Lamb. This topic needs to be treated with some delicacy since the impulse to remember wrongs can be very good, and there are multiple ways of understanding the forgetting that Volf is describing.

---

9 Walker, *Moral Repair*, 156.
10 For example, Miroslav Volf, *The End of Memory: Remembering Rightly in a Violent World* (Grand Rapids: Eerdmans, 2006).

Esau's forgiveness is like God's because it is offered freely (without payment), meaning that the wrongs he had suffered at his brother's hand were no longer allowed to overshadow their encounter. The restoration of the estranged relationship is accompanied with exuberant joy and embrace apart from questions of justice (of how Jacob had wronged his brother). This doesn't mean that justice is unimportant. But those in the position of demanding justice, like Jesus himself, may hope that those demands will, in Volf's words, 'fail to surface'. They might be crowded out by all of the celebrating that is happening. Rather than being a payment for a wrong, Jacob's gifts are true *gifts*. They instrumentalize nothing; they don't bring about the forgiveness. But they do demonstrate his contrition for what he had done as well as his delight at being reunited with his brother. Volf's theological vision for victims is one in which, in glory, the offer and reality of forgiveness issue in such celebration that deserved justice and punishment simply don't come to mind. Jacob's offering had been drained of its status as payment, allowing it to be joyfully received.

In Jesus' parable of the Prodigal Son (Luke 15), the point is the same. The father is so overjoyed at the return of his son that it doesn't occur to him to punish him or exact some kind of payment. Instead, he calls for a feast and the slaughter of a fatted calf, something that those of a different mindset might have thought of as a sacrifice necessary for forgiveness to take place. The calf is slaughtered, but it plays a different role, indicating that true forgiveness redeems the very notion of sacrifice. This point was lost on the Prodigal's older brother, who was more interested in balancing the scales of justice than celebrating the return of his brother.

Forgiveness is therefore still a kind of sacrifice for the one who does the forgiving. In Chapter 3, we looked at what we give up – what we sacrifice – when we forgive somebody else. But if we are going to continue to use the language of sacrifice for forgiveness, it will need to be without the idea that a payment is being made. Instead, the sacrifice is in letting go of something that is owed to us, giving up something to which we may have a right. In linking forgiveness with sacrifice this way, I described God as leading the way by forgoing the obedience, honour and righteousness that humanity owes to him in order not to hold our sin against us. God goes beyond this, though. Not only does God's forgiveness mean not punishing us for our disobedience, but it also means staying with the disobedient ones, healing us and reconciling us to himself.

Nevertheless, the Christian tradition has not uniformly portrayed God as leading the way when it comes to forgiveness. A striking example of an alternative can be found in the thinking of St Anselm of Canterbury

(1033–1109). In a work called *Cur Deus Homo* ('Why God Became Man') that has had a profound influence on Western Christianity, Anselm is engaged in a pretend dialogue with a character named Boso. When Anselm argues that sin against God must be either paid for or punished rather than forgiven, Boso objects, recalling the Lord's Prayer:

> I cannot withstand your reasoning. But when God commands us in every case to forgive those who trespass against us, it seems inconsistent to enjoin a thing upon us which it is not proper for him to do himself.

In response, Anselm explains himself:

> There is no inconsistency in God's commanding us not to take upon ourselves what belongs to Him alone. For to execute vengeance belongs to none but Him who is Lord of all; for when the powers of the world rightly accomplish this end, God himself does it who appointed them for the purpose.

Anselm clarifies that some things are right for God to do but not for us (such as taking vengeance) and some things are right for us to do but not for God (such as forgiving). Boso says that he is satisfied with this explanation.[11] Anselm truly believed that there is no *need* for God to forgive us. If our sin must be either paid for or punished, the work that Christ performs on the cross pays a debt of honour to God that we, in our sin, are both unwilling and unable to pay. We therefore escape God's punishment but without being forgiven. However, this doesn't mean that we don't have to forgive others. It simply means that in commanding us to do so, God is asking us to do something that God is not doing himself.

I believe there are problems with this view. Anselm set the tone for a lot of Western theology, both Protestant and Catholic. God is imagined to be an inflexible lawgiver whose absolute demands will be met; otherwise God would suffer injustice, which is impossible. Love moves God to come to our aid, but in a way that doesn't compromise what he is owed. Some have thought that this primarily reflects a philosophical image of God that doesn't stack up against the God we see in the Bible.

In Anselm's partial defence, it can be insisted that Christ certainly suffers injustice at the hands of sinners in order that God the Father doesn't have to. Although Anselm doesn't say it this way, because the Son is also divine we might qualify our depiction of the rigid God who cannot suffer injustice with a reminder that God is triune and therefore in fact *does* suffer injustice for the forgiveness of sinners. Otherwise, Jesus' plea from the cross, 'Father, forgive them', simply makes no sense.

---

11 *St. Anselm: Basic Writings*, trans. S. N. Deane (La Salle, IL: Open Court, 1962), 204.

Even so, some contemporary theologians like Jürgen Moltmann are not satisfied. The suffering of the Son does not protect the Father from suffering. Instead, like any human father who watches his son suffer, the Father experiences his own suffering as his Son suffers on the cross. Indeed, it is precisely his Son that the Father gives up in forgiving us. Notice, though, that this is very nearly the inverse of Anselm's understanding. Strictly speaking, Anselm had a non-forgiving God for whom the death of Jesus was the payment of a debt which God accepts on our behalf. Writing against Anselm's view, contemporary theologian James Alison insists that it is humanity rather than God who insists on sacrifice. This mechanism of expiation is one that we have already rehearsed in an earlier chapter. Alison cites Romans 8.32: 'He who did not withhold his own Son, but gave him up for all of us, will he not with him also give us everything else?'

Alison believes that, in writing these words, Paul had in mind a story from 2 Samuel 21.1–9. In this text, King David appeases the Gibeonites for something the previous king of Israel, Saul, had done. When David asked the Gibeonites 'How shall I make expiation?', they demanded the death of seven of Saul's sons, which David provided. Alison observes that there are two significant differences with the story of Jesus. First, whereas David handed over Saul's sons but not his own, God *did not withhold his own Son*. As Moltmann also argues, the Father doesn't accept the sacrifice of someone else, but gives something up to make it. Second – and this is crucial for grasping the critique of Anselm – David is being compared with God, and all of humanity is playing the role of the Gibeonites. If so, then God is not the one demanding sacrifices; we are! God is the one giving something to us, suffering injustice at our hands, propitiating us, because this is what we demand in order for there to be peace. We are wrong about that, of course, which is why the resurrection of Jesus is what ultimately does this. The contrast between these views is stark, even though both can use the language of sacrifice. The trick is in noticing how they are functioning quite differently.

Reconciliation

God's vision for humanity's future isn't only for there to be no violence or for all people to be forgiven. It is not enough to be forgiven if the wrong for which I am being forgiven remains a part of me and continues to alienate me from others and from myself. Forgiveness is just the first step; the ultimate goal is reconciliation. Other practices like reparation will usually need to come first. If a person steals my car and asks for forgiveness, it doesn't mean much until he or she gives my car back. That alone won't suffice to repair the harm done to our relationship, but it's hard to imagine anything positive happening between us without it.

In the same way, if one who claims to forgive me doesn't also take part in reconstructing the relationship that I have harmed, there is going to be little content to forgiveness. An exception to this would be a situation when the one forgiving me is a judge with whom I have had no relationship other than being one who is subject to the law that he or she applies. Judges act on behalf of others, but not themselves. I mention this exception because Western concepts of salvation have often focused on this *juridical* image of forgiveness: God, acting as judge, saves us from punishments that we are bound to suffer as guilty offenders in the face of divine law. This is an incomplete picture, though. It wrongly sets God's justice against God's mercy and it misconstrues the nature of the God–humanity relationship. We will consider a few ways of describing what we may hope is a more genuinely Christian picture.

First, we need to shift our focus on to other images and metaphors for when wrongs are done, forgiveness is offered and reconciliation is achieved. Especially important are relational images and metaphors. Christians will often talk about humans enjoying friendship with God or being made his children through adoption. In most relationships, especially intimate ones like friendship or kinship, law plays no role whatsoever. When one friend wrongs another, offering forgiveness will not only mean forgoing punishment, but also making amends of some sort and offering gestures that over time will restore trust. These amends, though, are not reducible to economic metaphors or economic realities (such as making payment) any more than they are reducible to juridical ones.

With a friend, the point is neither recompense nor punishment. What has been lost is the character of the relationship – trust has been broken, goodwill has been squandered, the spontaneous expressions of camaraderie that used to come freely and without thought are now muted. Acts are now guarded and careful; very few things are shared and in common. Being reconciled means focusing on what has been lost and broken, restoring and mending it. Unfortunately, much of the time, the path toward reconciliation after injury cannot begin with even this straightforward step since what has been taken cannot always be restored through a simple act of reparation. The fact is that more has been taken than can be restored by returning something like a stolen object. Promoting healing after a physical injury is important, but still might be considered minor in the light of the other injuries inflicted if they were inflicted by another person out of contempt, jealousy or neglect. These are the serious cases where reconciliation is most difficult.

In the previous section, we tried to make sense of the fact that forgiveness may involve some gift, some 'sacrifice', even though the more it functions as a payment, the less it will serve forgiveness. The Christian practice of *penance* has this quality. Acts of penance do not restore but can be an expression of remorse, of responsibility-taking and thankfulness for God's mercy. I want to return to a discussion of St Anselm to expand on these ideas. Even though he is often associated with a dangerous separation between justice and mercy, there is an alternative way to read at least part of his argument.

Because our offence against God is infinite, no act of penance can restore what has been lost. And because humanity already owes everything to God, there is nothing in addition to what is already owed that we can then offer to make up for what we have taken. As Anselm thinks of it, then, humanity as a whole is in the very predicament that makes day-to-day reconciliation between offenders and victims so difficult. For most of his exposition, Anselm can be read (as we read him above) as requiring an exact payment of debt, as in our example of returning a stolen car. But we know that returning the stolen car doesn't repair the relationship; reconciliation requires something further. Here, a sympathetic reader of Anselm will find the answer in his conclusion to *Cur Deus Homo*.[12]

Before turning to Anselm's conclusion, however, a strong case can probably be made for the idea that some atrocities are so heinous that they are quite simply 'unforgivable'. Margaret Urban Walker writes that when people say this, they mean that the outrage we feel at an extraordinarily evil act is important to hold on to for moral reasons. 'They must be punished,' she writes, in language that should remind us of Anselm's description of humanity's state. 'But no punishment could pay their debt.'[13] Nor should it, because the memory of the evil must constantly be kept alive in order to make sure our moral condemnation of it never stops. This is the force of Holocaust victims' cries of 'Never again'. When Archbishop Desmond Tutu of South Africa visited the Holocaust museum in Jerusalem and asked 'But what about forgiveness?', he was judged and condemned (until a decade later when his question carried with it his own experience with overcoming apartheid).[14]

---

12 David Bentley Hart, 'A Gift Exceeding Every Debt: An Eastern Orthodox Appreciation of Anselm's Cur Deus Homo', *Pro Ecclesia* 7.3 (1998): 333–49.
13 Walker, *Moral Repair*, 189.
14 Desmond Tutu, *No Future without Forgiveness* (New York: Doubleday, 2000), 267.

Walker wants us to see that, at the limits of what we normally consider morally commendable behaviour (forgiving people when possible), this sentiment runs out and is replaced with something that we might still be able to understand, but on different moral terms. Those who have committed unforgivable atrocities have stepped outside the usual moral relations we have that can recognize strain that needs attention and repair. Theologically, mercy runs out when its threat to justice appears to be too great. But Walker goes further, arguing that 'unforgivable' begins to name the failure of morality itself. Moralities that call for forgiveness and reconciliation and are usually admired by people now appear frail and naive. For (other) moral reasons, in these cases justice seems to require that we remain firmly fixed on the past rather than hope in an uncertain future that is simply too risky for those who have already suffered deeply for being vulnerable.

I am not sure whether calling some things unforgivable truly means we reach the limits of ethics. Perhaps what is happening is that a knot of sorts is being discovered within a culturally dominant ethic that *both* wants to affirm mercy and justice *and also* lacks a meaningful way to keep them together when things are extreme. Walker identifies that this is the point at which hope and trust no longer sound appealing in any way; they are now a moral liability and threaten the coherence of the moral community. 'We define a moral community both by what and whom it comprehends and what it marks as beyond the pale.'[15] If unforgivability sets some people permanently outside the moral community, it is a good reminder that forgiveness is never an absolute moral obligation. We never *have to* forgive. Forgiveness can only have meaning when there is hope in an uncertain future that prompts a risky offer that may well include those the community decides are beyond the pale.

This discussion, I believe, significantly raises the stakes for when we revisit Anselm. The idea that no punishment can pay the debt created by wrongdoing, especially when the offence is grave, should ring true. This is the predicament of humanity, as Anselm conceives of it. If there is going to be a constructive Christian ethic of justice and mercy, forgiveness and reconciliation, at the extremes, it will be found here. In response to humanity's predicament, Anselm concludes that God interposes his Son, but not to meet the exact requirements of God's justice with strict precision. Instead, God's love is greater than our offence against God. Even though Anselm's theology is thought of as a 'satisfaction' view of salvation,

---

15 Walker, *Moral Repair*, 190.

in his conclusion he appears to be claiming that God is *more than* satisfied ('he has earned a reward greater than all debt'[16]). We must not think about the Father demanding something that the Son begrudgingly gives. Rather, the Son lovingly agrees with the Father to be the Father's gift to humanity. Since God's love is overflowing, it exceeds the bounds of what is strictly speaking required, as we discussed above with the example of the Prodigal Son: the excessive love of the father is the focus of the story and its good news. Out of compassion, God shows mercy on humanity. Here, also, because Christ's offering of himself is also made in love, the offering is excessive.

There is some debate about whether this reading fully captures Anselm. But regardless, it is instructive for us when we turn back to the needs for reconciliation that are created when one person harms another in some way. The problem isn't just that sometimes it's impossible to return what was taken (in our example, perhaps the car was wrecked after being stolen). It is that the complexity of relationships means that more is required. Now we can say that this 'more' isn't tangible or monetary. If there is something tangible that can be given and this will help, it probably should be. So should reparations when there has been a serious injustice. But no payment of this sort achieves reconciliation if it is offered without love. By its very nature, love is excessive and doesn't count the cost in order to hold itself back or mete out only the required amount. Like the Prodigal's father, love runs ahead of spirits that calculate, weigh and measure. Love hopes for an embrace and is inherently sacrificial, knowing that an offer of love might be rejected, yet offering itself anyway. We intuitively know that anything less than these things shouldn't count as love (though perhaps it will be called 'charity' in the modern sense of the word).

Christian ethics isn't content only to describe what God is like. It will ask about how people ought to embody this 'more'. There is a real risk of sounding as though 'Love is the answer' is somehow an adequate response to atrocities so grave that it leads some to leave whole moralities behind. There is clearly the talk of coming to terms with a deeper and different (possibly offensive) kind of love that insists that even those beyond the pale of human community can be brought within it. This love is chief among the Christian virtues and, as Thomas Aquinas taught, faith, hope and love are 'infused' by God. They are gifts that can be sought through prayer and expressed in life, but do not come to us the same way that other

---

16 *Cur Deus Homo*, Book II, XX, in *St. Anselm*, 286.

virtues do (by habit). At the same time, reconciliation is one of the key Christian practices woven into the Church's liturgical life. When infused with love from God, the Christian life will more perfectly reflect God's life.

At its centre, Christian practice involves a shared meal at which reconciled sinners eat with each other and feast with God. This love feast or eucharistic meal assumes that a good deal of preparation goes into it. Traditionally, a Christian service also includes rites of reconciliation leading up to it. One of the first elements in Christian worship is the confession that we are sinners in need of God's grace. This corporate confession is followed by the offering or assurance of forgiveness, followed in turn by an exclamation of joy (the Gloria) in thanks for the mercy God has shown us. Just before the Eucharist, Christians offer the peace of Christ to one another, an act of reconciliation that follows the pattern Jesus taught in the Sermon on the Mount:

> So when you are offering your gift at the altar, if you remember that your brother or sister has something against you, leave your gift there before the altar and go; first be reconciled to your brother or sister, and then come and offer your gift. (Matt. 5.23–24)

This text shows that, at the time Matthew was written, Christians were already following the basic structure of liturgy. It forbids approaching the altar (offering and communion) without first seeking reconciliation with brothers and sisters. Paul writes similarly to the Corinthians when he warns them against eating the bread or drinking the cup of the Lord in an unworthy manner, that is, without examining themselves (1 Cor. 11.27–32). Where there is a need to be reconciled, the liturgy itself makes room for this. This doesn't mean that people must wait until a church service to seek reconciliation. Liturgy is given to us as a pattern for all of life, which means that all of its elements cohere when the total context of one's individual and corporate life is centred on the right worship of God.

The liturgy instructs us in many things by building habits through its practices. We learn the right relationship we ought to have toward ourselves, confessing that we are sinners and rejoicing in God's forgiveness. We learn the right relationship we ought to have toward wealth and possessions, offering them to the service of God and receiving back all that we need to be sustained. We learn that we are responsible for each other's well-being, seeing that our gifts meet the needs of all. At the Eucharist, God plays host for the gifts we have brought (bread and wine) and nourishes us with them as his very body and blood. We learn the right way to deal with conflict, setting them within Christ's peace.

It is significant that the central practice here is eating *together*. In Chapter 10 when we discuss reconciliation between different races, we will look closely at how the question of who eats with whom was a key challenge to early Christians. For now, it is important to understand that with all of this focus on eating together, the Christian meal is primarily the *goal* of reconciliation. We know things are better once estranged parties are able to sit down and share a meal together. But meals can also be the *means* of reconciliation. Especially when the meal is a proper feast, there is an enormous amount of work and preparation that goes into it. The whole community may get involved, bringing everyone's different talents, means and abilities into its service. This is at least symbolically enacted when Christians gather for a meal that both nourishes and celebrates. (A church 'bring and share' or 'potluck' supper might do so as well.) Worshippers bring their gifts, which are transformed into different gifts the host gives back. As nourishment, the Christian meal acknowledges that God feeds us out of the same love we hope to share with one another. The Christian practice commits those who take part in it to receiving God's life-giving sustenance as well as giving it to others. There is no gospel where the necessities of life are neglected.

Even so, the celebratory aspect of the meal has been our primary focus here. There first needs to be something to celebrate. There is plenty to celebrate in receiving God's mercy, but even more when it is offered to others as we receive it. If it is withheld from others, there is something wrong and it is questionable whether we have really understood what mercy is.

9

Justice from above (order)

In this chapter and the next, we look at justice in two very different senses. They not only differ from the perspective of who is looking at it, but also in the meaning of justice itself. When justice is sought from above, it tends to overlook a lot of the pain and misery of life that is brought on by the exercise of power. This is understandable since this perspective on justice really is the one that people with power have.

The nineteenth-century German philosopher Friedrich Nietzsche was a severe critic of all religion, especially Christianity. The main problem with Christians is that they are hypocrites. He illustrated the worst hypocrisies by reflecting on a well-known painting by the Renaissance painter Raphael. The painting is of the Transfiguration (see Figure 1), an event

Figure 1 Raphael, *The Transfiguration* (1520)

in the Gospels in which Jesus is lifted up in shining glory before some of his disciples and a voice from heaven admonishes them to listen to him (Mark 9).

Nietzsche noted that the painting is basically in two halves. A bright upper half shows Jesus lifted up in light – things are clear, beautiful and divine. The darker lower half shows the ugliness of human reality with a child writhing in pain, his concerned father and an anxious crowd. Observers of the painting, Nietzsche thought, do exactly what Raphael wanted – their eyes are drawn upward, toward Jesus and away from the gritty reality of human existence. This is the problem with religion, he argued: it causes people to neglect the world and instead contemplate eternity. One of the characters below points up to Jesus while another points to the contorted boy.

In my own view, it is important to take Nietzsche's critique seriously, especially when we discuss justice. For most of its history, Christian scholarship has asked moral questions *from above*, trying to discern God's view of things from the heavens and, in the process, smoothing out the rough road of everyday life. Doing this makes the work of ethics simpler, in a way, since it is purified of many of the difficulties of life that complicate the moral task. But it is also artificial and operates on a certain amount of neglect.

The topics in this chapter all assume that the moral agent – the one asking the moral questions – is in charge and holds power. The dominant traditions of Christian thinking about judgement, punishment and war ask about what rulers should do with their power to do these things. They have assumed that however the questions get answered, there will be armies, judges, jailers and executioners who can carry them out. This is a limited picture, of course, since it is possible and maybe even better to ask about these topics from the perspectives of the victims. This is what we will do in the next chapter where I will argue that, indeed, addressing justice from below is truer to the gospel's own perspective.

Judgement and punishment

The Bible recounts the message of the prophet Amos who prophesied in the Northern Kingdom of Israel, condemning the wealthy leisure class for their exploitation of the poor and perversion of justice in the courts. Around 750 BC, Amos warns that Israel will be conquered by the Assyrians as punishment. About a century later, Habakkuk bears a similar message in the Southern Kingdom of Judaea (probably in Jerusalem), only this time the warning is against the Babylonians who violently destroy whole nations without mercy while growing wealthy. In both cases, we read strongly worded warnings of judgement that are linked to threats of punishment. Violence, that is, is linked to justice. The specific prophecy of Habakkuk is instructive:

> O LORD, how long shall I cry for help,
>   and you will not listen?
> Or cry to you 'Violence!'
>   and you will not save?
> Why do you make me see wrongdoing
>   and look at trouble?
> Destruction and violence are before me;
>   strife and contention arise.
> So the law becomes slack
>   and justice never prevails.
> The wicked surround the righteous –
>   therefore judgement comes forth perverted.
>   (1.2–4)

> Dread and fearsome are they;
>   their justice and dignity proceed from themselves.
>   (1.7)

> O LORD, you have marked them for judgement;
>   and you, O Rock, have established them for punishment.
>   (1.12)

> But the earth will be filled
>   with the knowledge of the glory of the LORD,
>   as the waters cover the sea.
>   (2.14)

In these passages, we notice that 'justice' is a word that Babylon probably uses of and for itself, as indeed every unjust scheme and regime does. But Habakkuk says it is a perverted justice. True justice comes from God and is counted as the knowledge of God and punishment of the wicked. 'I wait quietly', Habakkuk says, 'for the day of calamity to come upon the people who attack us' (3.16). Calamity surely conjures up images of violence even while it is the violence of the Babylonians that is Habakkuk's chief complaint. Elsewhere, the Bible understands Babylon's attack on Jerusalem to be the outcome of Israel's unfaithfulness to God (see, for example, Jer. 2—3). Taken together with Habakkuk, especially, even though Babylon might have fulfilled this role, this doesn't mean it will be spared its own punishment.

Growing up, all of us learn our original moral concepts through a system of rewards and punishments. Behaviours and actions that please our parents or teachers are encouraged to continue and it is made clear to us that the displeasing ones should cease. In Chapter 2, we saw how this kind of system is ideally meant to fade away over time. It should no longer be necessary to instil morality using rewards and punishments once better, more stable and more meaningful reasons can be given. When we discussed the law of the Old Testament (of Moses) and the gospel of freedom from the law that Paul preached – freed as we are to follow the law of love, the law of the spirit – the law's function as a 'disciplinarian' (one who punishes wrongdoing) was only an analogy. Now we must take up the topics of judgement and punishment again, only this time as proper topics on their own.

Imagine scenarios in which it seems right or good to punish another person. Indeed, the punishments of the Babylonians were thought of this way by the ancient prophets. But we might also think of a child who needs to be taught a moral lesson, whether for propriety or his or her own safety or the safety of others. We might also think of criminals whose punishments probably serve similar ends. If we ask about the purposes of punishment in general, then, we already have some answers before us: moral education, which is the disciplinarian function; and protection from harm.

Moral education. Perpetrators too are confronted with the seriousness of their offence by undergoing the punishment associated with it. Ideally, this will result in their moral education, making them less likely to re-offend in the future. When this works and if it is a genuine aim of punishment, it is because a society or authority counts on the person learning the consequences of one's actions. But this hardly qualifies as morality or ethics on its own since it requires no change of will or attitude, only of behaviour. Parole boards want to see a changed person, not just be assured that a person is no longer a danger to society. The way the Bible speaks of punishment is strangely foreign to modern penal codes. There the glory of the Lord is demonstrated by the divine impatience with wrongdoing, and God's righteousness is highlighted through the demand for justice. Growing in the knowledge of the glory and righteousness of God, we might say, constitutes a moral education for some biblical texts. Whatever the idiom, though, so long as punishment has the goal of moral education, it needs to have an end in sight. There needs to be a time when there is no more punishment to make room for the full expression of a morally educated life. The harshest punishments we have (especially death) don't have this end built into them. It's obvious that no one is going to live better – more righteously and with more virtue – as the result of the punishment of death. Admittedly, this reflects a conviction that punishment applies to individual wrongdoers who are also to be the objects of moral education, a conviction the Bible doesn't always share. For example, David is punished only indirectly as the result of his sin involving Bathsheba and Uriah, as the prophet Nathan declares: 'Now the Lord has put away your sin; you shall not die. Nevertheless, because by this deed you have utterly scorned the Lord, the child that is born to you shall die' (2 Sam. 12.13–14).

We notice that David is forgiven but is still punished, though indirectly. It seems likely that this punishment is part of David's moral education, although an argument might be made for God's vengeance. Either way, it is important to note that David is not subject to the justice of human institutions (not least because he was the king). Instead, God's justice may at best offer an analogy for thinking about human justice. When we consider God's justice in the work of Jesus Christ below, this will become even more important.

Protection. In order to prevent dangerous people from causing harm, it is necessary to separate them from others. Even though contemporary penal systems emphasize 'correction' (gesturing toward the moral education of offenders), they also keep inmates 'off the streets', protecting the innocent. With adequate prisons, it is not usually necessary to enact physical violence in order to keep offenders separate from the rest of the population.

Other goals of punishment include deterrence and vengeance.

Deterrence. Deterrence refers to the effect that punishing a person has on other potential wrongdoers. When a person is punished for doing wrong, the hope is that others will associate the crime with the punishment and will be turned away from committing the same crime themselves. This is related to the goal of moral education, but in this case the one being educated is not the one being punished. The punishment is a *demonstration* of what will happen to others who follow the same path. The first-century Roman writer Quintilian wrote that the purpose of crucifixion was to act as a deterrent to others: 'Whenever we crucify the guilty, the most crowded roads are chosen, where the most people can see and be moved by this fear. For penalties relate not so much to retribution as to their exemplary effect.[1] This strictly utilitarian goal of punishment faces difficulties if it is not accompanied by moral reasoning in other ways. The reason is that if the sole goal is to deter other similar crimes, there is no theoretical upper limit to the harshness of the punishment. In practice, it is very difficult to determine whether capital punishment in the United States actually has a deterrent effect. Historically, the most effective punishments in this regard have been those that are swift, certain and harsh. These characteristics, though, also open the door for great injustices and abuse. Modern jurisprudence is usually not very swift, partly in order to ensure that innocent people aren't punished by mistake.

Vengeance. Christian thought has nearly always excluded *revenge* from counting as a serious aim of punishment. Vengeance is God's, writes Paul (Rom. 12). And he means by this that it is not for us to exact or require it. Currents in Roman Catholic theology, for example, oppose most instances of the death penalty since it considers most cases to be retributive in motivation. There is an allowance for killing an offender for a utilitarian purpose like protecting the innocent if all normal means of doing so (such as imprisonment) fail or do not exist.[2] For centuries, Catholic (as well as Protestant) thinkers defended the death penalty for various crimes; its mainstream condemnation is modern.

It must be said that quite a lot of Christian ethics mimics secular accounts of justice by making either a deontological case in which everyone receives the same punishment for the same offence (eye for an eye), or a consequentialist case in which the punishment is said to serve a positive end for the offender or the wider society in terms of deterring others. But little of this is distinctly Christian. In particular, since Christians believe that the work of Christ – in his life of full obedience, his death, resurrection and promised return – enacts the justice of God, then however this is understood, it radically reframes secular accounts of what justice is. The work of Christ is God's justice in that it achieves reconciliation between God and humanity. Classical, secular justice often doesn't attempt reconciliation between victim and offender, but only focuses on what 'justice' should be given to the offender.

---

1 Quintilian, *The Lesser Declamations*, N. 274, quoted in Donald Senior, *Why the Cross?* (Nashville: Abingdon, 2014), 3.
2 See especially the 1995 encyclical *Evangelium Vitae*.

Related to the way that Jesus reframes justice for Christians is how the Christian gospel resists the common separation of justice from mercy. In fact, God doesn't 'pay back' humanity for killing his Son, but instead shows us mercy. Yet this is not an act that bypasses justice, but one that redefines justice *as mercy*.

It is no coincidence that we came to this point via Christian theology. Today a focus like this, often called **restorative justice**, is not always explicitly linked with Christian ideas and practices, but it is rooted in them. South Africa's Truth and Reconciliation Commission (established 1995) is hailed by many as a modern example of this kind of justice in action. Its goal was to help the country move on together after the period of apartheid in which blacks were segregated from whites and violence on both sides was common. Desmond Tutu (b. 1931), Archbishop of Cape Town, chaired a process of hearing the truth of several hundred crimes committed over the course of decades in exchange for requesting amnesty or forgiveness, determined by the commission. Tutu has become a world leader on the topic of reconciliation and forgiveness, not only on the personal level, but also on the much less-tried level of societies, ethnic groups and nations. Tutu is up front about the Christian origins of this kind of justice.

I have been describing a version of justice that equates to mercy: justice *without* punishment. But this lack of punishment doesn't exclude acts of penance that attempt to mend what was broken or restore what was lost. Critics of the Truth and Reconciliation Commission argue that granting amnesty did not sufficiently meet the demands of justice. Mending what is broken, of course, is not always possible. In the case of a murder, there is no way to restore the life of the victim. Taking the life of the murderer might do some things that many will consider to be justice served, such as the substitution of one life for another. Some Christian thinking has argued that Jesus' death is itself a substitute for a punishment humans deserve, although a great many scholars dispute this understanding. The idea is present in the Gospels as rationale that Caiaphas the Jewish high priest uses for handing Jesus over to death. Caiaphas responded to worries that the Jesus movement would provoke the Romans to destroy Israel by introducing the idea of substitution: 'You do not understand that it is better for you to have one man die for the people than to have the whole nation destroyed' (John 11.50).

The kind of punishment Caiaphas has in mind seeks justice *with* punishment, although the punishment is carried out on someone else. We have already described anthropologist René Girard's concept of the scapegoat mechanism, which has the effect of uniting the community around the exclusion of a single person or smaller group. The Jewish leadership hoped that scapegoating Jesus would 'gather into one the dispersed children of God' (John 11.52). In Luke's account of the same events, scapegoating Jesus had the effect of making Herod and Pilate friends where before they had been enemies (Luke 23.12). Girard notes the same pattern in a lot of ancient myths and stories. In Euripides' *Electra*, for example, the sacrifice of Clytemnestra's daughter, Iphigenia, would have been justified if it had the effect of preventing the sack of the city, saving human lives.[3] What is distinctive about the story of Jesus is the way it turns this on its head. The Gospels and Acts refuse to accept Jesus' death as this kind of sacrifice (since Jesus' death is depicted as unjust killing) in the same way that it refuses to accept that this 'justice' is true justice.

Justice that punishes, it seems, can have many goals and effects. Weighing and considering them is part of the work of 'justice from above'. On the other hand, asking about the place of victims in justice belongs to 'justice from below' and will be taken up in the next chapter. If all punishment makes new victims, rightly or wrongly, then the account of God's mercy described above – justice without punishment – already directs us to look below for a different set of questions than the main ones asked here.

War in the Bible

What does the Bible have to say about war? This question represents the opposite problem from those issues on which the Bible is silent. Here, the Bible seems to have far *too much to say* about war, especially at the level of narrative. What makes the question complicated is that much of what the Bible says about war seems contradictory. When the children of Israel are led out of Egypt by Moses, they are depicted as a conquering army, from 'plundering' the Egyptians of silver and gold to their number coinciding with a standard military unit (Exod. 12). Their escape is not without violence – against the firstborn of Egypt and against the Egyptian army which drowns in the Red Sea. But the Hebrews do not do the fighting; God does. Soon after, Moses tells the people, 'The LORD will fight for you, and you have only to keep still' (Exod. 14.14). When the Amalekites attacked the Israelites in the Sinai wilderness, the Israelites fought back, but were successful only so long as Moses had his arms raised (Exod. 17). Aaron

---

3 René Girard, *Violence and the Sacred*, trans. Patrick Gregory (Baltimore: Johns Hopkins University Press, 1977), 11.

and Hur held up Moses' hands when he got weary. The message is that the people of Israel will succeed militarily only when God fights for them.

Joshua's conquest of the Canaanite cities continues to make this same point, although it makes for especially uncomfortable reading for modern people if they assume that an ethic of war is to be found there. The book of Joshua describes what we would today call ethnic cleansing of the promised land and utterly indiscriminate killing of innocent civilians (women and children) and animals. If read literally and normatively, it violates nearly every historic convention for just warfare in the West. Yet this is not just a modern sentiment. From early on, Christians insisted that these depictions of warfare must be interpreted spiritually and not literally. In the third century, Origen of Alexandria made this point strongly:

> Unless those physical wars bore the figure of spiritual wars, I do not think the books of Jewish history would ever have been handed down by the apostles to the disciples of Christ, who came to teach peace, so that they could be read in the churches. For what good was that description of wars to those to whom Jesus says, 'My peace I give to you; my peace I leave to you,' and to whom it is commanded and said through the Apostle, 'Not avenging your own selves,' and, 'Rather, you receive injury,' and, 'You suffer offense'?[4]

Origen is clear: Christians should read wars in the Old Testament *spiritually*. For him, this means understanding language like 'battle' and 'war' to be analogies to the struggles the Christian soul has against sin and evil. For this reason, Origen points to Paul acting like a military leader in calling Christians to 'Put on the whole armour of God, so that you may be able to stand against the wiles of the devil' (Eph. 6.11). Likewise, in his *Homilies on Judges* (9.1), Origen also talked about Christ as the 'chief of our army' who says to his soldiers, 'If anyone is of a fearful and timid heart, do not come to my wars.' This way of reading the Old Testament figuratively has long been a Christian custom and other ancient writers such as Clement of Alexandria (*c*.150–*c*.215) follow it as well. St Augustine taught that, generally speaking, the Bible ought to be read literally unless a literal reading doesn't lead toward a more holy life or to sound doctrine; in these cases, one should read these passages figuratively.[5] Yet Augustine and Origen approached the relationship between the Old and New Testaments differently. Augustine worked much harder to offer literal and normative readings of the Old Testament. He argued, for example, against Faustus

---

4 Origen, *Homilies on Joshua*, trans. Barbara J. Bruce (Washington, DC: Catholic University of America Press, 2002), Homily 15, p. 138.

5 Augustine, *On Christian Doctrine*, III.x.14.

the Manichaean that Moses and the Israelites were not wrong to wage war since they did so under the authority of God.

Augustine's determination to offer this kind of interpretation of war in the Old Testament then affects how he interprets the pacifistic-sounding passages in the New Testament. Tertullian (160–220) had claimed that 'The Lord, in disarming Peter, ungirt [disarmed] every soldier', referring to Peter's attempt to use violence to prevent Jesus' arrest in the Garden of Gethsemane (Matt. 26.52–53). But Augustine said that Peter's mistake was not the use of the sword, but acting hastily and without proper authority (*Reply to Faustus*). Likewise, rather than taking Jesus' command to turn the other cheek (Matt. 5.39) at face value, Augustine argues that Jesus isn't really teaching a bodily response, but an interior one – Jesus is concerned with the disposition of the heart.

Therefore, even though Augustine (like Origen) was prepared to interpret parts of the Bible spiritually or figuratively, especially when no useful ethic could come out of a literal reading, he nevertheless reads war in the Old Testament literally (unlike Origen). As a consequence it is then the challenging New Testament passages (like the command to love one's enemy) that he reads spiritually.

It's useful to contemplate what is going on with Origen and Augustine since the difference between them illustrates the effects of a decisive shift in the history of Christianity: the conversion of Emperor Constantine in the early fourth century. All Christian writing we have from the period before Constantine is decidedly pacifistic and Origen's work is typical of this. Once there is a Christian emperor, however, the best-known theologians begin to reflect this new alignment of power in how they read and interpret biblical texts about war. But Origen's spiritual reading leaves out additional theological themes that are also worth considering.

Another way of reading Joshua is to try to understand its theological themes, thus approaching the text alongside Origen, but with some differences. One of the complications that comes with reading Joshua historically is that it conflicts strongly with accounts of the same events in the book of Judges. But when Joshua and Judges are both understood to be theological narratives, that is, narratives that convey a certain theology, something different from an ethic of war emerges. Some scholars have referred to the kind of theology in these books as **Deuteronomic theology**. They display narratively the same theological concepts that the book of Deuteronomy presents in the form of commands, warnings and promises. These can be summarized this way: obey the Lord and you will be blessed; disobey the Lord and you will be cursed.

Even though Joshua and Judges tell their stories very differently, both uphold a Deuteronomic theology. In the case of Joshua, Israel is successful in its military campaigns so long as the land is being cleansed of idols and every possible temptation that, if left, will eventually lead Israel into false worship. The exception in Joshua proves the rule: when Achan takes booty from Ai rather than destroying everything (all the townspeople and their possessions were *herem*: 'devoted for destruction'), he is found out and killed. Israel's successes return immediately. In the case of Judges, the book begins by summarizing the conquest of Canaan under Joshua, but in this telling, the direction Israel takes is different. The Israelites are said to enslave rather than destroy the Canaanites. 'When Israel grew strong, they put the Canaanites to forced labour, but did not in fact drive them out' (Judg. 1.28). While this narrative is slightly more palatable to modern readers (since we consider death worse than slavery), the author of Judges believes the opposite since he strongly disapproves of the practice. The continued presence of Canaanites leads Israel to worship their gods:

> Now the angel of the LORD went up from Gilgal to Bochim, and said, 'I brought you up from Egypt, and brought you into the land that I had promised to your ancestors. I said, "I will never break my covenant with you. For your part, do not make a covenant with the inhabitants of this land; tear down their altars." But you have not obeyed my command. See what you have done! So now I say, I will not drive them out before you; but they shall become adversaries to you, and their gods shall be a snare to you.'
>
> (Judg. 2.1–3)

The temptation toward idolatry is a major Deuteronomic theme. So, despite their differences, both the Joshua and Judges narratives underwrite Deuteronomic theology. Joshua shows that obedience leads to blessing; Judges shows that disobedience leads to curses. These are two sides of the same coin. It is likely that this sometimes simplistic theology was part of the way that the people of Israel made sense of the fact of exile at the hands of the Babylonians. As they struggled to understand how God would allow exile to happen, these two narratives made the theological point that their current suffering was the result of their disobedience.

It should also be noted, though, that other parts of the Bible strongly challenge this theology, particularly once the mindset is in place that reverses the logic of Deuteronomic theology to a point where a person who seems blessed must be righteous and a person who appears cursed must have done something wrong. The Wisdom books of the Old Testament (especially Job) are the strongest rebuttal to this belief. But so is the angst in so many of the psalms in which the writer cannot understand why the wicked prosper and the righteous suffer – if Deuteronomic theology were true, how could this be?

What does this discussion have to say about war? I have been trying to show that war narratives are part of a set of theological claims that are contested by other parts of the Old Testament. This means that even the theology these stories uphold needs to be read alongside other theologies such as Job's refusal to attribute suffering to disobedience. In this respect, the question about war can be turned around. Instead of those who wish to make war asking the Bible whether it is all right to do so, this tension over Deuteronomic theology has something to say to those who suffer from the war-making of others. It doesn't excuse or justify war, but, rather like the Bible's complicated response to the question of suffering in general, it is not content with the standard or easy answers. As modest as this sounds, it comforts the defeated exiles.

We should also note some of the perils in reading Old Testament wars as licence for war-making today. For one thing, a common biblical theme is that God brings victory and defeat. These two outcomes are the result not of the strength of armies, but of God's will. In Judges, for example, the Israelite military commander Gideon is told to wage war using a very small army:

> [Gideon] responded, 'But sir, how can I deliver Israel? My clan is the weakest in Manasseh, and I am the least in my family.' The LORD said to him, 'But I will be with you, and you shall strike down the Midianites, every one of them.' (Judg. 6.15–16)

Today's Christians in powerful countries who wish to take instruction from wars in the Old Testament need to reckon with this, since it argues against rather than for a strong military.

A more theological case against reading wars in the Bible as morally normative explicitly links at least many of these wars to sacrifice (we have partly dealt with sacrifice already in Chapter 3). Joshua's wars against the Canaanites were *herem* warfare, ritual acts of sacrifice and worship carried out in the light of God's warnings against forgetting about the Lord in the new land and following other gods. This can be a disturbing link to observe for modern people. But in the scope of the Bible as a whole, however, one witnesses an undercurrent *against* sacrifice that in due course within the prophetic tradition of the Old Testament swells to become a dominant theme. Linking sacrifice with war-making makes sense of the prophetic theme of peace that also accompanies the end of sacrifice. A number of biblical texts illustrate God's own discomfort with sacrifices:

If I were hungry, I would not tell you,
for the world and all that is in it is mine.
Do I eat the flesh of bulls,
or drink the blood of goats?
(Ps. 50.12–13)

Sacrifice and offering you do not desire,
but you have given me an open ear.
Burnt-offering and sin-offering
you have not required.
(Ps. 40.6)

I hate, I despise your festivals,
and I take no delight in your solemn assemblies.
(Amos 5.21)

For I desire steadfast love and not sacrifice,
the knowledge of God rather than burnt-offerings.
(Hos. 6.6)

With what shall I come before the LORD,
and bow myself before God on high?
Shall I come before him with burnt-offerings,
with calves a year old?
Will the LORD be pleased with thousands of rams,
with tens of thousands of rivers of oil?
Shall I give my firstborn for my transgression,
the fruit of my body for the sin of my soul?
(Mic. 6.6–7)

The prophetic theme throughout these texts is that sacrifices are not the way to please God. God wants mercy, love, obedience and justice instead: *morality and ethics*, to use non-biblical words. Isaiah even links commanded sacrifice with unacceptable sacrifice – and even human sacrifice – in order to reframe the commands: 'Whoever slaughters an ox is like one who kills a human being . . . whoever presents a grain-offering, like one who offers swine's blood' (Isa. 66.3). Over time, the Bible is unseating the assumed place of violence as it relates to justice. Both sacrifice and war, I am arguing, play a role in the long-term overturning of this assumption, even before we get to the New Testament. Moreover, in the course of the unfolding of the Old Testament narrative, the concern over remembering the Lord and offering exclusive worship is recast through the language of a new covenant, a theme we explored in Chapter 2.

When Jeremiah talks about a new covenant in which law is written on the hearts of the people (31.31–34), we should read this as a strong contrast to the concerns of Moses in Deuteronomy and of Joshua. Piety and spiritual devotion to God and God's law will not require external reminders; the heart will bear God's imprint and knowledge of God will be unmediated.

What does this mean for war? Between the new covenant and the prophetic correction of Israel's common misunderstanding of sacrifice, war can no longer function as *herem* and it is possible that it never should have. For Christian readers, especially, who read the old covenant in the light of the new, my view is that the wars in the Bible ought to have no place in an apologetic for war.

In turning to the New Testament, we quickly see that there are no wars. When there is violence, the Christians are on the receiving end and the texts typically relate Christian suffering at the hands of others to Christ's own suffering. This is evident in the persecution of the apostles in Acts and in the interpretation of the resistance Paul faces in his Gentile mission (e.g. Acts 9.15–16). Political authorities are never Christian in the New Testament, and Christian instruction on how to behave in the face of violence is always given to those who are potential or actual victims of others. If we focus only on the New Testament, there is very little we would describe as 'justice from above' exercised approvingly by governments or other authorities. The people exercising this authority from above abuse it and are locked in confrontation with God's justice: these are Herod, the Sanhedrin, the Roman governor in Jerusalem and the high priest. In Acts there is a transfer of true authority from the priests at the Jerusalem Temple to the apostles, to those they anoint and also to Paul.

Many looking for something to do with war in the New Testament have noted Paul's language of spiritual warfare. Here the sword of the Spirit (which is the word of God), the shield of faith, the breastplate of righteousness, the belt of truth and the helmet of salvation are well-chosen rhetorical *alternatives* to actual implements of war. All of these things are defensive except for the word of God, the sword, which points to the decisive shift away from real swords, reflecting Paul's conviction that the Church's enemies are not flesh and blood but are spiritual powers (Eph. 6.12). Martin Luther King made a similar shift when he described non-violence as a sword that heals. There is no need to be naive here. Paul certainly knew that Christians had flesh-and-blood enemies. But the Christian struggle is not with them since Christians have been commanded by Jesus to lay down their swords and to turn the other cheek. By invoking metaphorical warfare language, Paul creatively disarms the ordinary force of these words and ideas. Now they are transposed into instruments of peace, righteousness and truth as genuine alternatives to war-making.

Just war theory

We have already observed the way that Christian thinking about war shifted once Christians gained political power, both symbolically and actually with the conversion of Emperor Constantine to Christianity in the early fourth century. A set of disciplined reflections on the morality of war developed, initially most notably by St Ambrose and St Augustine. Although these, and especially Augustine, are considered the Christian fathers of the just war tradition, the name given to the tradition can mislead. The purpose of this reflection, especially in the beginning, was not to justify war, but to limit it by issuing safeguards to make war less likely and less destructive when it was judged to be necessary. Augustine initially formulated his thoughts on war within the context of the Church's discipline of heretics. He worked out what may sound to us like tough love: love and war aren't always at odds with each other, he said.

> Love does not preclude a benevolent severity, nor that correction which compassion itself dictates. No one indeed is fit to inflict punishment save the one who has first overcome hate in his heart. The love of enemies . . . does not exclude wars of mercy waged by the good.[6]

Ideally, violence serves a compassionate purpose of justice and correction of the wrongdoer. It is not only possible to love one's enemy while carrying this out, but the love of one's enemy is positively required to ensure that the violence is not vindictive. Augustine insisted that peace is the goal of war and violence which must be waged in the spirit of love and for the eternal salvation of enemies of peace. The Church may therefore engage in 'a righteous persecution, which the Church of Christ inflicts upon the impious'. Augustine's motivation to use force to persecute heretics is something modern people have difficulty sharing. But it certainly reflects his ethos in which the power of the Church had become strongly associated with political power. On one hand, ecclesiastical disputes posed real threats to the unity of the Empire; on the other hand, church leaders now had much stronger tools at their disposal.

War was now being waged by Christian leaders. Augustine taught that for a war to be considered just, it must be declared by a legitimate

---

6 Cited by Roland H. Bainton, *Christian Attitudes toward War and Peace: A Historical Survey and Critical Re-evaluation* (Nashville: Abingdon, 1960), 97.

authority; this sets it apart from gang rivalry or feuding between private citizens who are not authorized to use force for their own purposes (apart from the common good). His requirement that war should also defend the weak and oppressed also reflects the shift in power by the time he was writing. Previous generations of Christians had no strong allies to call on when persecuted. Now Christian thinkers theorized about the strength of the faith. Augustine also insisted that a just war must be one in which no innocent people are killed; the innocent are to be protected. Nor may priests and monks shed blood.

According to Augustine, war is the product of sin, not of virtue. This means that it should be fought with a 'mournful' or 'sorrowful' attitude. No Christian ought to glorify war. This aspect of just war is particularly in contrast to modern war-making which is often celebrated and its soldiers honoured. Since the modern war-making with which readers will be most familiar is so closely aligned with nationalism rather than service to God, the churchly practices of confession and repentance have no real place. The only option is to try to feel good about fighting in war.

Today, discussion of just war is sometimes reduced to a mere checklist of criteria to meet before entering a war. A striking example of this is a letter sent by several American Christian leaders to President Bush in 2002 approving of war with Iraq. The so-called 'Land Letter' (named after its lead author, Southern Baptist Richard Land) listed each of the just war criteria and briefly told how each was met in that case. An implication of using just war this way is that anyone can use it, as though it can be applied as a theory to any concrete case. Against this kind of use, theologian Daniel Bell (b. 1966) and others have insisted that it is important to be reminded of just war's much richer history, particularly how its original context was not the state or empire but the Church.[7] It was meant to be used by church leaders in order to discern whether Christians could participate in a particular war. It was not supposed to be a tool of statecraft whereby political leaders could justify their war-making. Although it developed away from this original use in time, the fact that the Church used to be at the centre of just war can be shown in some instructions given to medieval confessors for how to handle penance for parishioners who had killed in battle. If it's true, as Augustine said, that war is the result of sin (John Wesley, the founder of Methodism, was more blunt: war simply *is* a sin), then anyone who kills in war needs to do penance, even those who killed in a just war.

---

7 Daniel M. Bell, Jr, *Just War as Christian Discipleship: Recentering the Tradition in the Church Rather Than the State* (Grand Rapids: Brazos, 2009).

The Bigotian Penitential stipulated that killing in war merited 40 days of penance. The Old Irish Penitential required a year and a half for killing in battle or ambushing the enemy. Another, the Penitential of Theodore, required a person who had killed to stay away from the church for 40 days. Fulbert, bishop of Chartres in the eleventh century, imposed a one-year penance for killing in war. Following the Battle of Hastings, a Penitential Ordinance required one year of penance for every man killed; archers, who kill at long range and often don't know how many they kill, were given a flat penance of three years. The seventh-century Penitential of Cummean requires that:

> He who by a blow in a quarrel renders a man incapacitated or maimed shall meet [the injured man's] medical expenses and shall make good the damages for the deformity and shall do his work until he is healed and do penance for half a year.[8]

The penitential response expected of soldiers returning from war is, again, in contrast to the modern practice of celebrating soldiers and veterans. Fighting in a just war has never meant that all bets are off or that killing doesn't still affect the soul of the soldier. Psychological trauma of soldiers returning from war has always been common, yet modern practices are surprisingly ill-suited to restoring them to the community and civilian life. Today's veterans often feel more at ease with other veterans who know the reality of war. Well-intentioned civilians may express their thanks but are not usually prepared to help restore them to a normal life. As strange as the medieval penitentials may sound to modern people, they should be seen as a way that earlier Christians have recognized the deep wounds that killing creates for people and which take a long time to overcome. One of the casualties of just war's drift from Christian to secular hands has been the loss of praxis and liturgy for helping people respond to war.

Most accounts of just war separate the requirements into two categories. *Jus ad bellum* criteria must be met before entering into war if it is to be judged a just war. Once a war has begun, *jus in bello* principles govern the justness of the fighting itself in the style of rules of engagement.

Chief among the *jus ad bellum* principles is **just cause**. Not all causes are just when it comes to war-making. A just cause must be one that the enemy can reverse or stop; it is never just to push for the unconditional surrender

---

8 Cited in Joseph J. Fahey, *War and the Christian Conscience: Where Do You Stand?* (Maryknoll: Orbis, 2005), 93.

of the enemy nation. When Iraq invaded Kuwait in 1990, the United States military, aided by the United Kingdom, Saudi Arabia and Egypt, went to war against the Iraqi army. Many considered the violation of Kuwait's sovereignty to be a just cause; the goal was to get Iraq to leave Kuwait. When this happened, the fighting stopped, as it should according to just war. If coalition forces had continued to pursue the Iraqi army back to Baghdad or to topple the Iraqi government, this would have violated just war since the aims of the war would have exceeded the cause. Furthermore, fighting for causes that are stated as abstract ideals – freedom, justice – cannot satisfy the principle of just cause since it is not clear what the enemy must do (short of being defeated) in order for the war to stop. Some critics have pointed out that the United States was wrong to push for the unconditional surrender of the Japanese in the Second World War. Just cause insists on concrete, real-world actions that one's enemy must carry out in order to avoid war. Likewise, critics of the so-called 'Bush Doctrine' adopted after September 11, 2001 that sought to justify pre-emptive strikes (*anticipatory* self-defence) have argued that this is not allowed under just cause. A related requirement of **right intention** states that a nation must intend peace as the goal of war. It cannot intend economic gain or expansion of its land or power.

The requirement of **last resort** states that the use of lethal force can only be contemplated once all other peaceful means have been tried and given a legitimate chance to work. Critics note how common it is to rush into war without giving serious consideration to diplomatic negotiations. If truly followed, just war would not only require better good-faith efforts to avoid going to war. In the United States, members of the peace movement have occasionally proposed a cabinet-level Department of Peace whose role would be to promote, fund and pursue peacemaking initiatives comparable to the work of the Department of Defense (called the Department of War until 1947).

Another requirement called **proportionality** has two aspects, one which applies to *jus ad bellum* and the other which applies to *jus in bello*. First, when considering the justness of a war, it must be asked whether more good than harm will come from the war. This, as one can imagine, is notoriously difficult or impossible to assess ahead of time; when guesses are made, they tend to underestimate the damage war will cause, especially when it comes to a war's long-term effects such as disease related to unclean water that results from destroyed infrastructure. Moreover, there is an implicit requirement that the nation contemplating waging war be stronger militarily than its opponents. This is because no clearly weaker nation could possibly answer the question about whether more good than harm will result if it is likely to lose, even if fighting in defence. This has led some to refer to this aspect of just war as a bully principle – the moral consideration sides with stronger nations from the outset.

The second aspect of proportionality has to do with the manner of fighting once a war has begun (*jus in bello*): are the weapons and tactics proportional to the goal being sought? To invoke a domestic example that Thomas Aquinas used, consider an armed intruder entering your home. The goal of defending your family would be just, according to Aquinas. But this can be accomplished in lesser and greater ways, from disarming and incapacitating the attacker to killing him or her. Proportionality requires the least amount of force required to stop the attack; fighting must stop once the attacker is no longer a threat.

There are two more *jus in bello* requirements worth discussing. Augustine's insistence that war be declared only by a **legitimate author-ity** has largely been taken, in modern times, to mean that nation-states are the entities that can do this. This is complicated in cases of civil war as well as in situations involving failed states where the very reason for war is tied to the loss of the state's legitimate claims to sovereign power. Beyond this, though, theologian William Cavanaugh argues that it is the Church rather than the state that ought to be the locus of judgement about war, discerning the various realities in the light of the requirements of just war and then directing its members accordingly. This is because the Church is larger than nations, and the civil authorities in Christendom were, in the words of John Figgis, 'the police department of the church'.[9] Armed forces and civil servants, then, ought to serve the aims of the Church – including justice and peace – rather than the Church offering its willingness to aid in achieving the aims of the state.

Since its beginning, just war has insisted on **non-combatant immunity**, meaning that innocent people (those who are not soldiers) cannot be the targets of intentional attacks. But in modern wars, civilian deaths often count for about 70 per cent of a war's total casualties and this propor-tion appears to be increasing. In the First World War, 40 per cent of total deaths were civilians; in the Iraq War (according to the organization Iraqi Body Count), it was 77 per cent. One of the key factors in this increase is the technology of war. Weapons have become more destructive and less

---

9 John Neville Figgis, *Political Thought from Gerson to Grotius: 1414–1625* (New York: Harper, 1960), 5.

discriminating. The phrase 'casualties of war' hardly seems appropriate when the percentages of civilian fatalities are so high.

In the thirteenth century, Thomas Aquinas formulated a principle called **double effect** that is used in moral reasoning about the unintended deaths of innocent civilians in war.[10] (We will discuss double effect again in Chapter 12 when discussing human embryos and euthanasia.) Double effect states that a single action can have two outcomes or effects, one of which is intended and one which is not intended. We might think about bombing a military base that is near a school. The action (bombing the base) would have the intended outcome of destroying the base, but the unintended outcome of also destroying the school. As a rule, the unintended outcome needs to be incidental – the destruction of the school cannot be part of the plan to immobilize the military base in any way. Aquinas put a very high premium on intention, arguing that we know whether or not to call an action moral based on what intentions lie behind it. Aquinas was a brilliant theologian and double effect has a long history in just war. For example, it helps us to understand that when the United States carpet-bombed Tokyo and dropped atomic bombs on Hiroshima and Nagasaki in 1945, these must be declared immoral acts according to just war. The reason is that civilians were intentionally targeted and only after a great deal of mental wrangling could anyone claim that the killing of innocents in these cities was unintended.

This problem is largely the result of indiscriminate modern weapons. In our example with the school and the military base, the proximity of the school is only a problem because the bombs in question destroy so widely. If the operation involved a different tactic – soldiers on the ground armed with daggers, say – the school would certainly be safe. One practical outcome of just war reasoning is therefore a tactical one: insisting on the least destructive means. Many have concluded that nuclear war can never be just for these reasons.

It must be said, though, that Aquinas and double effect have their critics. The main criticism is that, in practice, it can be very hard to distinguish between intended and unintended outcomes. Is it enough to say 'We wish the school wasn't there, but it is' in order to intend justly? Or does the presence of the school demand a more robust search for a military alternative? Moreover, because of self-deception and self-ignorance, we aren't always aware of our own real intentions. Psychological experiments clearly show

---

10 Thomas Aquinas, *ST*, II-II.64.7.

this.[11] More generally, critics of the rule about non-combatants worry that it does more harm than good. By continuing to insist that it is part of modern war-making, while the civilian death rate is often three times that of combatants, are we merely comforting ourselves with the *thought* that we have acted morally? Would we be better off being honest about what is really going on?

Just war is a significant way that Christians have thought about the ethics of war, but it is only one among several ways. Not only does just war become thinkable only after Christians get a taste of political power (recall that we are looking at 'justice from above'), but also the shifting place of the Church in political life throughout the centuries has led to changes in just war itself. We have noted that just war risks reduction to a mere checklist in the absence of disciplined Christian practice. A continuing question for Christian just war ethics, then, has to do with the virtues that are necessary to wage a just war. Are the churches able to produce soldiers who would rather die than kill unjustly? What kind of moral instruction forms people in this way? Or have the churches largely supported whatever the state asks of its soldiers? How ought churches send off, pray for and welcome home soldiers? In some ways, these questions assume that war happens elsewhere. What about when war is happening at home? What role do the churches play? The larger Christian tradition of just war reflection has resources for answering these questions; the modern, secular versions of just war do not.

---

11 See the discussion of this critique in Philip A. Reed, 'The Danger of Double Effect', *Christian Bioethics* 18.3 (2012): 287–300, who ultimately still defends double effect. Dana Kay Nelkin and Samuel C. Rickless argue that it's always possible to identify a person's intention in some way that evades the charge that he or she is intending harm, and so distinctions between intending and foreseeing harm are of no moral importance. See 'So Close, Yet So Far: Why Solutions to the Closeness Problem for the Doctrine of Double Effect Fall Short', *NOÛS* 49.2 (2015): 376–409. Nelkin and Rickless point out that Jeremy Bentham preferred to think of foresight as just another kind of intention.

10

Justice from below (liberation)

Unlike the previous chapter, justice in this chapter originates from below. 'Below' points to people and actions that do not wield sovereign power. Recalling Raphael's painting of the Transfiguration discussed at the beginning of the previous chapter, we now shift our focus on to the lower half of the painting – toward the painful, contorted human realities of oppression that a great many forces, including religious ones, attempt to draw our attention away from.

Nevertheless, I want to preserve some irony in these terms 'above' and 'below' since these are also theological words. Christians speak of God above and the world of here below. We are God's creatures and God reigns over it all – God is sovereign. What is ironic, then, is the sense that justice conceived from below usually claims God's justice as warrant for pursuing it. And while this doesn't differ from justice 'from above' in how it appeals to God's justice, it does think of *its own relationship* to God's justice quite differently. To claim, for example, that God is on the side of the poor and not on the side of the rich is to loosen the grip that wealth traditionally has on the power that it believes justifies it. After all, the rich believe God is on their side too and will speak of their wealth as God's blessing.

Justice from below talks of God as dwelling with us in Jesus Christ, becoming a slave for our sakes and giving up the privileges of sovereign power. This is crucial because it means that Jesus shares the experience of the poor, the despised, rejected, reviled and disinherited in order to bring good news – indeed life – to the darkest areas of human existence.

The topics addressed in this chapter differ from the last. This is because the categories of class, race and gender are the chief domains for discussing the liberation of people that the gospel brings. If justice from above 'sets things right' by restoring balance and order to the way society was, it defines this narrowly. Order often means returning power to the powerful and it usually requires some coercion or violence.

The liberation discussed in this chapter as justice from below sees 'setting things right' as deliverance of oppressed people, often from the very orders that justice from above seeks to establish. And while these two perspectives are not always at odds with each other, they often are. Jesus was unpopular with rulers because of his words and actions in support of justice for the oppressed. He preached good news to the poor as himself a poor person welcoming God's deliverance from the bonds of servitude to economic and religious systems that benefited the people at the top.

By our own day, both the oppression and the liberation of various groups can sometimes be seen as the work of Christian belief and practice. So part of this chapter's task will be to identify the tensions internal to Christianity itself on class, race and gender, and offer an account that liberates rather than oppresses.

Class

We have seen how important the poor are to Christianity. Even though the Bible doesn't explicitly use the language of class, it often speaks about people using categories of rich and poor. According to Jesus, the gospel is good news for the poor. This is because when the kingdom of God comes, it is the poor who rejoice. In this, Jesus is continuing the message of prophets like Amos, Isaiah, Jeremiah, Habakkuk, Micah and Hosea who all bear a message that links justice with the knowledge of God. When Mary hears that she will bear the Messiah, she gives thanks for God's goodness, in part anticipating what the arrival of the kingdom of God will mean for the poor, weak, and politically and economically disenfranchised:

> [The Lord] has brought down the powerful from their thrones,
>> and lifted up the lowly;
> he has filled the hungry with good things,
>> and sent the rich away empty.
>
> (Luke 1.52–53)

This was nothing new, but should be seen as the culmination of the Bible's long story of deliverance. God's creation of the Hebrew people was through an act of liberating them from slavery and violent oppression. The truth of God's message throughout the Old Testament often came through persecuted prophets who bore a dangerous message of confrontation against powerful elites. The idea that God in fact sides with the poor against the rich reaches a climax in the Incarnation of Christ. As incarnate, Jesus' perspective is not only as human but as a poor human, politically powerless in Roman-occupied first-century Palestine. Hailed as king and himself acting to restore the Davidic kingship, Jesus nevertheless suffered a humiliating death, thus recasting worldly notions of kingly power from the perspective of those who not only don't have it, but who have become accustomed to being its victims.

Even so, a Christian concern for the welfare of the poor doesn't usually stand alone. Along with it comes longstanding concerns about the souls of the wealthy. As we saw in Chapter 2, Jesus' encounter with the rich young man in Mark 10 is based on a question about what he needed to do in order to inherit eternal life. When he is instructed to sell all of his possessions and give the money to the poor, it is evident that his many possessions had become an impediment to his own salvation. The disciples, too, worry about Jesus' comment that it is easier for a camel to go through the eye of a needle than for a rich person to enter the kingdom of God. But the rich *can* be saved by using their wealth to benefit the poor. Part of the good news is that releasing the rich from their love of money provides the poor with material benefit. Not to be overlooked as well is the language Jesus uses in this encounter to talk about salvation. It is put in terms of having treasure in heaven (not on earth).

This same image – treasure in heaven – is elaborated within the early Christian tradition. It's most noticeable in the first- or second-century writing *The Shepherd of Hermas*, which some early theologians considered to be canonical alongside the texts in our New Testament. *The Shepherd* is very concerned that Christians not live as though this world is their home: 'You know that you who are the servants of God dwell in a strange land; for your city is far away from this one.' The Christian readers are challenged not to spend their wealth on houses and land in this earthly city as though they are making permanent preparations for themselves. This teaching is accompanied by an awareness that they were regarded with suspicion by their neighbours and pagan authorities. If they were constantly at risk of being banished for breaking the laws of the land, why put energy into set-tling in, focusing on possessions that can be easily lost?

The alternative course that *The Shepherd* instructs is:

> Instead of lands, therefore, buy afflicted souls, according as each one is able, and visit widows and orphans, and do not overlook them; and spend your wealth and all your preparations, which ye received from the Lord, upon such lands and houses.

Here, the words 'lands' and 'houses' are being used to refer to widows and orphans, which serve as a kind of investment for one's heavenly future. The text goes on to describe the very reason for wealth to begin with:

> For to this end did the Master make you rich, *that you might perform these services unto Him*; and it is much better to purchase such lands, and

possessions, and houses, as you will find in your own city, when you come to reside in it.[1]

In contrast to the ways that unbelievers spend their money, this kind of expenditure is made with joy. It is also ultimately for the salvation of those who learn to spend their wealth on behalf of the poor. Economic justice, then, is about the salvation of both the poor and the rich.

In the twentieth century, a number of Christian scholars from the Global South sought to retrieve this ancient emphasis on economic justice. Latin American **liberation theology** was the first and best-known version of this retrieval. Many scholars enlisted Karl Marx's critiques of capitalism, insisting that capitalism had blinded the Church to the idolatry of money. Wealth and poverty were the primary emphases of liberation theologians, the first of whom were from Latin America and reflected the economic condition of that continent's poor. What they offered was a Christian critique of the dominant Western forms of Christianity. Their accusation was that Western Christianity had come to favour the rich by neglecting the body at the expense of the soul, meaning that the faith had become consumed with otherworldly realities. The otherworldly message to the world's poor was to seek salvation in Christ in pursuit of heavenly, rather than worldly, well-being. It is a comfortable though certainly condescending message for the rich to tell. Most damning, though, was the liberationist observation that poor Christians had come to believe it too. Those who followed Marx most explicitly were able to identify the way that this form of religion had become *ideology*.

According to Marx, the dominant realities of any society can be thought of as a house – the portion above the ground called the **superstructure** with the **base** referring to the portion below. Marx taught that the most important realities in a society are the economic ones that nevertheless get buried and not addressed directly. These include the ways the upper classes exploit the poor, particularly in the form of cheap labour, and the fact that the working poor do not own the land, tools, machines and materials that are needed to produce wealth; instead, both the wealth and means of production belong to the rich. Even though these are enormously important, the superstructure of the society (media, politics, religion, culture) keeps these things buried.

Marx wrote during the Industrial Revolution and his insights are most directly applicable to industrial settings which are now spread throughout

---

1 Emphasis added.

the globe, with new global dynamics governing the flow of wealth between rich and poor countries. Of concern here is how the various superstructure elements of a society include religion, which Marx famously said functions as an opiate to the masses: it keeps them complacent since it so effectively keeps the people's focus away from their economic exploitation. Marx discussed **ideology** as ideas that function to justify or distract in this way. I think that we can get a handle on what Marx meant by thinking about the fans of professional sports teams. Marx would have understood as ideology how working people might put no effort into understanding or resisting being exploited by their employers while expending enormous energy being fans of a team and believing that their team's rivalries are very important. In the same way, any societal force is part of the superstructure if it functions to legitimize the base, not only not to call it into question, but also to ensure that it doesn't receive a lot of attention (see Figure 2).

To Marx, religion is like this, especially religion that promotes escapism, that values the soul over the body, and eternal life over material existence.

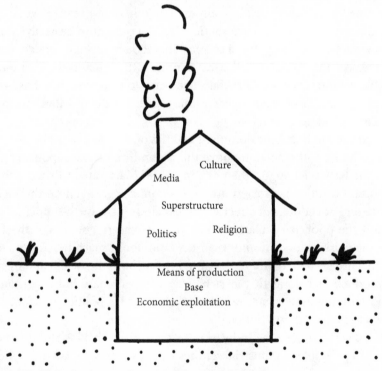

Figure 2 Karl Marx's concept of a society's base and superstructure
The base determines and shapes the superstructure while the superstructure legitimizes and maintains the base

Liberationist followers of Marx thought his critiques simply applied to the *dominant* traditions of Christianity that had developed over the years, but weren't true of Christianity in its true essence and as practised in the spirit of its founding. They argued against spiritualizing the Gospel texts relating to wealth and poverty and insisted that the primary interpretations ought to be materialist.

José Porfirio Miranda, in *Marx and the Bible* (1977), argued that the practice of almsgiving should be thought of as economic redistribution rather than charity. Miranda was a liberation theologian from Mexico who studied in the United States and Germany. To make his case for redistribution, Miranda considered the parable of the Unjust Steward from Luke 16. In this parable, a steward who had been working for a wealthy man is about to lose his job. To secure a future for himself, he reduces the debts owed to the wealthy man so that the debtors will be grateful and act toward him with kindness when he is out of work. Jesus concludes that his followers ought to 'make friends for yourselves by means of dishonest wealth so that when it is gone, they may welcome you into the eternal homes' (v. 9). Miranda renders the phrase 'dishonest wealth' as 'money of injustice' and interprets it to mean that *all money* comes from injustice. He then links this teaching to the tradition of almsgiving:

> The act which in the West is called almsgiving for the original Bible was a restitution that someone makes for something that is not his. The Fathers of the early Church saw this with great clarity . . . [Quoting St Jerome] 'And [Jesus] very rightly said, "money of injustice," for all riches come from injustice. Unless one person has lost, another cannot find. Therefore I believe that the popular proverb is very true: "The rich person is either an unjust person or the heir of one."'[2]

Miranda sees a clear connection between Jesus' teaching in Luke and Marx's analysis. His point is that the reason almsgiving is commended within Christianity has nothing to do with the generous spirit it demonstrates on behalf of the giver (that would be the gospel from the perspective of the rich). The reason it is commended is because it restores to the poor what has been stolen from them. According to Miranda, this is what the Bible calls justice. If we step back from some of the specific questions like the one involving Luke 16, we can see that whether one reads the Bible from above or from below can lead to different interpretations. For example, Miranda's analysis of this text differs somewhat from the attitude of

---

2 José Porfirio Miranda, *Marx and the Bible: A Critique of the Philosophy of Oppression* (Maryknoll, Orbis, 1974), 15.

The Shepherd, which we looked at earlier. Recall that *The Shepherd* was directing its teaching to people who had wealth at their disposal. They at least were faced with choices like whether to spend their money on land and houses or whether to 'buy afflicted souls'.

Liberation theology doesn't just teach that the poor are valued and are to be valued by those who are not poor – this perspective says that the Church is *for* the poor. Even more important is the idea that the Church is also the church *of* the poor. This means that the viewpoints of the poor should be given more weight, that it matters how the world looks from the perspective and experience of people who must struggle to survive and who know first-hand the misery of oppression.

Liberation theology is not only known for its strong focus on economic themes. It is also celebrated for its method, the way it insists that the entire theological enterprise ought to begin with praxis. We looked at this concept in Chapter 2. Praxis is a way of describing how people actually live, what conditions characterize their daily lives. Whether someone is rich or poor will shape how he or she views almost everything else. Liberation theology begins with the praxis of the poor and works from there to theory. Historically, most theology has not done this, especially as it has tended to be produced (since Constantine) by those who can be said to benefit in some way from connections with political power. Theology from that perspective, according to liberationists, cannot help but be coloured by these connections, which will often mean downplaying difficult economic teachings and messages of material good news for others. Instead, liberation theologians have tended also to produce their theology in the midst of grassroots work. They are, to use Antonio Gramsci's phrase, 'organic intellectuals' whose feet-on-the-ground approach seeks to uncover theology that is already at work among the people and in popular movements. And since they have also often been trained at elite institutions, many liberation theologians then translate grassroots theology into the categories being used by the academy.

One of the best examples of starting with praxis can be seen in the work of Ernesto Cardenal, a Roman Catholic priest in Nicaragua who served among peasants (*campesinos*) in an archipelago called Solentiname in Lake Nicaragua in the 1970s. During this time, Cardenal didn't preach sermons, but instead led dialogues based on the Gospel reading among his parishioners. Over 100 of these dialogues have been transcribed into a book called *The Gospel in Solentiname.* 'The *campesinos*' discussions were often more profound than those of many theologians,' writes Cardenal, 'but they reflected the simplicity of the gospel readings themselves. That is not surprising. The *gospel*, or good news (good news to the poor), was written for them, by people like them.'[3] The book is clearly different from modern academic commentaries on the Bible, which try to understand texts by locating them in historical and theological contexts. The *campesinos* of Solentiname brought their own experiences to their reading and sought to understand the gospel in the light of it.

In their conversation about Mary's song, the *campesinos* rejoice that Mary is so obviously on their side. When they discuss Jesus' encounter with the rich young man, one of the speakers, Olivia, comments that 'Even the rich can be saved, if they share, but not if they don't. And it's God who through a miracle can make the rich share and also be saved.'[4] Then Cardenal interjects a note about the way all things will be in the end: 'There won't be any poor people to distribute the wealth to, because with it all distributed there won't be rich and poor. That's the kingdom of God.'[5] Another, Alejandro, is struck by the way the disciples point out to Jesus that they have given up everything to follow him. Alejandro then insists that holding on to wealth isn't just a problem of the rich since the poor also have things they have a hard time giving up, such as homes and loved ones. Olivia agrees, 'Yes, we poor can also be selfish and just hang on to the four hens we have.' Laureano goes back to Cardenal's point about the end of the distribution of wealth in the kingdom of God. He then thinks about all of the people who are frantically buying and selling in the marketplace and tries to put it in this perspective. 'They don't know that afterwards they won't need to go around selling like idiots crying their wares in the street.'

Adan responds, 'Maybe nobody's shown them the Gospel.'

Race

We will consider the topic of race in terms of justice. There are certainly other things that can be said about race, some of which will also be touched on here. For example, where do our ideas of race come from? As we tend to

---

3 Ernesto Cardenal, *The Gospel in Solentiname*, trans. Donald D. Walsh (Maryknoll: Orbis, 2010), xi.

4 Cardenal, *Gospel in Solentiname*, 498.

5 Cardenal, *Gospel in Solentiname*, 499.

use it, the concept of race is a modern social construct that is imposed on human beings and classifies them. The ancient parallels are not identical. The Old Testament Jewish conception saw humanity comprising God's chosen people (the Jews), held by God's covenant with Abraham, and the other nations or Gentiles. The story of the Bible depicts God overcoming this division between Jew and Gentile by bringing Gentiles within the household of God through circumcision and keeping the law of Moses. Paul produces a Christian variation on this in which baptism 'into Christ Jesus' takes the place of circumcision and other acts of obedience to the law. In Romans 11, Paul explains that Gentile Christians are being grafted into the olive tree of God's covenant with the children of Abraham. The Church exists at the intersection of Jews and Gentiles who confess Jesus as the Messiah.

This is the basis of Paul's declaration that there is no Jew and Greek in Christ (Gal. 3.28). Theological discussions of race often point to this verse to highlight the distinctive contribution that Christianity brings to relativizing the racial categories we have received. But it is important to recognize that modern ideas about race do not map very well on to the Jew–Gentile distinction. This is a distinction that is primarily about covenant rather than what we think of as ethnicity. In fact, covenants with Abraham and Moses *create* a people who were not previously constituted as such, since the Bible understands Jews to be children of these promises.

The Jew–Gentile relationship has sometimes been used very poorly in Christianity's history of thinking about race. In Chapter 6, we looked at Willie James Jennings' argument that Western colonialism was aided by some mistaken theological ideas. The Church in the West had forgotten that it was largely a church of Gentiles but still hung on to the idea of election, which it transferred on to categories of race. We don't need to rehearse all of Jennings' argument here, but it's an important example of how poor theology can be displayed in real history with disastrous results. Setting things right is unfortunately never as simple as correcting the theology and then hoping for the best. But some believe that part of the way forward involves revisiting the kind of reconciliation that originally sought to overcome the distinction between Jews and Gentiles in the first place. Coming to terms with this specific form of reconciliation presented the Christian Church with two of its most difficult initial challenges, both closely related and told in the book of Acts.

In the first, Acts 6 shows something of a fall from the somewhat utopian communal gatherings of the Jerusalem church in which all needs were met. The church members had been gathering daily for prayer, worship, instruction by the apostles and a communal meal. But as their numbers grew, the Greek Jewish widows were being overlooked in the distribution of the food in favour of the Hebrew Jewish widows. In general, needs would have been greatest among widows regardless of whether they were Greek or Hebrew. Yet this early tendency to show favouritism has theological roots, and the solution to it – establishment of the office of deacons to focus on congregational service – set the Christian trend going forward, both in church practice as well as in its theology. At stake was one of the key purposes of eating together: providing concretely for the hungry. As long as Hebrew and Greek widows were treated differently, not all of these needs could be met. They needed reconciliation in order for the meal to work.

The second challenge is related to the first, but it takes on a different quality once the theological questions are made explicit. Acts recounts the start of the gospel mission to Gentiles by depicting the Christian movement quickly becoming multi-ethnic and going out from Jerusalem into non-Jewish regions. Whereas the Jews (including Jewish Christians) in Jerusalem probably all kept the traditional dietary laws, the growing Christian movement shifts away from this. Practically speaking, if Jewish Christian missionaries are going into Gentile areas equipped with both a message and a meal of reconciliation, eating together should not be a barrier, as a concern over unclean foods surely is. Peter receives a vision in Acts 10 instructing him to eat unclean foods, breaking down a potential barrier between himself and Cornelius, the Italian centurion whom he was about to meet. The message given to Peter – 'What God has made clean, you must not call profane' (Acts 10.15) – goes beyond food and refers to Gentiles in general. The meal of reconciliation is a microcosm of the gospel's function to reconcile people to each other and to God. At the same time, people of all time periods who are in conflict find it very difficult to eat together. Peter's conclusion confirms the key issue with the widows as well: 'I truly understand that God shows no partiality' (Acts 10.34). When this approach to Gentiles is concretized at the Church's first council, Peter's plea to the Jewish leaders is the same: 'In cleansing their hearts by faith [God] has made no distinction between them and us' (Acts 15.9).

The work that establishes and clarifies the biblical and theological principles of equality between people is obviously important. But the history of race is a history of inequality and therefore calls for more than equal treatment. Like liberation theology, black theology emerged in the twentieth century with this focus on praxis and with the goal of liberation from oppression tied to race. The best-known scholar of black theology is James

Cone (b. 1938), an African American from Arkansas who published *Black Theology and Black Power* in 1969 and has served as a professor at Union Theological Seminary in New York City since 1970. Cone links his consistent priority on the liberation of oppressed people with the idea of Israel's election, which he argues is inseparable from Israel's exodus liberation from bondage to the Egyptians. As with Jennings' argument, Cone understands that the idea that some people are elect can be dangerous when it is lifted out of the story by which God creates a people. (Fully developing this point would take us too far afield, but we could cite a lot of additional examples, such as the way that the idea of being a chosen people animated a lot of early American thinking, including that which approved of the displacement of native peoples.[6]) Black theology is done by and for the oppressed community which theology serves to liberate; liberation is a theme Cone documents throughout the whole Bible. Key to understanding black theology is Cone's claim that God isn't colour-blind, but instead takes the side of the oppressed. In class terms, as we have seen, this means that God has a 'preferential option for the poor'. When it comes to race, a colour-blind God is at best an abstraction that ignores the history of racism. At worst, it is a way of separating God from his concern for justice:

> To say God is color-blind is analogous to saying that God is blind to justice and injustice, to right and wrong, to good and evil. Certainly this is not the picture of God revealed in the Old and New Testaments. Yahweh takes sides. On the one hand, Yahweh sides with Israel against the Canaanites in the occupancy of Palestine. On the other hand, Yahweh sides with the poor within the community of Israel against the rich and other political oppressors. In the New Testament, Jesus is not for all, but for the oppressed, the poor and unwanted of society, and against oppressors. The God of the biblical tradition is not uninvolved or neutral regarding human affairs; God is decidedly involved. God is active in human history, taking sides with the oppressed of the land.[7]

To Cone, the words 'black' and 'blackness' aren't just descriptions of skin tone or ethnic heritage. They are words that describe a status of oppression by 'white' and 'whiteness'. He therefore uses the term 'white theology' as black theology's counterpart to describe conceptions of God and other theological topics that sanction oppression. Cone's analysis is deeply connected to the history of slavery in the United States and his language often

---

6 See, for example, Robert Bellah, *The Broken Covenant: American Civil Religion in Time of Trial* (New York: Crossroad, 1975), especially chapter 2 titled 'America as a Chosen People'.
7 James H. Cone, *A Black Theology of Liberation* (Philadelphia: J. B. Lippincott, 1970), 25–6.

reflects this, such as when he uses words like 'master' to describe the white role in oppression. Yet apart from the areas of life we normally think of as contributing to oppression (economic and political access, for example), there are the thought forms of the oppressor or master which oppressed people are forced to adopt in order to get by. Adopting them means undergoing the ways that the master defines, locates and fixes the meaning and significance of the lives of oppressed people. As Cone uses the term, white theology describes some of the thought forms used by masters to enslave blacks.

Because it is nevertheless black *theology*, Cone's argument points to an even deeper need to liberate theology itself from whiteness. Enslaved Africans who turned the master's spiritual instruction around into ideas about liberation were finding subversive strands within white theology. 'The task of Black Theology', writes Cone, 'is to take Christian tradition that is so white and make it black, by showing that the white man does not know really what he is saying when he affirms Jesus as the Christ. He who has come to redeem us is not white but black; and the redemption of which he speaks has nothing to do with stabilizing the status quo.'[8]

Cone is aware of objections to his usage of 'white' and 'black'. For example, the term 'black theology' can be heard as too narrowly focusing on the oppression faced by one group. In response, Cone clarifies that blackness should be thought of more generally to point to victims of oppression. But he believes that the reactions the term sometimes provokes are instructive and useful for isolating the real concerns of his readers. The concerns often turn out to be worries about the revolutionary potential in talk of liberation rather than a genuine concern to include all of the oppressed. Cone also knows that not every person with white skin represents whiteness or white theology. Far from dismissing all theology by white people out of hand, he shows his appreciation for any theology that is written with reference to oppression and names Karl Barth, Dietrich Bonhoeffer and Reinhold Niebuhr as examples. The problem is that white theologians have generally had the luxury of not writing from a black perspective. This is not a fact found at the level of a person's skin, but in the embodied history of modern racist societies.

For this reason, black theology takes a selective approach to what is commonly thought to comprise the highlights of the Christian tradition. Before the abolition of slavery in Britain and the United States, for example, many black preachers and some white preachers had a level of moral

---

8 Cone, *A Black Theology of Liberation*, 29, n. 4.

clarity about slavery's evils not universally shared. These, Cone says, represent more significant figures in the tradition than do Martin Luther and John Calvin. A similar approach is taken to the Bible, recognizing that every community of Bible-readers will in practice highlight some parts of the Bible and neglect others. What determines this is some set of theological principles most valued by the community; its focus will follow. The experience of oppression, Cone maintains, closely connects the concerns of today's black communities with some of the most significant concerns of the communities that produced the biblical writings. This is especially true for texts like Exodus and others that counsel remembrance of God's liberating acts in bringing justice to members of a society in which those deeds have faded from view.

More complicated, Cone teaches, is allowing the Bible to instruct oppressed people beyond what first jumps out as useful for liberation. 'Whatever [black theology] says about liberation', writes Cone, 'must be said in light of the black community's experience of Jesus Christ.'[9] Martin Luther King's message of non-violence resonated well with the black Church in America when more radical figures struggled for the same audience. Cone believes that the message of black power might have more immediately served the needs of the black community for liberation, but King was able to address the soul of the black Church and its tradition of seeking an authentically Christian liberation. Cone is not critical of King for this, but he is aware that white theology will sometimes also teach non-violence for different reasons. White appeals for non-violence might not serve the purpose of liberation at all, but instead serve to keep the status quo relatively unchanged and keep revolution at bay. In our day, this is no doubt the purpose when governments approve of protests as long as they are non-violent. Such protests are less likely to change things.

If black theology can play the role of helping liberate theology from whiteness, as I suggested above, the distinction it helps us see between white non-violence and black non-violence is surely part of this. Non-violence taught and practised by the oppressed differs from non-violence taught (and not practised) by oppressors. In fact, as Gandhi and King believed, non-violence can expose the hidden violences of oppression. These will include double standards about the use of violence (such as what is used in 'keeping the peace' and 'maintaining order' versus 'disturbing the peace' and 'disorderly conduct'). But non-violence will also expose something

---

9 Cone, *A Black Theology of Liberation*, 77.

even more subtle, namely, the hidden agendas behind some proposals for non-violence itself.

What Jennings calls 'the racial condition' as we know it is as much the product of Christianity as it is something a more faithful Christianity must oppose. It is the condition of dignifying and rewarding certain kinds of achievements (behaviours, attitudes, moralities) with the label 'white', a concept that has historically been quite fluid. Some societies that today consider Italian, Greek, Irish or European Jewish immigrants to be white did not do so in the past, especially when these groups were taken to pose some kind of threat. The racial condition is a social and cultural phenomenon and doesn't just arise out of nature. The social and cultural practices that produce and sustain it might be resisted through a more robust Christian practice.

We have seen that baptism is meant to disrupt settled identities. Jennings describes one purpose of baptism as breaking up homogeneity and inviting multiplicity. Race will not magically disappear. In fact, some attempts to make race disappear are just disguised ways of reasserting white sovereignty and ignoring or disguising oppression. Christians have used baptism in this way too – to reinforce the status quo rather than to challenge it – in quite the opposite way from what it is meant to do. Slave-owners in seventeenth-century colonial America hesitated about evangelizing their slaves because they worried that if slaves were baptized, they would need to be freed. But in September 1667, the Commonwealth of Virginia declared that 'the conferring of baptism does not alter the condition of the person as to his bondage or freedom'.[10] Baptism was made an innocuous sacrament that does nothing to liberate the person nor to enrich the Church. But Jennings argues that race can be put in its place relative to the new, *mixed* people that God is continually creating by joining many different people who have different ways of living and different visions of life in God.[11] The waters of baptism are not meant to blend the newly baptized into a unity that more or less leaves the Church unmoved, only bigger. Rather:

> This child or adult enters through the waters of baptism the body of Jesus filled with different bodies, spanning space and time. The newly baptized are set on a journey that will bind them to peoples they have not seen, to ways of life they have not known, and endow them with a holy desire to love other

---

10 Virginia Slave Laws Digital History: <http://www.digitalhistory.uh.edu/disp_textbook.cfm?smtID=3&psid=71>.

11 Willie James Jennings, 'Being Baptized: Race' in *The Blackwell Companion to Christian Ethics*, 2nd edn, ed. Stanley Hauerwas and Samuel Wells (Oxford: Blackwell, 2011), esp. 288.

people different from the people who brought them to those waters. This is the fire born of baptism that they will carry.[12]

Gender

In order to continue the theme of justice from below, we will consider issues related to gender and Christian ethics in terms of justice. Indicating that this is my plan tips my hand, however, since it shows my own belief that the most important questions regarding men and women have to do with the pursuit of equal dignity, treatment and expression within the lives of Christian families and congregations. This is an *egalitarian* view of the sexes. More conservative scholars and traditions argue for a *complementarian* perspective in which men and women are expected to play different roles that complement each other, while leadership ('headship') roles are reserved for men. Vocal advocates for change in the all-male priesthood of the Roman Catholic Church emerged in the 1960s. Mainline Protestants spent a lot of energy on questions about the role of women in the Church in the 1960s and 1970s in response to the advances made by the women's movement. Evangelicals debated it about a decade later.

By now, the respective camps are pretty well entrenched and, on the whole, debate on this topic isn't as lively as it once was. Progressives see the issues of gender having to do with equality, freedom and justice in which some secular values of social reform place a good pressure to hear God's fresh voice speaking to today's churches. Conservatives see the issues having to do with faithfulness to strict readings of the Bible and a refusal to accommodate to shifts in the surrounding culture. In this sense, the difference is pretty much a version of the older fundamentalist–modernist split from the 1920s. In truth, it is not just a debate about women's roles, but it is secondarily also about the nature of the family, the place of children, the workplace and the nature of the Church. In this book, we deal with some of these matters in other chapters.

The debate is often waged on biblical grounds by puzzling over whether elements of biblical cultures that we have called patriarchal have any *morally normative* force for Christians in other cultures. And because no culture is static, how should Christians assess, not to mention assist, movements away from patriarchy when some of the Bible's teaching appears to reinforce it? Protestant complementarians mostly look at Paul's writings in

---

12 Jennings, 'Being Baptized: Race', 286.

the New Testament to make a biblical case for different gender roles in the household, society and Church. Catholic complementarians often appeal to natural law as Thomas Aquinas did when arguing that the order of the human family depends on women being 'governed by others wiser than themselves' such that 'by such a kind of subjection woman is naturally subject to man, because in man the discretion of reason predominates'.[13] Throughout the centuries, many other male theologians also assumed the inferiority of women.

Some of the key Pauline texts seem clear enough, rooting gender roles in creation by appealing to the story of Adam and Eve or by appealing to God's very nature:

> Let a woman learn in silence with full submission. I permit no woman to teach or to have authority over a man; she is to keep silent. For Adam was formed first, then Eve; and Adam was not deceived, but the woman was deceived and became a transgressor. Yet she will be saved through childbearing, provided they continue in faith and love and holiness, with modesty.
>
> (1 Tim. 2.11–15)

> But I want you to understand that Christ is the head of every man, and the husband is the head of his wife, and God is the head of Christ . . . For a man ought not to have his head veiled, since he is the image and reflection of God; but woman is the reflection of man. Indeed, man was not made from woman, but woman from man. Neither was man created for the sake of woman, but woman for the sake of man. For this reason a woman ought to have a symbol of authority on her head, because of the angels.
>
> (1 Cor. 11.3, 7–10)

Feminist scholars object to automatically taking Paul's words on board for a Christian ethic today. Elisabeth Schüssler Fiorenza (b. 1938), a Roman Catholic theologian at Harvard Divinity School and author of many works on feminist theology, including *In Memory of Her* (1983), argues for a **hermeneutic of suspicion**. Approaching the Bible this way means trying to detect what is going on with a text beyond the words written. Fiorenza says that if texts like the ones above tell us about Paul's attitude toward women more than they offer a substantive ethic for Christians to adopt, then it is especially interesting that Jesus in the Gospels sounds so very different. Her point isn't just that Jesus didn't bother to say such things, but that the purpose of the Gospels – and perhaps the purpose of Jesus' mission more generally – on this point goes in a radically different direction.

---

13 Thomas Aquinas, *ST*, I.92 Article 1, reply to objection 2.

It is true that egalitarians and feminists point to Jesus and his dealings with women in order to make a case for how attitudes in the day were being recast in the light of the kingdom of God. Jesus especially took time in his ministry for women and children, such as when he heals a woman with a haemorrhage through his touch, indicating that her unclean status in that society didn't bother him. In Mark 5, that story is portrayed as an interruption that temporarily kept Jesus from performing a healing for someone deemed much more important, a leader of the synagogue, whose ill daughter dies during the delay, but whom Jesus later raises. Stories like these show Jesus' disregard for status in the light of the kingdom of God which orders things very differently, putting the last first and the first last.

The role of women in the kingdom of God is most dramatically shown in the role women play as witnesses of the resurrection. Women were legally disqualified from acting as credible witnesses, but in this case were the first to carry the Easter message. The point is probably twofold. On the one hand, the nature of the good news is best served by 'discredited' witnesses since belief in the resurrection depends on the eyes of faith rather than a legal argument. The idea is that no person should be argued into belief, which is more about the heart's trust than the mind's agreement. On the other hand, the women *as women* are blessed to be the first entrusted with the Easter message since their status will need to be reconsidered by the new society that the resurrection creates. The Church will henceforth play the 'womanly' discredited role when it comes to its main mission and message. In a setting where legal credibility and a greater degree of rationality are assumed to belong to men, a feminine way of knowing is made to be the way of the Church's own witness. This critiques a culture's stereotypes at a deeper level.

To Fiorenza, it is significant that the New Testament appears to be challenging traditional gender roles in some areas (the Gospels) while upholding them in others (Paul's letters). It shows that even the New Testament itself isn't uniformly comfortable in all corners with Christianity's radical re-evaluations. Still, depicting this disagreement as Gospels versus Paul is too simple, since surely the most frequently cited evidence that gender difference (like race and economics) undergoes a radical reconfiguration in the light of the gospel is Paul's declaration that 'There is no longer Jew or Greek, there is no longer slave or free, there is no longer male and female; for all of you are one in Christ Jesus' (Gal. 3.28). This is a reference to baptism as the means by which a person is baptized 'into Christ', being received corporately into his body, the Church. Since Christ is the Saviour of all, women and men don't need separate saviours – it is his humanity that is important, not his maleness.

Nevertheless, there is a danger in stopping after just declaring that gender differences don't matter in the light of Christ. It is a danger that is similar to claiming that God is colour-blind with regard to race. Cone's argument, which we saw above, was that God sides with victims of injustice against oppressors. This means that God cannot be colour-blind, but must be one who recognizes when injustice falls along race, gender or other lines. To those who insist on male headship, though, God doesn't make a distinction between these groups when it comes to salvation; yet when it comes to gender, a distinction still needs to be made in leadership roles.

Seeing gender in the light of redemption means recognizing God's vision for all his creatures to express all of their gifts in freedom and joy. Many churches testify to women displaying gifts in areas that have sometimes been reserved for men, itself an indicator that the Holy Spirit may be challenging traditional roles. Arguments *for* the traditional roles that are based in creation are surely stronger than those based in custom and culture, which change over time. But some of the arguments given in support of traditional roles appear in Genesis as clear *departures* from God's intent in creation since they appear as part of the curse that follows the sin of Adam and Eve. It is in this context that God declares to Eve, for example, 'your desire shall be for your husband, and he shall rule over you' (Gen. 3.16). Given that this is part of a curse, this text automatically foreshadows a drama that will unfold to overturn it. Without a hermeneutic of suspicion, it's not obvious what becomes of New Testament texts that appear to reinforce male headship.

Some biblical analogies are gendered, raising interesting additional questions of interpretation. The image of God's relationship between himself and Israel or the Church is often described as a marriage. As with all analogies, if they are to be helpful in bringing moral clarity, we need to ask what it is doing and how it works. In particular, we need to be careful in identifying the ways the two things being described (here the relationship between the Church or Israel and God is being compared to the relationship between spouses) are alike and where they differ. Even more basic is the way that this particular analogy draws upon an image of a male God, which feminist theologians have strongly opposed when it is taken too literally. After all, not every element of an analogy can be pushed successfully; when it becomes ridiculous, we know we have gone too far.

If we consider the metaphor of God as Father, we can quickly notice that there are some ways in which God is father-like and other ways in which

God is not. Sallie McFague (b. 1933), a feminist theologian who spent 30 years at Vanderbilt University Divinity School, has written a lot about how metaphors for God work. She writes that 'metaphors of God, far from reducing God to what we understand, underscore by their multiplicity and lack of fit the unknowability of God'.[14] McFague warns in a chapter titled 'God as Mother' that focusing too much on the image of God as Father can be a form of idolatry.

The metaphor of God as Father breaks down once we get into aspects of human fatherhood that clearly don't apply to God, such as maleness (since God has no gender), physical procreativity (since God has no body) and having at least one child who is younger than oneself (since Christianity confesses that God's Son is 'eternally begotten of the Father'). None of these things should surprise us or distress us, as though they take away from the practice of calling God Father. This practice is perfectly acceptable as long as we are clear about the points at which the analogy breaks down. If it never broke down, it wouldn't be an *analogy*, but an *identity*, which obviously 'Father' isn't when it comes to God.

McFague uses the term 'models of God' to describe the various metaphors in order to show how the language we use brings other concepts along with it. The Father model can wrongly imply that God is domineering or that God is an absolute monarch who stands over or above the world and enacts punitive justice. For some, these ideas come along with images they have of fatherhood or of men in general; calling God Father transfers them on to God. Because of the way that metaphors work, language models will potentially end up saying more than was first intended by using them. Paul's description of God as the one in whom 'we live and move and have our being' (Acts 17.28) works very differently; we are in God as a fish is in water. Jesus uses a motherly image to express his hope that he might gather the children of Jerusalem together 'as a hen gathers her brood under her wings' (Luke 13.34). The best course to take is to employ many different models of God, loosening the grip of the most common ones and thus reducing the risk of idolatry.

Still, it is worth clarifying the Fatherhood of God theologically. If God is triune, then Father-language is most at home when describing relations *within* the Trinity. The Father is the father of the Son, not in the sense that he was biologically begotten (biology can't apply since God has no 'bios' as this is a quality that creatures have). Rather, the Father is father of the

---

14 Sallie McFague, *Models of God: Theology for an Ecological, Nuclear Age* (Philadelphia: Fortress, 1987), 97.

Son in *resemblance* ('Whoever has seen me has seen the Father', John 14.9), *unity* (or *essence*, 'The Father and I are one', John 10.30) and *inheritance* ('everything you have given me is from you', John 17.7). 'Father' names a triune relation that is unlike all other relationships. Christians pray 'Our Father' because we are brought within God's family. There are a lot of ways Father-language functions, but the point is never to project male as opposed to female characteristics on to God.

This discussion of metaphors or models of God matters for ethics and not just for theology. As it is sometimes claimed, if God is male then male is God. Where feminism stresses male and female equality using liberal political (Enlightenment) concepts, the idea that men are more advanced in their capacities for using reason is opposed by showing that women are equally capable in this way, especially once educational, domestic and other inequalities are addressed.

A different strand of feminism highlights the ways that 'feminine' qualities have taken a back seat to 'masculine' qualities in the household, the workplace and in society. In Christian ethics, the masculinity of violence and war, for example, might be said to account for why it ever seemed right to offer reasoned defences of them. A feminine approach might never have dignified war in this way in the first place. Likewise, **ecofeminism** notices an association between the domination of women and the exploitation of the environment. Women are associated with nature and the earth, and men are responsible for creating cultures that separate us from our materiality. The idea is that the masculine exaltation of reason functioned not only to separate humans from the other animals, but also to alienate our minds from our bodies. Feminine is more bodily, emotive and intuitive than intellectual, analytical and calculating. McFague experiments with thinking about the world as God's body as a way of overcoming the opposite tendency to link God with masculine transcendence.[15] Unlike a liberal feminist focus on equality that stresses similarities between men and women, this approach depends on differences. And while it can feel as though gender stereotypes are being upheld rather than challenged, the point is to offer a much more complex picture of God and humanity than has usually prevailed.

---

15 McFague, *Models of God*, ch. 3.

11

Sexuality

Christian tradition has drawn attention to several goods of sexuality. The most obvious is procreation, which is good because God declared creation to be good and invited us to be participants in the process. Procreation and the unity that sex brings between two individuals in the best of cases are two sides of the same coin. The language is important here. 'Creation' is terminology for the having of children that is most at home for Christians. It is in contrast to, say, 'reproduction', which has a secular ring to it, drawing as it does on a mechanical and industrial image that is non-participatory.

In the best of cases, and by design, human procreation is strongly connected with love. Just as love itself grows as there are more things to love, procreation isn't to be driven by any lack. Love literally loves new things into existence for the purpose of the further exercise of love. This is the best way to think about God creating the universe. The eternal communion of the Holy Trinity was so full of love that it overflows, bringing forth creatures to share in the love, delight and joy of God. People do not play the role of God by having children since all children are further creatures God creates in order for his love to be expressed.

The joy of celebrating new life is thus worlds away from the experience of fulfilling a command or directive. 'Be fruitful and multiply' is given as permission to humanity, not requirement. Indeed, nothing that arises from love can be tied to need without undoing itself in the process. Where necessity is removed, true joy can flourish. One of the main arguments of this chapter will be to frame sexual and non-sexual relationships as demonstrations that God has created us in love and for joy.

Related to this, we will need to establish that sexual virtue – the right ordering and living of sexual selves – is not unique to sexuality. This is especially true of sexual faithfulness, which is only one expression of faithfulness in general. Virtues such as constancy are about keeping commitments and following through on promises, even when there appear to be good reasons to break them. These are not unique to sexual relationships but are nurtured and enriched through Christian practices that include all believers.

Departures from these themes – negative attitudes about human sexuality; sex without love; anxiety about having children, marriage and singleness; objectifying marriage and the family; unfaithfulness – become clear once sexuality is properly and adequately framed.

Singleness and divorce

It may seem strange to begin the sexuality section of this book with a discussion of singleness. But even though a lot of contemporary Christian discourse emphasizes the importance of the family, Christian ethics has long highlighted the role of the single life. Jesus, of course, was single, as were most of his disciples (perhaps all were, although Peter had a mother-in-law, cf. Matt. 8.14, implying that he either was or had been married). Paul the apostle seems also to have valued the single life and begrudgingly commended marriage for those whose sexual desire will prove to be too much of a distraction (1 Cor. 7.9). Ancient and medieval Christian traditions also speak about the priority of virginity over marriage. Single people have the practical advantage of not being tied down with the domestic responsibilities of those with families. This relative freedom is of great interest for the Church's mission and may explain why the New Testament seems to assume that singleness is the norm and not a special calling for just a few. St Augustine argued that singleness is the greater good compared to marriage. Those who marry have the burden of proof.

Those who are part of the Church but who never marry prompt Christians to give an account of their unique role. There are two main reasons Christian tradition gives for why singleness may be preferable. (We should be clear that 'singleness' is here a way of signalling a lack of sexual relations and not only a lack of a marriage partner.) Augustine mostly represents the first, which links sex with **concupiscence** or lust, even within marriage. The idea is that sexual desire overwhelms the will and because all sin is disordered desire, according to Augustine, lust should be thought of as disordered sexual desire. Perhaps rightly ordered sexual desire was originally a possibility in the goodness of creation, but this changed as a result of the Fall. This doesn't make procreation wrong, but it is how Augustine understood original sin to be passed down from generation to generation. Jesus was free from original sin because he was conceived without concupiscence. His mother conceived him as a virgin by miracle by the Holy Spirit.

Augustine wasn't alone in thinking about human sexuality in these essentially negative terms. But associating sexuality with sin is only one of the two main reasons for valuing singleness. The second is a positive one that looks on singleness as a special vocation that aids in the Church's mission. One thing that the reality of singleness within the Church does is loosen the grip Christians might otherwise have on their familial relationships. We have already seen how, in baptism, all Christian identities are reconfigured. Those once considered strangers to each other are brought within the same family where fraternal bonds (one's new brothers and sisters in Christ) become more significant than one's biological kinship ties. The mission and practices of the Church are to be carried out by all people according to the gifts God has given them, which the baptized receive apart from the roles they have in their families. All Christians are to imitate Christ. When Ephesians 5 instructs husbands to love their wives and wives to be subject to their husbands, the point isn't to counsel a subordination in line with roles taken in ancient marriages, but to urge Christians to strive to imitate Christ in all things, including in the marriage relationship. But because this call isn't unique to marriage, all of the baptized are to pursue mutual subordination, roles available to both married and single people because the Church establishes the first context for renewed human relationships.

Moreover, singleness demonstrates something about what probably ought to be a relaxed Christian attitude toward having one's own children. A single person gives up many things that are available to the married person, including sexual fulfilment. But the primary thing a single person forgoes is children. In the Old Testament, the plight of barren women is tied to the deep desire to establish oneself as part of a great line of descendants that will carry on through time (in addition to the economic advantage that children tend to bring in an agrarian setting). God's covenant with Abraham included the promise to make of him a 'great nation', a promise that generated a considerable amount of tension in the subsequent narrative every time that line was threatened with being interrupted by barrenness. The tension began immediately with the inability of Abraham to have children with his wife Sarah until God provided Isaac in their old age. The line was then imperilled again when Abraham was asked to sacrifice Isaac. In all of these cases, the narrative emphasizes God's intervention to open barren wombs and, in the case of Isaac, spare him from sacrifice.

All of these stories point to what Karl Barth called the 'anxiety about posterity' in ancient Israel.[1] God's covenant promise was practically expressed

---

1 Karl Barth, *Church Dogmatics III.4: The Doctrine of Creation*, ed. G. W. Bromiley and T. F. Torrance (London: T&T Clark International, 2004), 240–85 (266).

as itself a blessing through land and children. But, Barth argues, the birth of Jesus the Messiah fulfils (and therefore ends) the need for the covenant to yield children. We encountered this emphasis in an earlier chapter when we noted Jesus' shocking declaration: 'Do not presume to say to yourselves, "We have Abraham as our ancestor"; for I tell you, God is able from these stones to raise up children to Abraham' (Matt. 3.9). Christians have long understood that what Jesus is doing is addressing the way that he is himself the fulfilment of the Abrahamic covenant. We should not think primarily of lots of biological offspring from the one man Abraham. God will bring others within this family, including those outside Abraham's strictly biological family tree. In fact, once again we happen upon the struggle to understand the inclusion of Gentiles within the first Jewish churches, which became a heated controversy and, it is fair to say, the first serious theological debate that Christians faced.

Even so, Barth goes beyond simply agreeing with Paul and the other early Christians that Gentiles are welcomed by God and are being grafted into the Jewish family. Barth also thinks that anxiety about posterity has been removed. There is just no more need to have children after Christ has come – the Son of God given to humanity, the one through whom we are adopted into God's family as his brothers and sisters. After all, thought Barth, these are *God's children*, not, in the end, the children of Abraham. And if God isn't anxious any more, nobody should be.

Nevertheless, Barth didn't think that people should simply stop having children. Instead, they shouldn't feel *anxious* about having children. Any children will bring joy for a different reason now, one that is not tied to any need, but whose existence is part of the non-necessary enjoyment God wants for his creatures. Now 'the fruitfulness of a marriage does not depend on whether it is fruitful in the physical sense'.[2] Not only are children released from the burden of fulfilling a need that their parents may have for them to be or do something in particular; parents are also free to relate differently to their children. They are even free from needing to justify their marriage through the having of children. The command to Adam and Eve (and thus seemingly to all humanity) to 'be fruitful and multiply' is, according to Barth, no longer in effect. Humans may still be fruitful and multiply, but it will be a joyous case of receiving permission to do so rather than the need to obey a command.

It is partly within this context that singleness makes some theological sense for Christians. Augustine had a similar view to Barth about how

---

2 Barth, *Church Dogmatics* III.4, 266.

Abraham's covenant was fulfilled in Christ, but was quicker to dismiss marriage as a result of his conclusions. Barth is more nuanced: releasing marriage from the need to be 'necessary' to fulfil a covenant that, on the surface, relies on procreation actually frees marriage to be something much more significant. It also releases singleness from the shadows of marriage. If singleness rises in dignity once the pressure to procreate is off, then so do marriages that are likewise non-procreative, whether by choice or not. If there is no need to secure a legacy or secure heirs whose endurance grants a kind of eternal life even after one dies, the interest Christians place on the growth of the kingdom of God turns out to be accomplished through conversion rather than primarily through procreation. This is a risky situation for the Church, which is called to give up its desire for self-preservation and instead to trust that God will bring in the harvest as the gospel spreads among those who do not believe. It is much easier to grow the Church by having children than making disciples (although, of course even children born into the Church must learn to become Christ's disciples too). There is no place in Christianity for securing one's legacy by seeing one's family as a possession. Like all possessions, one's family (actual or potential) must be given to God, as the Hebrew firstborn were always ritually dedicated to God – if they were kept, it was only because they were first given *back* to God who had given them in the first place. So the practice of having children is not, strange as it seems, theologically very different from not having children. Both take the human temptation to claim our possessions as our own creations (and by extension, the temptation to want to be the creator) and acknowledge God's sovereignty.

Because the spirit of this acknowledgement involves letting go of ties we would want to control, preserve, maintain and hold on to, the practice of adoption can be appreciated for its deep theological rationale. Indeed, the growth of the Church's family is more akin to adoption than procreation anyway. God only has one *begotten* Son, and that is Jesus Christ. All others who are brought within God's family are adopted, whether Jews or Gentiles (Rom. 8.15; 9.4). In the best cases, people who are adopted into other families are shown that they belong there, that they will not be treated differently from non-adopted siblings and that nothing will be held back from them that might be given to others. This loosening of the grip on 'natural' (biological) relations is a useful model for discerning the role of childless single or married people within the Church with regard to the children of others. After all, parents and their children are equally adopted into God's family, as are the other members of the Church who are therefore baptized into something of a parental role to other people's children.

The approach we have been taking so far has the effect of destabilizing conventional ways that marriage and family, but especially singleness, play out in many modern societies. I have been highlighting an ethic that is rooted primarily in vocation and mission and not in creation. It is useful to think about divorce in a similar way. More common is to begin with the ideal of marriage and then discuss divorce as a departure from it, often in conjunction with other threats to marriage such as adultery. It must be said that this approach is useful too. Biblically, the case against divorce is strong on deontological grounds, as in Jesus' teaching that a man who divorces his wife causes her to commit adultery (Matt. 5.32). The exception built into this teaching – that rather weakly appears to approve of divorce in cases of unchastity – doesn't dignify divorce very much since in the exception the wife has *already* committed adultery. Christian justifications of divorce tend not to be deontological but consequentialist, compassionately siding with an abused or wronged person, or realistically recognizing that the marriage has died.

For our purposes, however, divorce can be thought of as a return to singleness. And despite what we have been saying here about the dignified, even default, vocation of singleness within the mission of the Church, many single and divorced people feel pressure to marry or remarry. In response to Jesus' teaching about the permanence of marriage, he was asked why Moses allowed divorce if the woman is given a certificate of dismissal. This, Jesus says, was a condescension to the hard-heartedness of the people (Matt. 19.3–9, referring to Deut. 24). In a patriarchal culture, the practice in which a man might send his wife away for a variety of reasons makes the woman (and not the man) deeply vulnerable. A certificate of divorce was a provision made for a dismissed woman to find social and economic security in a new marriage. Much better is to change the expectations within the culture so that the husbands will feel a deeper level of commitment to their wives. But this still leaves marriage as a saving institution in patriarchal settings. Better still is Jesus' vision in which the kingdom of God includes, dignifies and provides for all people, regardless of marital status.

There are parallels, then, between the burdens and troubles that threatened divorced women in ancient Israel and the tragic unravelling of normal life that many divorced people in our day experience. There is the further parallel that some single people feel in which there is no 'settling down' unless and until they marry. This settling down often brings along with it strong social esteem and acceptance for choosing an acceptable form of life. Where the Church's mission is already busily destabilizing what passes for an acceptable form of life, it will not only be a haven for single and divorced (and widowed) people, but may even take its cues from *their* forms of life.

In some cultural settings, of course, marriage is becoming less common in favour of cohabitation and other arrangements. Here a cultural preference for singleness is probably at odds with a Christian ethic, as when there is a desire to have sexual intimacy but also the freedom of being single, or when there are children whose parents value a freedom that could compromise the care they need. Then again, in these cultural settings, marriage will not magically increase a couple's commitment to one another or to their children apart from formalizing the legal ties that bind them. As I have been arguing throughout this section, getting a Christian ethic of singleness right as a dimension of the Church's mission will also reframe how we think about divorce, children, parenthood and marriage itself.

Marriage and family

Today, many attempts to discuss marriage and the family by appealing to the Bible come with a caution against unwittingly (perhaps) underwriting ancient practices of patriarchy. This is a particular concern when dealing with creation accounts in Genesis, which are often presented with normative force: this is the way things were meant to be. The opening chapters of the Bible certainly deal with the creation and origin of many things, not only the material universe, but also human practices like marriage and keeping the Sabbath. They also offer an original account of realities like temptation, disobedience, pain in childbirth, difficult physical labour and at least some dimensions of patriarchal social arrangements.

When we deal with the environment and stewardship in Chapter 13, our approach to language in Genesis about humans having dominion over other parts of creation will be to argue that this has sometimes been wrongly understood to license exploitation. The references to the origins of marriage are unfortunately open to being used in a similar way. They are used to justify male dominance over women, particularly in families, though it must be admitted that such texts function differently once the traditional arrangements have undergone significant challenge, as they have in our own time. In particular, these early texts have often been challenged by other, later texts that are also in the Bible. The Gospels portray Jesus to be positively anti-marriage; Paul sometimes also writes this way. Scholars who see a theological development of marriage within the Bible itself must reckon with the fact that this development doesn't seem linear.

Some of the last texts we have seem to revert to more traditional patri-archal formulations. These are sometimes called 'household codes' and are listed in Ephesians 5.22—6.9 and Colossians 3.18—4.1. They give instructions for wives to submit to their husbands, husbands to love their wives, husbands and wives to submit to one another, children to obey their parents, and slaves to obey their masters. One solution is to attribute these later texts to writers who were working within the tradition of Paul, but were not faithful to his spirit of radically re-evaluating social norms in the light of the gospel. From the perspective of Christian ethics rather than the historical study of biblical texts, these instructions can seem disap-pointingly conventional and indeed have been used extensively in the past to justify slaveholding. As with most topics, then, Christians are likely to adopt a canon within the canon, or a set of texts we will focus on and those we will largely set aside when constructing a way forward. The key concern is not to counsel disobedience rather than obedience, but whether the con-ventional structures of authority ought to be reproduced into the future without fundamentally questioning them, especially when other parts of the Bible do just this. Is it true, for example, that 'a little child shall lead them?' (Isa. 11.6) or should we continue to look to the same (adult) lead-ership that, in one form or another, always appears to be running things?

On the specific topics of marriage and family, it goes without saying that concepts and forms of marriage and family are neither unique to Christian cultures nor universal. Some developments in marriage practice within the Bible – such as the move away from polygamy – probably say more about wider cultural trends than anything that is religiously significant. Even so, some other developments are clearly significant beyond cultural trends. Perhaps most important is that in the Bible, marriage is often the chosen image or metaphor to describe God's love for humanity. In particular, it is a love formalized by the specific kind of promise called covenant. When the promise of faithfulness is broken by one side, marriage describes the enduring constancy of the other. This is dramatically shown in the book of Hosea (chs 2—3) in which the prophet is told to take a prostitute as his wife, illustrating God's commitment to his covenant despite Israel's unfaithfulness.

A marriage covenant gives meaning to acts that violate it, such as acts of unfaithfulness. On analogy with God's relationship with Israel, this is significant theologically because it means that for those relationships that matter (such as marriage and friendship), it is not enough to think of them as rule-governed, as though the rule 'Don't be unfaithful' could stand on its own. In the same way, before speaking a word of judgement against the

people of Jerusalem for abandoning the Lord, God tells Jeremiah to speak
to them about a love now grown cold:

> I remember the devotion of your youth,
>> your love as a bride,
> how you followed me in the wilderness,
>> in a land not sown.
>
>> (Jer. 2.2)

Further on, the marriage metaphor continues:

> Can a girl forget her ornaments,
>> or a bride her attire?
> Yet my people have forgotten me,
>> days without number.
>
>> (Jer. 2.32)

Like a long marriage whose spark must occasionally be reignited, the
prophet addresses the tendency of Jerusalem's inhabitants to allow the passing
years to eclipse their initial enthusiasm. Jeremiah is speaking the prophet's
version of 'You don't bring me flowers any more' on behalf of God. This
is a critique of the way that romantic love can be mistaken for all of what
love is, leading to love's covenant being forgotten. This should strike many
people today, given that personal intimacy and romance is made to bear so
much of marriage's meaning. These biblical pictures point to a better way.

For one thing, as we have seen in our discussion of singleness, not all
faithfulness is sexual since of course God's love for humanity is not a sexual one. It is worth repeating that sexuality is not able to be reduced to
sexual intercourse. On the other hand, elements of the Christian tradition
have used erotic language and images to portray the human encounter
with God's love. Well-known examples include Bernini's sculpture *Ecstasy
of Saint Teresa* and John Donne's sonnet 'Batter My Heart' with the memorable and paradoxical couplet directed toward God, 'Except you enthrall
me, never shall be free / Nor ever chaste, except you ravish me.'

I showed in the previous section that some Christian thinkers have elevated the life of singleness above the married life. Part of the rationale for
this was that the begetting of children, after Christ, is no longer either a
sign of nor a requirement for being within God's promise to Abraham. But
as we said before, this is not a reason not to have children; it is a signal that
children do not need to *have a reason to be had*! God's inclusion of all people
within the divine household through his Son decisively reconfigures the
Christian notion of family.

226

Since Christian identity is based in baptism, in a sense one's real family becomes the Church. We witnessed this transformation in an earlier chapter. To this we can now add that whatever previous notions of marriage we may have had, they are upset by the description of the Church as the 'bride of Christ', a common motif found throughout the New Testament. The Christian's inclusion within the Church is the most fundamental move of leaving one's mother and father in order to be wed (recalling Gen. 2.24) – but in this case wed to God. (Jesus' disciples are repeatedly reported to have left natural relations behind.) We should notice that this image isn't about individual Christians being called the brides of Christ. There is only one bride, just as there is only one bridegroom.

It is precisely here that we should locate a Christian understanding of the family. The natural relations – the ones given to us at birth or otherwise by biology: brother, sister, son, daughter, father, mother – are constantly being subverted. In addition to the other relations we have discussed, in the Bible, the firstborn status is upset in the story of Jacob and Esau; the claim to the father's inheritance does not pass through the normal lines. At the far end of the process of subverting the normal process lies **adoption**, the language used to describe how humans become part of God's family. In this light, the language of bride and groom used of the Church and Christ works the same way: these are not natural relations but ones of initiative, of invitation.

Not all Christian traditions refer to marriage as a sacrament. But the fact that many Christians have continued to get married and have children, even after Christ, shows a belief in marriage's sacramental character, in some sense. Traditionally, and especially in Roman Catholicism, a sacrament is both a *sign* and a *means* of receiving God's grace. If marriage were only a sign, but did not also impart grace, there might be little reason to participate in it. But God's faithfulness to humanity is partly made understandable to us through our experience of marriage, as the many examples cited above from the Bible indicate.

We should add, by the way, that other forms of relationships are based in covenant. This means that while marriage may be the main type of relationship for experiencing the difficulties and joys associated with long-term faithfulness, there are others, such as friendship, which Augustine taught has intrinsic value (unlike marriage, which may be an instrumental setting for a friendship to flourish). The grace of friendship can be experienced in relationships that may or may not depend on sexual difference, though friendships do not usually have the same formalized, exclusive status that marriage does. We will take up this theme somewhat in the next section when we discuss homosexuality and same-sex marriage. The point

I have been making here is that Christian marriage is an arrangement that requires the kind of commitment that God makes to us as humans. It is therefore sacramental in the sense that it involves married people in the kinds of dynamics in which their promises and faithfulness will be put under stress when times are difficult and will also be the occasion for the full flourishing of joy that can come with being in a close relationship over a long period of time. So marriage is a sign of God's faithfulness and also the opportunity to experience and to grow in faithfulness oneself.

The sacramental character of marriage, though, is not only for the married couple. Since all sacraments have their home within the Church *and* we have seen that marriage is itself language that involves God's special relationship with the Church, the love between married people will be a sign to the rest of the community. Other people will look on and celebrate how God's faithfulness to a couple can be seen in that couple's life together over many years. The reason that marriage is to be lifelong and exclusive does not have to do with commands that it be this way (deontology). But put in the language of a virtue-based approach, the reason is that the constancy and faithfulness that characterize the way that God loves is meant to be the highest and best form of human loving too.

So some of what can be said about the human practices of marriage generally are given a distinctive theological shape within Christian thought and practice. Similar things can be seen in terms of having children. Children are given to the community when they are baptized. The distinction between adopted and biological children means nothing to Christians. Within the Church, if the community takes seriously its identity granted by baptism, then infertile couples do not need to feel anxiety. A person's or couple's feeling that they *need* their own children is most understandable when people's experience of the Church as a family is less than it could be.

With this in mind, let us look at the Bible's attitude toward those who cannot have children. We will do this in a way that might strike some readers as obscure at first, by considering eunuchs and what today is that class of people born intersex. The Bible possibly has this latter group in view when, in one of his key teachings about divorce, Jesus also speaks about those who are eunuchs from birth (Matt. 19.12). This is a reference to people who are born impotent. Other eunuchs were made impotent later, whether by choice or not, through the crushing of genitalia (it is males that seem to be referred to exclusively as eunuchs in the Bible). Old Testament law excluded eunuchs as well as people born out of wedlock (even to the tenth generation) by barring them from Israel's public worship assembly

(Deut. 23.1–2). The first-century Jewish historian Josephus recorded that eunuchs are to be avoided and treated 'as if they had killed their children' since they are not able to fulfil God's command to procreate. Moreover, in depriving themselves of their manhood, both their bodies and souls have become effeminate. Eunuchs were treated similarly in the Roman world, excluded from public life.[3]

Nevertheless, the reality of law and practice was promised to be upended in the prophets, who describe a future in which eunuchs who are otherwise faithful and righteous will be included in God's Temple:

> Do not let the foreigner joined to the LORD say,
>   'The LORD will surely separate me from his people';
> and do not let the eunuch say,
>   'I am just a dry tree.'
> For thus says the LORD:
> To the eunuchs who keep my sabbaths,
>   who choose the things that please me
>   and hold fast my covenant,
> I will give, in my house and within my walls,
>   a monument and a name
>   better than sons and daughters;
> I will give them an everlasting name
>   that shall not be cut off.
>
> (Isa. 56.3–5)

> Blessed also is the eunuch whose hands have done no lawless deed,
>   and who has not devised wicked things against the Lord;
> for special favour will be shown him for his faithfulness,
>   and a place of great delight in the temple of the Lord.
>
> (Wisd. 3.14)

Notice that Isaiah's reference to the monument and name that is 'better than sons and daughters' promises the very things a eunuch cannot have. They will be better, in fact, since they are eternal. The New Testament has sometimes been thought to fulfil the prophets in this regard and overturn the law's teaching in the story of the apostle Philip baptizing a eunuch from Ethiopia (Acts 8), thereby including him in the newly formed assembly of Christians called church (*ekklesia*, which literally means assembly), overturning Deuteronomy 23.

---

3 Ulrich Luz, *Matthew 8–22*, trans. James E. Crouch (Minneapolis: Fortress, 2001), 501.

Unfortunately, the history of Christianity is uneven on this topic at best. The fourth-century Council of Nicea affirmed that eunuchs cannot become clerics and a version of this restriction is still part of canon law. On the other hand, Christians throughout the ages have tended to downplay the relevance of the Matthew 19 text as a general call to celibacy since the Church frequently worried about people taking ascetic practices to extremes. Eunuchs are chaste by necessity, whether through nature or a previous choice. Some church fathers concluded that those who choose celibacy who might not have so chosen (that is, non-eunuchs) are more highly prized. It wasn't until Reformation debates about clerical celibacy that this text again received attention.

There is undoubtedly something obscure and esoteric about this discussion of eunuchs. But for all of the discussion in Christian and Jewish tradition about the necessity to have children either in order to fulfil a mandate given at creation ('Be fruitful and multiply') or in order to fulfil the covenant to Abraham, the place of people who cannot have children is very interesting to think about. These people are a touchstone for prejudices related to family. By going out of its way to reverse the way that people think about them, the Bible is doing much more than redeeming eunuchs, barrenness, intersex and infertile people. It is describing a new reality that challenges basic assumptions about what it means to be human beings in God's world.

Homosexuality

Many contemporary discussions of homosexuality begin with the Bible even though no specific homosexual people are mentioned in the Bible, nor is homosexuality treated in the Bible as an identity or orientation since these are modern developments. Yet the Bible on several occasions mentions homoerotic acts, and its judgement on them is always negative. At the same time, readers are provided with no explanations as to why such acts deserve negative judgements; these must be deduced or guessed from the various contexts – theological, cultural, literary – of each passage. Those who are interested not only in what the Bible condemns, but also in *why it does so*, need to go deeper.

There are about five texts relevant to this discussion because they seem to mention homoerotic acts or those who practise them: Leviticus 18.22; 20.13; Romans 1.18–32; 1 Corinthians 6.9; 1 Timothy 1.10. Other texts having to do with the nature of marriage are relevant more broadly. There is considerable contemporary scholarship on all of these texts and many scholars draw widely divergent conclusions about them. Below, I will consider just two of them since they highlight two different kinds of challenges.

Leviticus 18.22 is very similar to 20.13. Both texts forbid sexual acts between males and the latter text commends the death penalty for it, the same punishment for other sexual violations listed: adultery, incest and bestiality. A few questions arise, some exegetical and some theological.

First is the question of how Christians ought to read this text as people who are being shaped by the good news of Jesus Christ. It's important to say that from the beginning, Gentile Christians have never simply cited and adopted Old Testament laws as binding. Many laws have to do with ancient Israel's ceremonial worship and were deemed by Gentile Christians to be irrelevant (this precise debate takes place within the New Testament itself; see Acts 15 and Galatians). Moreover, Jesus specifically called off the near execution of a woman caught in adultery (John 8), which at least qualifies the punishments listed in Leviticus.[4] Then again, in calling off the execution, Jesus wasn't justifying adultery. So, on its own, this story deals with the punishment but not the moral questions. Some behaviours condemned in Leviticus probably have to do with order rather than moral purity. This explains other commands such as not wearing clothing made of two kinds of material and not sowing a field with two different kinds of seed (Lev. 19.19). Christians, therefore, have at least two questions to consider when looking at an Old Testament law: (1) Did this have a specific meaning in ancient Israel that it no longer has, thus rendering it irrelevant to today? (2) Has this been overturned or fulfilled by Jesus Christ?

In addition, let us ask questions that the Bible nowhere seems to ask nor answer, but that are necessary in order to ask what it is about homoerotic acts if they are considered an abomination. For example, what is really meant by calling an action unclean (which is sometimes interpreted to mean *unnatural*)? One possibility that has a long history in Christian thought is that homoerotic acts are sex acts that are inherently non-procreative. As such, their sterility may be compared to that of several Old Testament women who lamented their barrenness (Sarah, Rebekah, Rachel, Hannah), remembering that the Bible is relatively unconcerned about goods of sex apart from procreation (Song of Songs is a notable exception). Likewise, a menstruating woman, who is therefore in a non-procreative state, is considered unclean for intercourse. Apart from the radical reversal that we looked at in the last section with eunuchs, one can discern a relatively consistent biblical concern that sex acts generate life.

---

4 A number of early manuscripts of John do not include this story.

Even though the Bible only mentions homoerotic acts on a few occasions, when they are mentioned it is always with a negative judgement. The connection of these acts to life and the generation of life is the most likely explanation, along with the closely related ideas of purity and uncleanness. It is, of course, one thing to come to an understanding of the Bible's attitude and quite another to consider whether Christians ought to adopt a similar attitude. For this, we need to look at another reason for the Bible's negative attitude toward homoerotic acts that has to do with the pagan practices of ancient Israel's neighbours.

Many Christians are content to give no thought to trimming a beard or getting a tattoo. Tattoos and beard-trimming were practices – probably religious practices – of the other nations against which Israel was determined to distinguish itself. In the Graeco-Roman world of the New Testament, other pagan practices linked to worship involved prostitution (cf. 1 Kings 14.24; 15.12; 22.46; 2 Kings 23.7) and pederasty (homoerotic acts between a man and a boy, both presumed heterosexuals by today's understandings). In the same way, a first-century cultural association between the plaiting of a woman's hair and ostentation and immodesty is probably the reason that two New Testament passages condemn plaiting hair (1 Tim. 2.9–10; 1 Pet. 3.3). What should Christians do, morally speaking, with these kinds of commands and statements in a modern culture that lacks those associations? It should be obvious that answers to this question will vary widely depending on different views of what the Bible is and how it ought to be read.

Romans 1.18–32 devotes an entire sentence to same-sex intercourse as part of Paul's elaborate theological argument about the human need for God's salvation. Paul is establishing that we are sinners and, in these specific verses, is showing that God's wrath can be seen in the Gentile world:

> For this reason God gave them up to degrading passions. Their women exchanged natural intercourse for unnatural, and in the same way also the men, giving up natural intercourse with women, were consumed with passion for one another. Men committed shameless acts with men and received in their own persons the due penalty for their error.　　(Rom. 1.26–27)

'They exchanged' is language of idolatry (cf. Ps. 106.20) and functions within Paul's indictment of the spiritual state of pagan Gentiles. Other Jewish sources from the same time period make similar condemnations, sometimes because the non-reproductive character of homoerotic acts produced anxiety about the continuation of the human species. 'Unnatural' assumes that homoerotic acts violate a person's natural desire for the opposite sex, a widely held assumption in the ancient world. It is worth repeating that the Bible knows nothing of the modern treatment of sexuality as an identity or condition of our humanity. It doesn't consider that there are some people who are gay or lesbian as people. If we were to force our modern way of speaking on to the Bible, we would say that it seems to assume everyone to be heterosexual, though it is aware of homo-erotic acts. If this assumption is wrong and it is something Paul shared, can it be let go of? Those who say yes will point out that the fact that Paul in Romans 1 is not giving moral commands, but instead building a much larger argument where this plays only a small part, makes it easier to set it aside. Then again, if one of Paul's points is that people shouldn't go against their nature, then even though it wasn't a thought of Paul's, a homosexual shouldn't go against his or her nature either.

Let us develop a couple of points in more detail. A great deal of the current debate in churches regarding homosexuality can be understood as: (1) differing views on whether the Bible's assumption of heterosexuality ought to be considered *morally normative* or whether it merely reflects a certain culture in ways that might yield moral principles but should not be used to offer timeless moral guidance on their own; (2) differing understandings of what exactly is being condemned and prohibited in the Bible when homoerotic acts are mentioned. We will look at these two items in turn:

1 There is much more to go on than a handful of verses that deal with homoerotic acts. The opening chapters of Genesis, for example, give an account of the origin of sexual difference (God made humans male and female) and of marriage (a man shall leave his father and mother and cling to his wife). Yet while the vast majority of people are born either male or female, some are born neither, as we discussed above (intersex or 'eunuchs from birth'). Perhaps the Bible is expressing the norm in a strictly numeric sense rather than a moral sense. This would mean the difference between thinking about intersex people as being a *violation* of God's design and their just being *different* from the majority of people.

2 A number of scholars have shown that the homoerotic acts the Bible condemns are those that are either exploitative or associated with pagan rituals, and doesn't have in view mutually assenting relationships of gay and lesbian people. In his article, 'The Bible and Homosexuality', Victor Paul Furnish (b. 1931), a professor of New Testament at Southern Methodist University, sets forth what he calls the law of diminishing relevancy, which says that 'The more specifically applicable an instruction is to the situation for which it was originally formulated, the less specifically applicable it is

to every other situation.'[5] For Furnish, the historical and cultural specificity of the Bible's references to homoerotic acts shows that they cannot be
appropriated as God's will for all times and places. In other words, certain
acts condemned by the Bible no longer have the pagan associations they
once did, so this key problem disappears.

We have already said a lot to address a misplaced anxiety about the continuation of the human species. An adequate account of the gift of children
unburdens every sex act from needing to be procreative. Christ is the only
offspring of Abraham that truly matters for God's promises to be fulfilled.
We have spent a lot of time on this theological point, but there is also
a point to be made that more closely resembles sociology. As contraception has become morally acceptable in the last century in many churches
(but not the Roman Catholic Church) and wider society, attitudes about
the necessity of procreation have changed, allowing for some of the other
goods of sex to play a more prominent role in overall thinking about sex
and marriage. As a consequence, concerns about same-sex acts being
non-procreative diminish.

A different kind of biblical argument doesn't look at specific verses
that address sexual matters, but instead draws analogies. In response to
its appointment of an openly gay bishop in 2003, the Episcopal Church
(USA) published 'To Set Our Hope on Christ', a long document that
defends the appointment by analogy to the early Christian decision on the
place of Gentiles within Judaism in the light of Jesus Christ (Acts 10—15).[6]
The apostles Peter and Paul made their cases for the inclusion of Gentiles
within God's salvation for the Jews, arguing that Gentiles do not need
to keep the law of Moses. This was an unprecedented innovation within
Judaism, but its advocates pointed to God's seeming acceptance of Gentiles
(by baptizing them with the Holy Spirit) who were not keeping the law.
Peter had earlier made a similar argument in favour of baptizing the family of Cornelius whom God had accepted apart from observing dietary
and other commands that were part of ordinary Jewish observance (Acts
10). What the apostles had been discovering with Gentiles, the Episcopal
Church had been discovering with gay and lesbian people: 'We believe that

---

5 Victor Paul Furnish, 'The Bible and Homosexuality: Reading the Texts in Context' in
Homosexuality in the Church: Both Sides of the Debate, ed. Jeffrey S. Siker (Louisville:
Westminster John Knox, 1994), 32.

6 <http://archive.episcopalchurch.org/documents/ToSetOurHope_eng.pdf>. On understanding this analogy, I recommend the work of John Perry, especially 'Vocation and Creation:
Beyond the Gentile–Homosexual Analogy', *Journal of Religious Ethics* 40.2 (2012): 385–400.

God has been opening our eyes to acts of God that we had not known how to see before.'[7]

Those who employ this analogy in arguing about homosexuality claim that God's clear use of gay and lesbian Christians in ministry functions like Peter's argument: let us not reject those whom God has accepted. Similarly, by referring to Gentile freedom from the law of Moses, advocates of the use of the Gentile analogy are addressing the strangeness of Christians appealing too strongly to certain commands within the law while ignoring others. As the Episcopal Church argued, the apostolic process of coming to terms with the new work of God 'has given us new eyes to read other passages of Scripture'.[8]

Critics of the analogy, however, point out that in order for it to work, being straight or gay needs to be the same *kind of status* as Jew or Gentile. Today, many people debate what kind of distinction gay and straight is, asking questions such as how much one's desires ought to constitute one's identity. If a person believes that there is no such thing as homosexual orientation, there is clearly no force behind drawing this analogy. Other critics appeal to the Acts text itself in which one of the stipulations of the compromise that the Jerusalem Council agreed to was to insist that Gentile converts abstain from sexual immorality – a stipulation that, for its lack of specificity (what 'immorality' did the council members have in mind?), hardly helps in this case. It is clear that there were meant to be moral entailments to being Christian that may have paralleled or summarized many of the commands found in the law.[9] Those who defend using the analogy insist that the text isn't being asked to weigh in on homosexuality (through a literal reading), but only on whether or not moral rules can change (through an analogical reading).

On the other hand, the force of the Jew–Gentile analogy isn't really about how well those categories match straight–gay categories. It has a *revisionist* force that hopes to find a pattern in the Bible and in theology for how teaching changes. As the apostles might say it, the point is responding openly when God does something new and surprising that goes against ideas and customs that people have held for a long time. Their argument that won the day was essentially 'Just look at God pouring his Holy Spirit out on uncircumcised Gentiles!' It's not even an argument, strictly

---

7 'To Set Our Hope on Christ', 9.

8 'To Set Our Hope on Christ', 6.

9 See Peter J. Leithart's response to 'To Set Our Hope on Christ': <https://www.firstthings.com/blogs/leithart/2005/06/to-set-our-hope-on-christ>.

speaking, but a way of directing the audience's attention toward the work of God among people others condemn.

Certainly most of the Christian tradition for most of history has condemned homosexuality. This is despite notable but small exceptions such as the presence of same-sex rites in pre-modern Christianity, which Yale historian John Boswell (1947–94) has documented.[10] Yet if 'justice from below' (see the previous chapter) is a matter of seeing and welcoming something 'new' (which may mean 'outside the main traditions'), resolutions to these difficult debates are not likely to come from greater and greater detailed exploration of biblical texts. But it is also hard to imagine resolution coming about without this. Gay and lesbian Christians are themselves divided about sexual ethics. Some advocate for celibacy. Others advocate for a conservative same-sex ethic that includes marriage and opposes promiscuity. Still others mount a much stronger opposition to traditional marriage, rejecting marriage altogether as an oppressive institution that limits sexual freedom.[11]

The debate in Christian ethics about homosexuality shouldn't be thought of as simply a yes–no decision on gay and lesbian identity, homoerotic acts or same-sex marriage. The debate is also among gay Christians who are working on articulating a consistent sexual ethic in much the same way that has occupied Christians for centuries. In this chapter, I have tried to approach topics of sexuality in a way that steers away from primarily focusing on naming sexual sins and instead looks to describe good relations and good love.

---

10 John Boswell, *Christianity, Social Tolerance, and Homosexuality: Gay People in Western Europe from the Beginning of the Christian Era to the Fourteenth Century* (Chicago: University of Chicago Press, 1980); John Boswell, *Same-Sex Unions in Premodern Europe* (New York: Vintage, 1994).

11 For a variety of perspectives from gay Christians, readers may want to consult the following: Wesley Hill, *Washed and Waiting: Reflections on Christian Faithfulness and Homosexuality* (Grand Rapids: Zondervan, 2010); Justin Lee, *Torn: Rescuing the Gospel from the Gays-vs.-Christians Debate* (New York: Jericho, 2012); Mel White, *Stranger at the Gate: To Be Gay and Christian in America* (New York: Simon & Schuster, 1994).

12

Vulnerable life

Attention to 'the least of these' (Matt. 25) is fundamental to the Christian moral task. These include orphans, widows and immigrants – groups long singled out for special treatment by ancient Israel's laws. It is easy to see why. These are vulnerable groups, people who lack power and a voice in the larger society. Without parents, orphans need to depend on the care of others; without husbands, especially in a patriarchal society, widows are financially vulnerable; and without connections and roots, immigrants must rely on the good will of the non-immigrant, native population for their survival. In Jesus' teaching, 'the least of these' specifies those who are hungry and thirsty, the strangers, the naked, the sick and prisoners. In his ministry, Jesus welcomed children, touched lepers and preached good news to the poor.

We have already seen the importance of many of these groups in an earlier chapter when we discussed justice from below. In this chapter, we look at instances of vulnerable life that have occupied quite a lot of attention in Christian ethics in recent years: abortion, the use of human embryos in scientific research, and euthanasia or physician-assisted suicide.

Abortion

Christians have nearly always condemned the practice of intentionally aborting a pregnancy. Even though the Bible never mentions abortion, early Christian writings mention it. The *Didache*, a Christian document from the early second century AD, teaches, 'You shall not murder a child by abortion, nor shall you kill one who has been born.'[1] The second-century *Epistle of Barnabas* commands the same thing.

Yet while abortion isn't a topic treated specifically in the Bible, this doesn't mean that the Bible can't still help to navigate contentious matters of the meaning of pregnancy, life at a very early age, childbirth and the place of people in the human family. For one thing, the Bible's near silence

---

1 *Didache* 2.2: <https://www.ccel.org/ccel/richardson/fathers.viii.i.iii.html>.

on the issue serves to indicate how different our modern, Western cultures are from the ancient Hebrew culture. The biblical scholar Richard Hays argues that there is no such thing as a 'problem pregnancy' in the Bible. Instead, the opposite is quite common. The Bible very often expresses the anguish of barren women who mourn their inability to bear children.[2] This is a significant theological theme throughout the Bible and is woven together with the very idea and reality of the promises God makes to make a people for himself. This is accomplished in the face of the serious biological obstacle of barrenness in all the cases of the wives of Abraham, Isaac and Jacob, the patriarchs to whom God's covenant promise is continually affirmed (Gen. 17.15–16; 25.21–22; 29.31; 30.1). The theological point here is not only that God hears and sympathizes with the plight of such women. It is that the creation of Israel as a nation set apart to be God's own people is a miracle for which God alone will take the credit and receive glory. One's ability to give thanks for new life is a deeper question than many of the modern debates over abortion since, when this happens, abortion simply doesn't come to mind.

Other biblical texts point to the dignity of unborn life. Pope John Paul II's 1995 encyclical *Evangelium Vitae* ('The Gospel of Life') discussed a number of these. For example, consider Psalm 139.13–16:

> For it was you who formed my inward parts;
>   you knit me together in my mother's womb.
> I praise you, for I am fearfully and wonderfully made.
>   Wonderful are your works;
> that I know very well.
>   My frame was not hidden from you,
> when I was being made in secret,
>   intricately woven in the depths of the earth.
> Your eyes beheld my unformed substance.
> In your book were written
>   all the days that were formed for me,
>   when none of them as yet existed.

John Paul II concludes that texts like these 'show such great respect for the human being in the mother's womb that they require as a logical consequence that God's commandment "You shall not kill" be extended to the unborn child as well'.[3] Connecting the sixth commandment to abortion

---

2 Richard Hays, *The Moral Vision of the New Testament: Community, Cross, New Creation* (San Francisco: HarperCollins, 1996), ch. 18.

3 *Evangelium Vitae*, sec. 61.

makes a deontological case against it, as indeed most contemporary arguments tend to be. This psalm, however, shows something different from issuing commands about how to treat the unborn. It comes closer to being useful in the debate over when life begins, but even that isn't its purpose. Instead, it describes God's tenderness and attentiveness toward the weak, vulnerable and easily ignored from a very early stage.

The Bible doesn't weigh in on the main ways that abortion tends to be debated today. There are some gestures toward questions of when life begins (as in Exodus 21, which we will look at below) and whether a foetus is a person, but nothing that constitutes straightforward teaching. What we primarily find are rich descriptions of God's loving concern for all human life regardless of accomplishment or any kind of instrumental value. God cares for everyone for reasons that are intrinsic to their status as his creatures and have nothing to do with actual or future successes, their contribution to society or the fact that they take up their role in a productive labour force. The opposite is the case for 'the least', who may serve none of these functions and so are the first to be thought insignificant in the wider society, a problem for those who must look after them or a drain on the system.

Many of the current debates over abortion are not actually debates over morality. Instead, they take the form of legal debates that ask questions such as whether pregnant women ought to have the choice to abort their pregnancies, at which stage a foetus ought to be protected, and so on. Questions about when life begins aren't, on their own, moral questions, although what lies behind them is usually the conviction that it is wrong to take innocent life. Even though these questions sound as though they might be answered by science, they belong more naturally to religion and philosophy. A number of ideas have emerged in the histories of Judaism and Christianity. Medieval Christians used Greek categories of metaphysics to understand that at some point during pregnancy (such as the fortieth day for males and eightieth day for females), the foetus becomes formed, up until which it had been unformed. The idea is that things have both an essence and a form, and the human person receives its soul as an act of being formed into something unique that we would probably call personhood. Earlier ideas took the complete person to be wholly present within the father (who provides the essence) prior to conception and then grown and shaped within the mother (who provides the form). Drawing on the biblical image of God breathing his spirit into Adam, animating him with life (the words 'spirit' and 'breath' are the same in Hebrew), Christians have sometimes wondered when this occurs. Such a process was known as

'ensoulment' – the soul coming into the body – which effects the formation of the unformed foetus.

It is important to understand that ensoulment is not necessarily identical to talking about when life begins since ensoulment might happen later
than conception. Even so, notable early Christian writers like Tertullian,
Clement of Alexandria and Gregory of Nyssa held a view called **traducianism** in which the conception and the entering of the soul occur at
the same time. Maximus the Confessor agreed and offered a christological
argument for it. Maximus pointed to the fact that the church councils had
affirmed that Christ was fully divine and fully human from the moment
of conception, meaning that we should also speak about his having a soul
from that same point. Christ would not be different from the rest of us in
this respect since his full humanity is something we share with him.[4]

Jewish law understands the foetus to be a full human being at birth.
Before this time, a foetus is considered part of the mother.[5] This reflects a
law in Exodus that seems to rank the value of the foetus's life differently
from the life of the mother:

> When people who are fighting injure a pregnant woman so that there is a
> miscarriage, and yet no further harm follows, the one responsible shall be
> fined what the woman's husband demands, paying as much as the judges
> determine. If any harm follows, then you shall give life for life, eye for eye,
> tooth for tooth, hand for hand, foot for foot, burn for burn, wound for
> wound, stripe for stripe. (Exod. 21.22–25)

In its teaching, and in this translation, the text appears to be quite clear. It is
drawing a distinction between harm (death) to the foetus and harm done
to the mother, with different penalties assigned to each. The text places a
different, lesser value on the life of the foetus. But there is a very different interpretation represented in the Septuagint and the writings of the
first-century philosopher Philo. The Septuagint is a Greek translation of
the Hebrew Bible that was in use at the time that the New Testament was
written. When citing the Old Testament, it was common for New Testament
authors to quote the Septuagint directly, since they too were writing in
Greek. The fact that the Septuagint offers a very different interpretation
indicates that this interpretation was in circulation among scholars at the

---

4 Lindsey Disney and Larry Poston, 'The Breath of Life: Christian Perspectives on Conception
and Ensoulment', *Anglican Theological Review* 92.2 (Spring 2010): 271–95.
5 David Michael Feldman, *Birth Control in Jewish Law: Marital Relations, Contraception, and
Abortion* (New York: New York University Press, 1968), 252–3. Cited in Disney and Poston,
'The Breath of Life', 279.

time. The Aristotelian distinction between an unformed foetus (without a soul) and a formed foetus (with a soul) was being used to interpret a Hebrew text with a rather different meaning. It should be clear that this text contributes differently to debates about abortion depending on how it is read. The original, Hebrew meaning in which the foetus is valued less than the mother is no doubt the more authentic one, even though it is also more at odds with subsequent Christian tradition.

Nevertheless, the public abortion debate is seldom this biblical. In the United States, for example, the debate centres on competing *rights*. Does the developing foetus have a right to life? Does the mother have a right to choose to terminate her pregnancy? In the famous *Roe v. Wade* ruling of 1973, the US Supreme Court decided that the language of 'personhood' used in the Fourteenth Amendment to the Constitution to discuss citizenship and other rights does not apply to the unborn. The ruling contains an admission, however, that if a case could be made that foetuses are persons in this technical sense, the whole case collapses. For this reason, demonstrating personhood has dominated anti-abortion arguments ever since. Additionally, the ruling concluded that the state nevertheless does have an increasing 'interest' in protecting prenatal life as the stages of pregnancy progress, although the language of '*potential* life' (as opposed to simply 'life') was deemed sufficient for the state to assert this interest.

Even though this rights-based debate can be quite intense, it is not clear that it can come to any resolution using the terms employed. Some Christian ethicists argue that the terms of the debate should be changed. Stanley Hauerwas says that Christians should not finally be concerned about rights at all, but that rights-language belongs to the world of political liberalism and is designed to work in societies that have lost all common moral language. Like any content-rich moral tradition, such as other religions, Christianity possesses moral language for dealing with issues of life and death, what we owe to others, what levels of care and concern are proper to loving, and what risks we take and ought to accept when we open ourselves to others and to God. But instead of debating questions about the common good – what kind of people we want to be as a culture, what it means to live a virtuous human life – Christians in liberal societies find themselves reaching for rights-language as a kind of lowest common denominator. Hauerwas says that this explains why the abortion debates simply go on and on. In order to weigh rights against each other and come to some resolution, we would need to talk about questions of value, of goods. But 'rights' is meant to function *in place of* discussions like this in recognition of the fact that people in a diverse society are not likely to agree on questions of value. If this is true, though, the impasse in the abortion debate is just one instance of a much larger intransigence that is built into the discourse itself. What, then, might be an alternative?

As is the case with any question in ethics, it is important to look into who it is that is asking the question. Christians are not just any people. We are a people whose existence is storied by a loving God who blesses his enemies by forgiving them and welcomes the least by making room for them. In place of arguing about rights, Hauerwas says that Christians have a different way of speaking about vulnerable life. 'The crucial question for us as Christians is what kind of people we need to be to be capable of welcoming children into this world, some of whom may be born disabled and even die.'[6] We notice that Hauerwas is working with a perspective on abortion that takes the focus away from the specific decision of whether or not to abort a pregnancy and also from legal debates about when a foetus becomes a person and what rights the mother possesses. Instead, he is urging Christians to remember that care for 'the least of these' is integral to the Christian mission. By focusing on showing hospitality to those whom others reject, Christians may avoid adopting the terms of the public debate that are ultimately foreign to the heart of Christian moral concerns.

Richard Hays, a colleague of Hauerwas at Duke Divinity School and a biblical scholar, offers a similar attempt to shift focus away from rights-language. He uses the biblical example of the parable of the Good Samaritan in Luke 10 to show that the language of rights can be a way of avoiding more serious questions. Jesus tells this parable in response to a lawyer who is trying to find a loophole in the law that states 'Love your neighbour as yourself.' The lawyer wants to raise a somewhat technical issue with Jesus by asking, 'Who is my neighbour?' He hopes that there are some people that this excludes. Surprisingly, Jesus tells a parable that shows that the neighbour whom we are to love includes all people, including strangers and even enemies. Indeed, Jesus explicitly teaches about the love of enemies in Luke 6. For Hays, asking when life begins and whether a foetus is a person with the right to life is much like asking 'Who is my neighbour?' The force of the question is meant to exclude rather than include. It is trying to get off the hook somehow, to limit my sphere of concern rather than expand it. But the Christian attitude, according to Jesus, ought to be very different. As Hauerwas puts it:

---

6 Stanley Hauerwas, 'Abortion Theologically Understood', *The Hauerwas Reader*, ed. John Berkman and Michael Cartwright (Durham, NC: Duke University Press, 2001), 619.

The Christian approach is not one of deciding when life has begun, but hoping that it has. We hope that human life has begun! We are not the kind of people that ask: Does human life start at the blastocyst stage, or at implantation? Instead, we are the kind of people that hope life has started, because we are ready to believe that this new life will enrich our community.[7]

We see here a virtue-based alternative to both deontological and consequentialist modes of moral reasoning. The theological virtue of hope stands out by taking the focus away from both what we know to be the case morally and what we think the future might hold. In this way, hope differs from knowledge. When it comes to elective abortion, a key challenge for Christians and Christian communities is to embody this hope and the risk-taking it will require in very difficult circumstances. It may well involve trying to see every pregnancy and new birth as a sign of God's goodness, to be welcomed and received by the community, sometimes at great cost to itself.

This section hasn't addressed the less common, but certainly no less trying, cases such as when pregnancy puts a woman's life at risk or where an abortion is deemed medically necessary to remove a uterine tumour. Instead, the focus has been on elective decisions that involve women contemplating abortion out of fear and other feelings of vulnerability (in addition, that is, to the vulnerability of the foetus) in which the future prospect of motherhood seems impossible to accept, such as when domestic and communal supports are missing. This is why we discussed the community rather than the individual woman as the moral agent that must take responsibility for the abortion decision. When communities intervene to overcome her vulnerability, the abortion decision may become less pressing.

Human embryos

In order to understand the current moral debate over the use of human embryos in scientific research, we need to talk a little about biology. In short, embryos are of some medical usefulness due to their abundance of embryonic stem cells, cells that can regenerate themselves and turn into a variety of other types of cells. Even though further research is needed in order to know whether embryonic stem cells might be able to cure diseases like Alzheimer's and Parkinson's, stem cells from other sources such as umbilical cord blood and bone marrow are currently being used therapeutically.

---

7 Hauerwas, 'Abortion Theologically Understood', 615.

Embryonic stem cells are derived from embryos created in a lab within about five days of fertilization. They are produced *in vitro* (literally 'in glass') rather than *in utero* ('in the womb') or *in vivo* ('in the living'). At the present time, these embryos are commonly left over from *in vitro* fertilization (IVF) treatment in which individual women or couples receive assistance with conceiving a child. The IVF procedure always generates more embryos than are transferred into the patient's uterus, and more are transferred than actually implant. Leftover embryos that have not been transferred from this procedure may be frozen for later use, donated to others, destroyed, or donated to scientific and medical use. Only a minority of couples who produce spare embryos in the process of fertility treatment are willing to donate them to others. The main reason is that they are uncomfortable with somebody else raising their biological children.

It is important to see that the moral questions raised by the scientific and medical use of human embryos go beyond the question of whether destroying embryos for a good reason may be justified. These are certainly important questions and they parallel, in many ways, the questions we raised above about the moral status of foetuses. But since a surplus of embryos is being created through IVF, we need to ask questions about whether it is justifiable to create embryos that we know will never survive. In order to discuss the use of embryos responsibly, we therefore need to start further back with the much less controversial procedure of IVF. It is true that *in vivo* fertilization (within the female body) very often results in a fertilized ovum that never implants in the womb, just as miscarriages at later stages of gestation also occur. What is different in the *in vitro* cases is that a surplus of embryos is *intended*.

At this point, we need to talk again about the principle of double effect, the very important principle in philosophical ethics we discussed in Chapter 9 in connection to warfare. We are coming back to it in order to deal with the problem of intending. You may recall that double effect was first defined by Thomas Aquinas (1225–74) in his discussion of self-defence.[8] Today, however, it is discussed in connection to a lot of different issues, some of them in the field of bioethics.

The idea of double effect is that some actions we perform may produce more than one effect, one of which is good and one of which is bad. In the case of IVF one good effect of the procedure is helping infertile women conceive a child. The bad effect is that spare embryos left over from the procedure will in many cases be destroyed. Aquinas's innovation was to

---

8 Thomas Aquinas, *ST*, II-II.64.7.

introduce a further consideration and ask what is intended. Is the intent of IVF to produce a lot of spare embryos? Of course not. The intent is to help patients conceive a child. So in addition to the action (which here is the IVF procedure) having both a good and bad effect, only one of the effects – the good one – is intended. The other, bad effect is not intended.

If we were to stop here, far too many things are able to be justified. Double effect does not only say that the intention must be good. There are two further conditions that must be met:

1 the good gained must outweigh the evil effect;
2 the bad effect cannot be the means to the good effect.[9]

Now we can ask whether IVF passes the test of these two considerations. First, does the good of helping an infertile couple outweigh the evil of creating unused embryos? This is hard to say. Certainly the benefit to the couple is greater. But we should also acknowledge that this is only one way of measuring the total good of IVF. Assessing the magnitude of the evil effect will largely depend on the moral status of the embryos. Second, is the creation of an excess of embryos (the bad effect, since they will be destroyed) the means of creating a child (the good effect)? The way the technology currently stands, it is not possible to have one without the other. If it were possible to create a child *in vitro* without the creation of spare embryos, this might instead become the practice. But of course the present practice is limited by current technology.

The reality of current IVF practice, however, is more involved than this discussion has indicated so far. The procedure is not limited to helping infertile women conceive. It is now also possible to choose the sex of one's child through Pre-implantation Genetic Diagnosis (PGD) and even to screen for genetic diseases. The ethical questions raised by PGD are multiple. First, unlike IVF, the *intent* of PGD actually is the destruction of some embryos – the embryos that are not selected for implantation are destroyed. This means that, in these cases, the bad effect (destruction of embryos) really is the means of achieving the good effect (the birth of the child who is chosen). So PGD runs into problems according to double effect because of the role it plays in helping to select some embryos for implantation and some for destruction.

When used to screen for genetic diseases, the good effect of PGD is often discussed as 'genetic vaccination'. The child born will not have the genetic

---

9 For a helpful summary of double effect, see William C. Mattison III, *Introducing Moral Theology: True Happiness and the Virtues* (Grand Rapids: Brazos, 2008), 172.

diseases screened for. This language, however, is not accurate. It implies that the procedure is somehow preventing the genetic disease. In reality, the only way to prevent the genetic disease for an embryo that has it is to ensure that that embryo never develops into a child. The same goes for sex selection. In order to achieve the desired result – the sex and genes that the patient wants in a child – other human embryos *must* be created in order to be destroyed. Some have proposed that doomed embryos might be 'adopted' since they otherwise have no future. This might be a moral path, but on its own doesn't change the moral questions associated with procedures like PGD.

Supporters of scientific and medical use of spare embryos from IVF procedures will point to the fact that doing something beneficial with them is preferable to simply destroying them without benefit to anyone. This shifts the moral responsibility for what happens to the embryos from those who *use* them (scientists) to those who *derive* them (the specialists working in fertility clinics). Does this argument work?

The social theorist Paul Virilio (b. 1932) points out that with every technological innovation there is also the unintended innovation of what he calls 'the accident'. If someone invents the train, he or she has also unintentionally invented the train crash. The scientists who invented nuclear reactors also unintentionally invented nuclear waste and the nuclear meltdown. Every technological innovation also includes unintended 'accidents'.[10] And there are also what we might call unintended *moral* accidents that come with every innovation. The point is this: the moral problem of what to do with spare embryos is not something that appeared out of nowhere. It is the specific consequence of technological innovations (IVF and PGD) even if it was not intended from the start. So to argue that it's better to destroy embryos for benefit than to destroy them for no benefit ignores the fact that this very choice was generated by a culture determined to advance technologically without considering that we would be faced with choices such as this. In other words, if we think this is our only choice, it is because we have already made more basic choices – technological ones – without understanding the moral accidents we were causing.

Critics of IVF and PGD in particular sometimes point to considerations beyond those strictly dealing with the life-status of embryos. Deciding that embryos are human lives is not on its own enough to settle the moral questions about what to do with them. After all, many moral schemes allow for taking human life under certain circumstances (such as in war). There are

---

10 Paul Virilio, *The Original Accident* (Cambridge: Polity, 2007).

deeper questions here about what the vast cultivation of human embryos says about a culture's attitude toward life and death. Over time, such a culture may become so desensitized to the value of human life that those who are most vulnerable become expendable in the service of those who are less vulnerable. We will encounter this point again in our discussion of euthanasia below.

The popular atheist writer Sam Harris expresses frustration with opposition from religious people to what seems to him 'utterly straightforward' and in no need of ethical debate whatsoever.[11] Harris thinks that showing any concern about using human embryos is 'one of the many delusional products of religion that has led to an ethical blind alley, and to terrible failures of compassion'. Harris is right to name compassion for current and future sufferers as the most decisive motive for approving of the therapeutic use of human embryos. He thinks it should be obvious, though, that compassion for embryos makes no sense.

Harris takes a strongly consequentialist approach toward the therapeutic use of human embryos. This approach focuses only on the positive consequences for the patient's health. Left out of consideration are the negative consequences for the medical and scientific communities that must generate or sustain a certain apathy toward vulnerable life and for the larger culture that must do the same. Rather than asking questions that are at the heart of the Bible and Christian tradition about the care for the least, a culture that countenances the destruction of human life for the therapeutic benefit of others is what Pope John Paul II described as a 'culture of death':

> This culture is actively fostered by powerful cultural, economic and political currents which encourage an idea of society excessively concerned with efficiency. Looking at the situation from this point of view, it is possible to speak in a certain sense of a war of the powerful against the weak: a life which would require greater acceptance, love and care is considered useless, or held to be an intolerable burden, and is therefore rejected in one way or another. A person who, because of illness, handicap or, more simply, just by existing, compromises the well-being or life-style of those who are more favored tends to be looked upon as an enemy to be resisted or eliminated. In this way a kind of 'conspiracy against life' is unleashed.[12]

---

11 Sam Harris, *The Moral Landscape: How Science Can Determine Moral Values* (London: Free Press, 2010), 171.
12 John Paul II, *Evangelium Vitae*, sec. 12.

The same conclusions hold whether the matter being discussed is abortion or the destruction of embryos. Foetuses and embryos are sacrificed for the sake of others, and since we are treating these topics under the heading of vulnerable life, it's worth noting that the beneficiaries are often themselves vulnerable. The more vulnerable are sacrificed for others who may also be vulnerable.[13] There is a warning in this: we will probably always find it easier to feel and show compassion for some people than for others. If people are more like us, our compassion more readily flows to them. But surely this indicates that what we feel as compassion can also be deeply bound up with self-interest. Catholic teaching, especially the 2008 document *Dignitas Personae*, insists that the lives of embryos are equal in dignity to those of older humans.[14]

There are deeper and related moral questions connected to this debate that have less to do with the moral status of human embryos as such. We are faced with the frailty that comes with being human, the inevitable reality that we will feel pain, suffer losses of ability, become injured and never fully recover, and die. Therapeutic use of human embryos aims not only to stave off death a little longer, but also to improve the quality of life for people in debilitating conditions. Arguments against such use can come close to justifying suffering. Yet a deeper way of having this debate needs to acknowledge that we will not always be able to ease suffering and postpone death. We do not bear ultimate responsibility for doing so. How are we going to live in the light of this recognition? The Christian bioethicist Gilbert Meilaender thinks we need to insist on continuing to ask the fundamental moral question of *how* we live, not *how long*.[15]

Indeed, Christians of all people must know what it means to live and even flourish in the midst of vulnerability. The temptation is to take control of the vulnerabilities that come with being human, in effect refusing to accept that we are as vulnerable a species as we appear to be. We are therefore faced with the strains that our societies put upon the medical profession, pressures to heal even at great moral cost. But there are costs, and they are precisely also vulnerabilities that come with being human. Some of these only appear tragic, such as when an embryo is shown to have a genetic disease. Screening it out, we need to remember, doesn't cure the disease. Others are simply the luck of the draw, such as the embryo's

---

13 G. McGee and A. Caplan, 'The Ethics and Politics of Small Sacrifices in Stem Cell Research', *Kennedy Institute of Ethics Journal* 9.2 (1999): 151–8.

14 *Dignitas Personae*, sec. 32.

15 Gilbert Meilaender, 'The Point of the Ban: Or, How to Think about Stem Cell Research' in *The Hastings Center Report* (January/February 2001).

sex. Of course, screening out embryos of a certain sex introduces choice into what has always been thought to be arbitrary.

There is a deep and deeply serious Christian sensibility that needs to be cultivated in which what others see as arbitrary is cherished as a gift. This involves being open to surprises, with the new possibilities, opportunities and even burdens that come along with gifts when the gift-giver is believed to be good and loving. As long as Christians continue to view children as gifts from God and not as creatures of our own making, we will make the most of receiving the bad with the good, especially when the alternative to receiving the bad involves taking control of the process to ensure a predictable, even 'good' outcome. Today, 90 per cent of people in the United Kingdom who learn that they are carrying a child with Down's syndrome abort it. The numbers are 98 per cent in the Netherlands and 100 per cent in Iceland.[16] But what would it mean to see a child born with Down's syndrome as a gift to be received, cherished and showered with love?

Whatever it would mean would also transform the burdens we feel toward people who are sick and dying. We won't feel as though our only way to help them is to cure them. We will be able to offer care and companionship in recognition that human vulnerability is an occasion to demonstrate the kind of presence God demonstrates to us in Christ. We also won't feel as though curing them is such an overriding requirement that it demands that we make sacrifices out of other, more vulnerable, embryonic lives. These too are gifts.

Euthanasia

Life is especially vulnerable when it is close to being lost. Attempts to gain or exert control over the manner of one's death, especially when life has become medically fragile, are what is usually meant by euthanasia (which is Greek for 'good death'). The routines of worship liturgy train Christians to think about their lives and deaths in terms of Jesus' life and death. The fact that Christians commemorate Jesus' death on Good Friday reflects some core beliefs about his death being, in some manner, good. What was good about Jesus' death? We first need to be clear about what was *not* good about it. It's clearly not good that we or anyone else dies. The Bible associates sin and death such that death enters the world through sin (Rom. 5; 1 Cor. 15), and salvation is depicted as freedom

---

16 <http://www.bbc.com/news/magazine-37500189; https://downpride.com/appeal-to-the-united-nations/>.

from both sin and death. We still die, and when others die it is something to be mourned just as Jesus joined Mary and Martha in weeping for their brother Lazarus (John 11). The good news of the gospel is one of hope in the face of death. Jesus raised Lazarus and spoke these words: 'I am the resurrection and the life. Those who believe in me, even though they die, will live, and everyone who lives and believes in me will never die. Do you believe this?' (John 11.25–26). Death is not itself good since it is at the heart of everything that God is overturning and overcoming in Christ.

Nevertheless, we can say that it is good to approach the deaths of others and of ourselves hopeful of God's consolation and expecting resurrection. Paul taught that there is a form of hopeless grief in the face of death that Christians have every reason to resist: 'But we do not want you to be uninformed, brothers and sisters, about those who have died, so that you may not grieve as others do who have no hope' (1 Thess. 4.13). For the Christian, we know that there are worse things than dying since Jesus himself and many Christians since him are honoured for their faithful devotion to God's mission in the world even though it cost them their lives. This is what Christians mean by calling a death good: a life is handed over to God's service so that death can be faced without fear, trusting that God brings resurrection and eternal life. Jesus taught that those who mourn will be comforted (Matt. 5.4). What comforts mourning people more than the promise that the one who died will live again? And this is not only a hope for individual people, but for all of creation, as some of the Bible's very last promises declare:

> [God] will wipe every tear from their eyes.
> Death will be no more;
> mourning and crying and pain will be no more,
> for the first things have passed away.
>
> (Rev. 21.4)

All of this points to the fact that Christians have a distinctive and very strong sense of what a good death means. For this reason, when Christians first established hospitals, they were meant to be places of rest and care. They were places where a person close to death would receive prayer and the ministrations of the Church, such as final communion and blessings. These goals were very different from those of modern medical practices that primarily seek ways to cure the patient and postpone death. In his book, *Western Attitudes toward Death from the Middle Ages to the Present*, Philippe Ariès describes how the idea of what constitutes a good death has changed significantly since the Middle Ages.[17] At that time, people wanted to die slowly and know that they were dying. This way they could prepare for their death, seeking reconciliation with friends and family, take time for the private spiritual devotion and entrust their final days to the care of ministers. A good death was slow and experienced in full awareness that one's life was drawing to a close. Ariès notes that most Western people today think that a good death is the opposite. They would prefer to die suddenly and in their sleep.

One thing that has changed is that we have mostly forgotten how to be ill with patience. When we are patient, we wait on God – and not only to cure us. We wait on God in order to learn how to suffer virtuously, how to endure hardship with hope: ultimately, how to die a good death. The biblical story of Job illustrates this. Job was a righteous man who suffered great loss for no apparent reason. When Job's friends saw him and how extreme his suffering was, they literally did nothing:

> Now when Job's three friends heard of all these troubles that had come upon him, each of them set out from his home – Eliphaz the Temanite, Bildad the Shuhite, and Zophar the Naamathite. They met together to go and console and comfort him. When they saw him from a distance, they did not recognize him, and they raised their voices and wept aloud; they tore their robes and threw dust in the air upon their heads. They sat with him on the ground for seven days and seven nights, and no one spoke a word to him, for they saw that his suffering was very great. (Job 2.11–13)

As the story goes on, Job and his friends tend to lose their patience. But when they do so, God judges them for lack of faith. But this story has been instructive for Jews and Christians who have sought faithful responses not only to suffering, but especially to *unjust* suffering – suffering that lacks explanation and is not deserved. The book of Job repeatedly counsels patience and waiting on God, not even speaking a word of explanation, but placing our hope in God's provision, comfort and deliverance. If we think that Christians are called on patiently to care for the weak, the suffering and the dying, we will probably find little support from a society whose first impulse is to deal with the problem and eradicate suffering out of impatience and desperation.

It is not natural to want to die. But death can indeed be faced in a number of different ways. Modern medicine is not equipped to talk meaningfully about death, and often the words spoken surrounding death in the

---

17 Philippe Ariès, *Western Attitudes toward Death from the Middle Ages to the Present*, trans. Patricia Ranum (Baltimore: Johns Hopkins University Press, 1975).

rest of society are well-meaning, but ultimately empty and shallow (one thinks perhaps of the messages found in sympathy cards). Euthanasia as we have come to know it is thought to belong to the sphere of medical practice. But since modern medicine has no way to talk about death, it must deny that it has anything to do with death. This sounds absurd, of course, since people die all the time in hospitals. But they are not supposed to, since as a discipline, medicine is devoted to dreaming up new ways of keeping death at bay. These are often desperate, costly, unnatural and inhuman.

As we have already discussed in this chapter, it can be easy to think that many of the ethical issues surrounding biomedical technology are givens. In fact, they are often symptoms of a *theological* problem or shift that we don't always notice. If modern medicine is dedicated to finding all manner of ways of staving off death through a kind of technology of salvation, then modern euthanasia is just its inverse: the hopeless admission that this project has failed in a particular case.

When euthanasia is the personal choice of the patient (this gets the technical name of 'physician-assisted suicide'), it joins an ancient (though not Christian) tradition of respecting deliberate, rational suicides that are elected after careful deliberation. In our day, these discussions focus almost entirely on relieving suffering. We most readily associate putting an end to mental suffering with suicide, which many people will try to understand but perhaps not justify. In the United Kingdom, these suicides were legalized in 1961.[18] On the other hand, putting an end to physical suffering is a topic that evokes a different response. There is currently much more pressure to approve of it, both morally and legally, as has been done in several countries of Europe and in Canada, in addition to a handful of states in the USA. Euthanasia comes up because of a concern that many have, especially in our day, not to be a burden on their loved ones. It reflects an autonomy that many have come to associate with modern life in the West. It is certainly a departure from the medieval concepts of a good death that we looked at above. When people are used to living their lives without depending much on others, the loss of this independence can be interpreted as placing burdens on other independent people. By contrast, cultures that have a higher degree of communal interdependence, such as when multiple generations of family members live together (sharing meals, rearing children and caring for the older generations), there is less independence to lose. Support for the elderly, sick and dying may already

---

18 Samuel Wells and Ben Quash, *Introducing Christian Ethics* (Oxford: Blackwell, 2010), 330.

be woven into household and communal practices. Apart from these routine, everyday practices of living, a society will view dying differently. Now being made to feel a burden on others has become a key part of the suffering many sick and dying people feel.

It is impossible to talk about the modern debate over euthanasia without talking about suicide. Dietrich Bonhoeffer pointed out that one thing that sets humans apart from the other animals is that we have the ability to take our own lives in freedom.[19] This freedom is used whenever someone commits suicide, but also when a person sacrifices his or her life for the good of others. Bonhoeffer, for example, wrote about a prisoner of war who kills himself rather than betray his country. We sometimes talk about a person 'taking a bullet' for someone else. These seem to be commendable actions that we might think of as resulting in a 'good death'. What, then, makes sacrifice different from suicide?

If someone sacrifices his or her life for others, it can be viewed as actually ultimately embracing life rather than rejecting it – the sacrificial person is embracing the life of others. Unlike the distinction we have made in previous chapters between good and bad sacrifice, and although in particular cases it may not always be possible to see the difference, suicide seems to have little to do with sacrifice. Even though we can usually get by keeping these two separate in our minds, it is possible to complicate them somewhat.

In the Bible, suicide is never specifically prohibited although there is clearly a general pattern of despair or indignity associated with the deaths of those who commit suicide. Judas, the betrayer of Jesus, is a good example of this. Even so, it is not always clear where the blame lies for the suicides. In Matthew, Judas somewhat repents to the chief priests for betraying Jesus and offers back to them his pay for doing so. But the chief priests reject his gesture of repentance whereupon he then kills himself. He dies unforgiven, as much of the tradition would say – his sins upon his own head. But notice that, if he had truly repented to the priests, their lack of forgiveness might actually have made them responsible for his death. There is an understandable reason that they didn't forgive Judas, of course. Doing so would have been an admission that there was something to forgive, that Judas had done something wrong when he betrayed Jesus, an act which they had supported, financially and otherwise.

So it is possible that the Bible is complicating the issue of suicide more than some people sometimes notice. Bonhoeffer maintains that suicide is

---

19 Dietrich Bonhoeffer, *Ethics*, trans. Neville Horton Smith (New York: Touchstone), 164–71.

often the attempt to justify one's life – to make it better, to give it a meaning that is greater than it seems to have, to come to terms with despair over the disconnect between one's hopes and reality. This is evident in the story of Judas when he realizes that Israel's priests are not going to fulfil their justificatory role. Bonhoeffer's response to this function of suicide is a theological one: only God can justify human lives; God saves us; we cannot save ourselves, even through suicide.

Now that we have considered the very broad questions of how to approach death with trust and hope, and why the concept of a good death has come to be what it is today for so many, we can look at some of the specific moral issues surrounding so-called mercy killing, or hastening the death of terminally ill patients. Chief among these is the question of whether there is a moral distinction between killing and letting die.

This distinction is sometimes described using the language of **active euthanasia** and **passive euthanasia**.[20] In active euthanasia, a patient is purposefully put to death by some means (in physician-assisted suicide, this is often done by the patient wilfully ingesting a prescribed barbiturate). In passive euthanasia, medical interventions are stopped and the patient is allowed to die of his or her illness. Debates about whether there is a moral difference between these two are important in settings where passive euthanasia is permitted but active euthanasia is not. The idea is that actively killing a person seems different (and worse). Then again, in both scenarios, not only is the outcome the same (death), but they also seem to involve the same motive. It is, after all, possible to have a motive for *not* doing an action, and not just think that we have motives only for acting. Sometimes it is possible to describe an apparent non-action in positive terms, such as when a person insults someone by not shaking his or her hand.[21] That person has done something (insulted) by not doing something (shaking the hand). So it's possible to kill someone by not doing something that could have prevented his or her death. This, one argument goes, shows that active and passive euthanasia are morally the same.

Of course, it's very difficult to know anyone's motive for action. In standard euthanasia cases, treatment might be withheld if it is deemed useless because the patient's death is imminent. Or treatment might be counterproductive, such as when a feeding tube is necessary for nutrition but its invasiveness is beyond what the body can handle at that point. These are

---

20 See James Rachels, 'Active and Passive Euthanasia' in *Euthanasia: The Moral Issues*, ed. Robert M. Baird and Stuart E. Rosenbaum (Buffalo: Prometheus, 1989), 45–51.
21 This example comes from Rachels, 'Active and Passive Euthanasia', 50.

examples of what James Rachels called passive euthanasia. In some of the cases, death results from the illness; but if a feeding tube is withdrawn, the patient dies from starvation rather than the illness. In other cases, though, compassion leads many to favour hastening the patient's death, especially where great pain and suffering is involved.

In practice, the legal possibility and availability of active euthanasia leads to the feeling in some ill people that because this option exists, it not only provides a way out of their own suffering, but will also relieve others of any possible burdens. What begins as a choice made available to a person can quickly feel like an expectation. Christians will need to counteract this pressure with a very clear message that we are to bear one another's burdens (Gal. 6.2) and willingly suffer with those who suffer (1 Cor. 12.26; Heb. 13.3). The reason is not that suffering is good or even that it 'means something'. Rather, Christians are called to see suffering in the light of the suffering of Christ. Doing this does give a kind of meaning to suffering, though not as a good. It acknowledges the opportunities that suffering presents for hospitable care and dependence.

While it is important to relieve suffering, what should be done when the only way to relieve a person's suffering is to end his or her life? Can this be called care of the patient? As before, the principle of double effect can help to address this question. We clearly have a case in which double effect might apply, were it not for one of its stipulations: the bad effect (here death) cannot be the means of achieving the good effect (here relief of suffering). Notice that the situation would be different, as far as double effect is concerned, if the pain relief involved administering a drug that, if taken long enough or in elevated doses, is foreseen to kill the patient. In this case, the bad effect doesn't bring about the good effect, but is only a consequence of acting to relieve the pain (that is, by administering the drug).

In most societies that permit active euthanasia, the patient must be diagnosed with a terminal illness that will soon lead to death (such as within six months). But we might wonder why a person in great suffering must have a terminal diagnosis in order to qualify for euthanasia. Once a society condones granting the choice of euthanasia to those who seek it on the basis of their suffering, there seems to be little stopping a slide toward approving of anyone seeking suicide in order to put an end to pain. It is not obvious why a person in great *chronic* pain could not argue for their hastened death through a very similar argument.

In the end, the strongest Christian responses to today's debates over euthanasia probably ought to focus more on the practices of living and care that make euthanasia less likely to be chosen. These responses will be practical rather than strictly philosophical or theoretical since they will make real differences in how people in our communities and in our churches experience their final days. This kind of focus might certainly have public policy implications, but will not set out to directly weigh in on policies. The current urge that so many feel for permitting active euthanasia or physician-assisted suicide reflects deeper anxieties about death and hopeless suffering that cannot be fixed by changes in the law.

13

Challenges posed by science and technology

In this book, we have often made the observation that the questions of ethics are not simply givens. We shouldn't imagine that a canonical set of pressing questions dropped from the sky and demands our attention. Many of the questions come and go according to what people and various groups consider to be most important. But considering some things to be more important than others is *also* the work of ethics since these are already matters of value, of the good. Scientific advances and technologies are responsible for generating many new challenges to ethics because newly discovered facts and newly devised machines, instruments, procedures, forms of communication and modes of transportation test the suitability of the customs and habits that people have generally relied on until now. The need to ask new questions of ethics when these arise is a need that humans create by valuing something else, and usually something new. In this section, we will look at three key areas in which science provokes ethics in general and Christian ethics in particular.

The first is a relatively abstract discussion about the role of science with respect to ethics. Can science tell us everything we need to know about morality, as some have argued? This move is sometimes framed as a way of getting rid of moral objections raised by non-scientists to what some consider to be crucial or promising scientific advances. It is not necessarily opposed to ethics per se, but it refuses to concede the sources of ethical reflection to disciplines outside the sciences. Responding to this move entails looking at the difference between facts and values as well as uncovering the origin and meaning of some of science's own deeply held assumptions.

The second area involves the relatively new biotechnologies of genetic engineering and cloning. Here the questions raised for us are especially pressing when they involve human lives that may be fabricated for the benefit of others. Various efforts to urge caution on this front appeal to justice and the principle of treating people as ends rather than means. Different understandings of 'playing God' are sometimes brought into this conversation in order to move us to consider the proper role we ought to play as God's creatures when it comes to engineering the building blocks of life.

The third area is the environment and human stewardship of it. Of course thinking about the environment isn't new. But the threats to the integrity of the earth's ecosystems, its role in sustaining human and other life, and the relationship of humans to other animals are just a few themes that are rapidly changing and seem to call for urgent moral responses. How are material things related to God? What do the sacraments have to teach us about environmental responsibility? How have the creation stories in Genesis been used and abused when talking about the ways humans interact with the earth?

Can science alone make us moral?

Most people are aware of some dramatic clashes between religion and science. Even if the clashes are sometimes caricatured, examples such as the Scopes Trial of 1925 that pitted Christian fundamentalism against secular science suggest to many people that there is a fundamental antagonism between science and religion. Not all examples are as colourful as the creation–evolution debate, however. In the Introduction, we considered an objection to the entire prospect of doing ethics that has to do with the feeling that it is hopeless. Science provides us with clear-cut answers to questions through processes of hypothesis-making, observation and experimentation. But it is generally understood that ethical positions cannot be verified or proven with anything like this level of confidence.

One option, then, is for new scientific ideas to be given freedom *from* moral constraints. With this approach, raising questions about the morality of, say, human cloning appears backward, unnecessarily moralistic and opposed to making advances that will benefit the human race. Even though this approach arises from an impatience with the fact that ethics is far from a pure science, it nevertheless relies on a form of consequentialism which the word 'benefit' in the previous sentence indicates. As long as a strong case can be made that cloning will provide a net benefit, what is the point of ethical reflection that more often than not seems to put the brakes on state-of-the-art progress? When we looked at the debate over therapeutic use of human embryos in the previous chapter, we phrased the force of arguments in favour of it in terms of consequentialist moral reasoning rather than in terms of the superiority of science. What sounds like science asking ethics to get out of the way is really the elevation of purely consequentialist considerations.

An approach that is more up front about how arguments for science rely on consequentialist reasoning is called **moral realism**.[1] This view insists that there are moral facts in the same way that there are facts about other things. These moral facts can be established through testing and proofs involving evidence in the same way that a scientist might arrive at the ideal human diet. Both cases, according to moral realists, fall within the realm of science since both are asking about what is good and best. This has led some proponents of this view to speak about a 'science of morality'.[2] The idea is that our knowledge of empirical facts (things that can be known by observation) is enough to make decisions about the good. The popular atheist writer Sam Harris holds this view, which he develops by asking consequentialist questions he believes can be answered through empirical science. Chief among these questions is: does acting this way as opposed to that increase human happiness and well-being or does it cause human suffering? Harris insists that answering this question is not subjective, that happiness isn't a subjective state that we need to ask people about. The scientific study of the brains of conscious creatures can tell us objectively what really promotes happiness. As a result, moral questions have objectively right and wrong answers.

In this section, we will look seriously at this proposal and indicate some problems with it. Most of the problems can be identified without the aid of a distinctly Christian ethic, although we will end up by giving a Christian account for why it emerged in the first place.

The version of moral realism I have briefly summarized attempts to overcome a distinction that philosophers have usually upheld, a distinction between facts and values. For centuries, philosophers have discussed this distinction, usually concluding that facts and values are two different kinds of things. Facts can be observed and proven, but values cannot, a position associated with Scottish philosopher David Hume (1711–76) who famously argued that it's not possible to move from *is* statements to *ought* statements. Today, most people would probably agree with Richard Dawkins, the contemporary critic of religion and advocate for science, that 'science has no methods for deciding what is ethical'.[3] But a counter-argument holds that

---

1 In this section, I present some arguments I develop at greater length in *What Makes Us Moral? Science, Religion and the Shaping of the Moral Landscape: A Christian response to Sam Harris* (London: SPCK, 2012).
2 Sam Harris, *The Moral Landscape: How Science Can Determine Moral Values* (London: Free Press, 2010).
3 Richard Dawkins, *A Devil's Chaplain: Reflections on Hope, Lies, Science, and Love* (New York: Mariner, 2004), 34.

what we think of as values and moral obligations are just more imposing ways of making factual statements. To take a mundane example, there may not be much of a difference between saying, 'Your car is being towed away' (an *is* statement), and 'You should go and do something about your car' (an *ought* statement). The first expresses a fact and the second expresses a value (the word 'should' tips us off) but you might react to both statements the same way – by rushing over to save your car! Then again, it's possible that you may not *value* your car. The two sentences only communicate the same thing if the value for your car is already in place and assumed, leaving the origin of our values untouched. The famed biologist E. O. Wilson (b. 1929) argued differently, saying that the way to overcome the is–ought distinction is by pointing to biological reasons (facts) – such as passing on our DNA – for why we value what we do.

In practice, we are usually dealing with multiple values at once. If a city's government is entertaining a particular proposal that would reduce levels of homelessness, it will clearly contribute to the well-being of the city's citizens in some sense. This will be judged by a value that says it is good for people not to be homeless and it is good for cities to have fewer homeless people. But if the proposal imposes a hefty tax burden on citizens, some will certainly oppose it for reasons that have to do with valuing *other* things as well (such as lower taxes). As with any form of consequentialism, making a judgement about whether a decision is moral based on how much it increases the total well-being of the world is not a simple calculation. How it gets calculated, and whether it is the kind of thing that can be calculated in the first place, will depend on ranking and ordering values. Is a city with lower taxes better or worse than a city with low rates of homelessness? The point isn't just that people will disagree on the answer. It is also that the fact of their disagreement reveals differences of value that can't always be overcome by gathering more empirical facts.

We are concerned here with the question of what *is* the case versus what *should be* the case. In addition to proposals like Harris's that claim that facts can tell us what to value, a good case can be made that the opposite is true: that how we describe what *is* is already shaped by our values. Harris clearly values what science claims happiness to be for a person based on a scan of his or her brain, regardless of what that person says or believes. But this only smuggles a value into the discussion under the guise of being a fact. Our values function as lenses that colour what we see.

Half a century ago, Oxford anthropologist E. E. Evans-Pritchard (1902–73) wrote about the Nuer tribe of Sudan. When a deformed child was born to the Nuer, it was not considered a human being, but a hippopotamus, which ought to be raised by its own kind. The baby was then placed in the river where it of course ended up dying. Most of us will be horrified by this practice and call it infanticide, even though it presents no moral problems for the Nuer.[4] It would be one thing to argue that the Nuer were simply wrong about the babies, which science can demonstrate are of the human rather than hippopotamus species. But what moral realism struggles to do is connect fact (the child is human) to value (even deformed humans deserve to live in human communities). If it seems obvious that establishing the humanity of all Nuer babies will take care of questions of how they ought to be treated, then we have skipped over a crucial step.

The Nuer described reality differently and so acted accordingly. But this doesn't need to mean that all descriptions are equal. It may well be that some descriptions of the way things are are better than others, but that the ways in which they are 'better' fall outside what can be established empirically. Christian belief is that the world is not just *nature* but *creation*, imbued with purpose, brought into existence by love and sustained by tender care. Yet this can't be known just by looking at it any more than (in an example Terry Eagleton gives) you can know whether a porcelain vase was a birthday present just by looking at it. Apparently equivalent factual descriptions – 'It is a vase' and 'It is a birthday present' – will communicate different levels of value since gifts are usually thought to have more value than non-gifts. Going further, gifts given for manipulative or unsavoury, ulterior reasons are obviously less valuable than gifts given as expressions of costly love. The point is that if no description of a simple vase is all that simple, the project of describing *the way things are* is always open to being challenged by factors that seem to fall outside empirical observation, strictly speaking.

This last point is particularly important when it comes to asking what values guide (and ought to guide) science itself. Does science depend on a big-hearted commitment to the betterment of our world? Some scientists may personally share this commitment, but it is difficult to argue that it is integral to science itself. Science names a commitment to a methodology for discovering facts which is usually thought to be value neutral since the achievements of science can obviously serve good or bad ends. It is one thing to say that our actions ought to promote the well-being of ourselves

---

4 Mary Douglas, *Purity and Danger: An Analysis of Concepts of Pollution and Taboo* (Harmondsworth: Penguin, 1970), 52. Douglas cites E. E. Evans-Pritchard, *Nuer Religion* (Oxford: Oxford University Press, 1956), 84. See also Stanley Hauerwas, *The Peaceable Kingdom: A Primer in Christian Ethics* (Notre Dame: University of Notre Dame Press, 1983), 116–17.

and others, but it is another to say that we ought to value well-being in the first place. It might seem to be a safe bet to assume that people will generally value their own well-being, which Harris argues should be as uncontroversial as the suggestion that we ought to value health instead of sickness. This sounds right except that people in fact make all kinds of choices that move them *away* from well-being, from smoking to eating poorly to taking part in risky relationships. Just knowing better isn't enough, since clearly most people will happily live with a certain tolerance of risk if it means receiving other benefits and pleasures that count toward one's total sense of well-being. People can also be deluded about what will bring about their well-being. When they are *wrong* about this, we mean that they are factually wrong. But does this also mean that they are morally wrong to be wrong in this way? Do we have a moral obligation to try to live without self-deception and face the truth about ourselves and our world?

One of the virtues of modern science is surely that it purports to answer yes to these questions, at least when it comes to its own rigorous investigations. Science is meant to be free from prejudice and subjectivism. The scientific method strongly depends on not ruling out certain findings in advance or privileging some outcomes because they will benefit the researchers, their institution or their grant-funding agency. In practice, of course, this kind of objectivity truly is threatened all the time and is evidenced by people's suspicions when, say, the tobacco industry funds lung cancer research. Even so, our ability to call conflicts of interest threatening or even wrong depends on values we already ascribe to an ideally practised scientific enterprise. We are matching science as an ideal up against science as it is actually practised. Ideally, we say, science should be practised objectively, perhaps without noticing that this ideal already is a value. The key question is where values like this come from. It is doubtful that they come from science itself.

In reality, the virtues of scientific objectivity, even when expressed only in ideal form, come from outside science itself. What lies behind it is a belief, even faith, in scientific truth that will sustain its dogged pursuit wherever it will be found. No supply of traditional answers will take the place of putting questions to the test. While modern science shares considerably in the Enlightenment's suspicion of tradition, the deeper roots were watered by Christian theological commitments. This is God's world and therefore the truth about it is valuable and reason can be trusted. Universities first gave theological reasons for justifying devoting the time it takes for all of the different disciplines to specialize in their own ways. Since all things cohere in the mind of God, there is a unity to all truth. But because truth is too complex to study all at once or in the same way, the different sciences could devote themselves to the study of different aspects of the universe, yet untroubled as to the importance of the respective projects in recognition that truth is a whole. As long as universities were associated with monasteries and linked with the Church (as was the case with the oldest universities such as those in Paris, Bologna and Cologne), non-theological topics were able to take their place alongside theological ones and share a rationale. Pursuing knowledge of God and God's world could be done in both empirical and non-empirical ways.

Today a lot of people mourn the 'siloing' of knowledges in modern universities. The specialization that once was made possible by a deeper coherence of the disciplines has mostly given way to specializations without coherence. The virtues that are necessary to sustain scientific enquiry come from outside science, but cannot be recognized without admitting that things may be more connected than we can now give an account for. The most dangerous outcome may be that science continues to have the confidence that was once given to it at a deep level by theology, but antagonisms toward theology for being non-scientific convert this confidence into a hubris that is resistant to moral guidance.

Genetic engineering and cloning

It took over a decade and roughly 3.7 billion dollars for the Human Genome Project to map the entire genetic code for human beings. It completed this work in 2003. Today, individual genetic maps can be generated much more quickly and cheaply. This section looks at some of the ethical issues involved beyond this knowledge of human genetics, strictly speaking, and focuses on what is being done with it, in addition to what might be done. Cloning is a specific type and outcome of genetic engineering, but both evoke similar ethical questions. Selective breeding in plants and animals has long been used both to encourage and to suppress different expressions of genes. Taboos against mating between close relatives in humans carry the force of morality, but at root may primarily be a way of preventing the undesirable expression of recessive genes. Various techniques of breeding to achieve desirable traits, a process known as *eugenics*, have in some famous examples included the forced sterilization of people who are deemed to have less desirable characteristics. Genetic engineering goes beyond all of these by manipulating the genetic material itself. Genome editing makes up part of this process and involves inserting, removing or replacing DNA in the nuclei of living organisms.

The strongest arguments for genetic engineering are medical and often therapeutic. Ill patients in need of a bone marrow transplant, for example, would be able to find an exact match in a clone. Genetic diseases could be engineered out of existence if corrected at the embryonic stage. In fact, many of the promises of these biotechnologies are the same as what we covered in the last chapter under the heading of 'human embryos'. There, as here, darker elements also accompany the subjects. Given humanity's history with human eugenics, would the ability selectively to enhance certain desirable traits be used to create a master race? Would current prejudices be magnified? For some, any discussion of these biotechnologies quickly turns into a list of warnings and cautions.

Some concerns are deontological, raising questions about the intrinsic rightness or wrongness of genetic engineering. Immanuel Kant is well known for insisting that people must always be treated as ends rather than means. It is wrong, Kant argued, to use people for some purpose, especially because this takes away their moral autonomy, their ability to make free choices about what to do with their own selves. This **ends rather than means** principle is deontological. With human beings, any time a therapeutic reason (for someone else) is given to justify genetic engineering and cloning, the human subject in question is being treated as a means to some end. Even short of engineering, this happens in cases of merely selecting an embryo out of many because it has certain genes that will produce a body that will help someone else. Umbilical cord stem cells can be useful in treating a sibling's disease as long as the genetics are right. As we discussed in the previous chapter, this kind of practice yields excess embryos that are usually destroyed, or at least raise moral questions about what to do with them. It is just a step further to engineer a genetic match for the ill patient, or else clone the patient's DNA.

Kant's principle of not using people as means is violated in all of these examples. This is because humans are being created with an instrumental purpose in mind. The child is needed and needs to be something in particular, a bearer of specific tissues, for example. But if human value is *intrinsic* (rather than *instrumental*) it is because, regardless of what a person can contribute to society or a family or an ill individual, there is worth in that life. Describing this worth comes easily and naturally to Christian belief that points to a life-giving, creative God who creates out of freedom (for no reason) and love (excessive joy, goodness and gladness). Kant's arguments were secular rather than religious and depended on linking human rationality with moral autonomy. Because we are rational, it is good (and therefore right) to use our reason freely by making our own moral choices.

For Kant, our intrinsic worth comes from our nature as rational. When some are used by others, this is a situation in which some rational and free beings are treating others in ways that don't respect their nature.

That said, it probably doesn't take very much philosophy to understand that we shouldn't use other people. But being able to articulate what it is that gives human life intrinsic worth is crucial since this principle becomes harder to hold on to once confronted with concrete instances of suffering. Making another human being serve a therapeutic function can be a strong temptation. Versions of this happen in organ donation from living and dead donors, but in both cases (though differently) obtaining prior consent from the donor strikes most people as morally right. As with everything, it is the extreme cases that truly test an ethic, such as when starving sailors lost at sea decide to eat the body of a member of the crew who has recently died. Here, the survival of the sailors as a promised outcome tests conventional morality at several levels (including the taboo against cannibalism). If the sailors justify their actions, it will be on consequentialist grounds. If they don't justify them but act anyway, they probably want to preserve the deontological quality of what they still believe deep down regarding cannibalism and consent but only under extreme duress are willing to suspend. I have used an extreme example, and yet cloning a human being and engineering a discrete life for the express purpose of saving another might be no less extreme. The point is that even if someone normally has a strong commitment to treating people as ends rather than means, it may not be enough to guide actual behaviour when faced with extreme situations. On the one hand, this is nothing new and is something we have looked at in previous chapters, especially when discussing the limits of ethics. On the other hand, therapeutic cloning and genetic engineering could easily become quite common and routine, making it much harder to live by suspending conventional morality. What is likely is simply that other justifications will be given.

One such justification that attempts to work with the means–end deontology makes room for the new life to be its own person with the exception of the therapeutic role its body is asked to play. If stem cells from the umbilical cord are what is needed, then the baby donor of it has completed his or her role once the child is no longer attached to it. An understanding that that life has intrinsic worth apart from donating the umbilical cord (which arguably belongs equally to the mother) would now need to take over to keep from concluding that, having served its purpose, there is no more need for this life. Most people's moral sense would be horrified at the prospect of ending a life once it has served a therapeutic purpose for someone else, even though the very thought of creating that life in the first place might have been dominated by these therapeutic considerations. The destruction of unused human embryos may or may not elicit this kind of horror since they are much smaller and at a much earlier stage of development. Pointing out these factors challenges what we really mean by calling human worth intrinsic. As above, the point is that if intrinsic human worth is deontological and it is being asked to sit alongside consequentialist justifications, something must keep it from being overwhelmed.

Critics of genetic engineering and cloning will usually double down on deontology by making it overriding and absolute. The argument is that without this, or apart from some way of chastening the lure of the consequentialist views that made these technologies appealing to begin with, there is a slippery slope away from the dignity, respect and sanctity that each life must be afforded. The debate over human cloning, for example, prompts legal and political questions about whether clones are persons possessing rights in ways that are related to the status of foetuses in the abortion debate. If these are lives with *only* instrumental value, then their status could be as copies secondary to the original.

Another, more religious-sounding deontological concern is raised by accusing the various synthetic biotechnologies of 'playing God'. Here, there is no need to focus exclusively on therapeutic technologies, as we have been doing. The claim that we are playing God – humans doing what it is only right for God to do – is often applied to a range of ways that genetic technology promises to take control of what has usually been thought to be uncontrollable 'variables' in human existence. It seems right to qualify the word 'variable' like this since one of the key roles science plays is showing that many more things are explainable than we previously thought. Still, the predicament of being vulnerable to fate, fortune, luck has for millennia at least provided such a rich background to how we think about what it means to be human that no religious view of the world would be complete without preserving knowledge and control of these things for God alone. It is commonly claimed that tinkering directly with a human being's genetic make-up is off limits because it puts humans in the place of 'playing God'.

Although one hears this phrase, it is very imprecise but probably points to something important about what we think a human being is. The eighteenth-century Scottish philosopher David Hume made an argument in favour of suicide and against the traditional Christian prohibition of it. In the course of his argument, he objected to the idea that suicide is a violation of something humans owe to God – that as creatures, we are to live the life God has given us and not take it under our own power. To Hume, this argument must have sounded like today's 'playing God' arguments. In response, he wrote:

> were the disposal of human life so much reserved as the peculiar province of the Almighty that it were an encroachment on his right, for men to dispose of their own lives; it would be equally criminal to act for the preservation of life as for its destruction.[5]

Hume's claim is that if bringing about one's premature death steps on God's toes, shouldn't we say the same about intervening in order to prevent it? There is something very crude about this comparison, as though taking antibiotics might violate God's function to bring both death and life. Hume didn't believe that, of course, but was merely trying to expose Christian inconsistency. Still, if his argument succeeds at all, a version tailored for our purposes will surely be much stronger: that life-enhancing and life-sustaining biotechnologies only extend interventions (like antibiotics) that we haven't felt the need to justify.

Theologian Ted Peters (b. 1941) is probably right that the phrase 'playing God' isn't very useful to theology. As people tend to use it, it functions to express warning, like saying 'Stop!' Peters wants a more careful way of proceeding. He writes, 'Caution is always good advice, to be sure. Yet the task before us is to be good stewards of the advance of genetic science and technology so that it contributes to human welfare without creating new injustices.'[6] Peters can be read as downplaying deontological concerns in favour of consequentialist ones. Promoting human welfare and avoiding injustice are worthy goals. But what is going to make people good stewards of biotechnology and keep these goals in view? Writing about genetic control in *Fabricated Man* (1970), Paul Ramsey insisted that we will know the usefulness of an ethic when we identify things that we *can* do but that we *ought not* to do. Yet at root the problem is theological, not ethical. He makes use of the idea of 'playing God' to indicate the adoption of a rival, godless theology complete with its own hopes. To Ramsey, the real issue has to do with idolizing a human-made future, attaching religious significance to an ultimate vision of humanity that science will create. Ramsey asserts that:

> whatever is reasonable in the heads of the molecular biologists is bound to become real. There is nothing to do but to yield to this cult's Providence.

---

5 David Hume, 'On the Naturalness of Suicide' in *Life and Death*, ed. Louis Pojman (Boston: Jones and Bartlett, 1993), 198.

6 Ted Peters, *Playing God? Genetic Determinism and Human Freedom* (London: Routledge, 2003), 2.

Men are to erect a 'good hope,' even an 'infinite hope,' over the 'corruption' of the existing world.[7]

'Playing God' is a description Ramsey uses for particular convictions about what it means to be a human being living in the world.

Learning to be human creatures does not exactly mean embracing every 'corruption' of the existing world. It means recognizing hopes that promise (or threaten) to tear us away from the virtues necessary to live with bodies that are limited. Where these hopes hold forth a notion of life that requires that bodies be transformed to more ideal forms, Christians are right to feel uncomfortable. Ramsey might have gone further than describing a rival theology; he could have pointed out a rival understanding of salvation. Early Christianity rejected ideas that took the material world to be a drain on the aspirations of the spirit and that sought salvation from the burdens of the world. Bodies are central to Christianity. We are saved in our bodies, not from them, and Christians undergo sacraments of baptism and Eucharist that both richly involve our material existence as we happen to be. Some bodies are utterly dependent on the care of other people, and others will eventually also be dependent in this way. The idea of having bodies perfectible through biotechnology represents a dream of independence for every person because of a cultural ideal that is probably, at root, moving in the opposite direction compared to where Christians move as they sacramentally enter the Church and are nurtured there.

It is important to say that, in the approach taken here, Christianity is involved in identifying surrogate theologies at work, not primarily to *heal*, but to *raise*. There is no question about the good of healing wounded bodies, praying for and tending to the ill, and ministering to the dying. What are deeply questionable are rival theologies essentially driven to look for the benefits of resurrection by removing undesirable biological qualities of human existence. If there is a kind of resurrection without suffering and death here, the point isn't that suffering and death are good. It is that pseudo-resurrections provide the wrong kind of answer to them. For example, bio-utopia can't include the massive sacrifice of human embryos in its moral calculation of the good it brings to others. Finally, Paul's reference to God's adoption which we wait for as 'the redemption of our bodies' (Rom. 8.23) draws attention to what Christians have been in the meantime, while we wait. The Church, Christ's body given for people, incorporates all bodies brought to it by signifying their worth as God's children

---

7 Paul Ramsey, *Fabricated Man: The Ethics of Genetic Control* (New Haven: Yale University Press, 1970), 144–5.

made in his image and it busies itself, while we wait for redemption, with the care of both souls and bodies.

This approach of identifying surrogate theologies also helps to highlight two further concerns in conclusion, both of which can be identified as consequentialist. First are worries about justice for weaker bodies. As knowledge of the human genome grows and the genetic make-up of individuals can also be known, some have raised ethical concerns about discrimination based on this knowledge. For example, will employers refuse to hire applicants based on health problems revealed by their genes? Will there be other, perhaps more dramatic ways of segregating superhumans from less adequate ones? Will seeking liberation from bodily flaws imprison those who have them? Who will liberate them? And will our current ethics of liberation serve us in this project? Christians attuned to watching for rival theologies will better spot rival displays of liberation and side with the weak, as God does.

Second are worries about economics.[8] Biotechnology is currently a big industry, propelled by capitalism. It seeks returns on its investments for shareholders and opportunities for creating new markets. Its everyday drives to experiment and develop in new areas are not likely to be tied to humanitarian concerns any more than pharmaceutical companies develop new drugs because they just want to help people. Moral objections will be viewed as troublesome more than they will be taken seriously. Short-term profits and other goals for stakeholders will propel research agendas rather than humanitarianism with long-term ends in view. The point isn't to be unduly cynical about these facets, but to be realistic about how little morality often has to do with the ways actual decisions get made. Christians attuned to everything about their faith that is stripped of instrumentality – from the practice of worship to church gatherings to resurrection – will better identify where things are being valued most for what they can gain for others.

Environment and stewardship

Christian environmental ethics is currently a subject of considerable urgency. Challenges posed by climate change, pollution of the world's oceans and food and water supply, deforestation, rapid species extinction and a host of related matters call for all people, and perhaps especially

---

8 See Samuel Wells, *Improvisation: The Drama of Christian Ethics* (Grand Rapids: Brazos, 2004), 194–5.

Christians, to confront the ways that we live on the planet. Do these ways express our God-given role as stewards? What are the pictures of our role and our connection with the earth and all material existence that shape our vision for living in our environments?

In fact, one unfortunate Christian habit throughout the centuries has been to elevate humans at the expense of the rest of creation. This was done with a supposed biblical warrant – God's direction in Genesis that humankind ought to have 'dominion' or rule over the other animals (Gen. 1.26, 28). Since humans were created last and in the special character as image of God, not to mention the fact that Adam named the animals, the rest of creation has sometimes been understood as existing merely for the benefit of human beings. In the thirteenth century, Thomas Aquinas followed Augustine in arguing that, unlike humans, animals lack reason which is a sign that they are 'naturally enslaved and accommodated to the uses of others'.[9]

An appeal to reason or intellect as the thing that distinguishes humans from the other animals has been very common. Here, Aquinas was primarily defending the killing of animals for food, but he was also reflecting a long tradition that goes beyond Christianity (Aquinas cites Aristotle) in which the purpose of animals is understood according to their usefulness to humans. As he writes elsewhere, 'animals are ordered to man's use in the natural course of things, according to divine providence. Consequently, man uses them without any injustice, either by killing them or by employing them in any other way.'[10] The point is clear: non-human animals exist for use by humans.

Two questions arise, one narrow and one broad. The narrow question has to do with the purpose of animals and whether humans can eat them. The broader question is about the place of humans within the whole created order.

In considering the purpose of non-human animals, it is important that the notion of dominion be stripped of its association with violence and mistreatment. Many Christians now prefer to use the English word 'stewardship' to describe how we should relate to animals and the rest of creation. A steward strives for responsible management of those things within his or her care. The creation of humans in the language of Genesis 2 is along these lines: 'The LORD God took the man and put him in the garden of Eden to till it and keep it' (Gen. 2.15). The fact that the paradigmatic

---

9 Thomas Aquinas, *ST*, II-II.64.1.
10 Thomas Aquinas, *Summa Contra Gentiles*, ed. Joseph Kenny (New York: Hanover House, 1955–7), XI.14.

humans are placed in a garden which is to give them their food (see 1.29; 2.16) has been evidence to some observers that the animals must ideally serve some purpose other than food for humans. Human origins are depicted with a vegetarian diet. Only after Noah's flood – that is, after the Fall – are humans told to eat meat: 'Every moving thing that lives shall be food for you; and just as I gave you the green plants, I give you everything' (Gen. 9.3).

These elements of the Bible's creation narratives suggest a recognition of the violence involved in eating meat. The theologically original and ideal state of creation has humans eating only plants and fruits. The Bible then introduces instances of human violence from the first animal sacrifice (Abel's) to the first murder (Cain's) to the widespread violence of the earth during the time of Noah. As we have seen in previous chapters, the relationship between violence and sacrifice in the Bible is complex. The way it is associated in the story of Cain and Abel is instructive. There is no indication of why God accepted Abel's animal sacrifice but not Cain's grain offering. But René Girard suggests that the story partly serves to explain the origin of sacrifice as violence that is condoned religiously. God rejects Cain's murder, of course, condemning the act but sparing Cain's life. This might be a way of signalling that there is a sacrificial mentality that lies at the heart of our violence. On the flip side, we are prone to neglecting a lot of our own violence with the help of concepts like sacrifice. As Girard reads the story, Cain's jealousy of his brother indicates the lack of a 'sacrificial outlet' which he then seizes through committing fratricide.[11]

Perhaps we are being shown that humans require some kind of sacrificial outlet. We kill in the hope of making things better. We justify violence in the name of goodness, justice and peace. As the opening stories of the Bible move along and violence becomes the norm, as in the time of Noah, God essentially sacrifices the whole world and enlarges the original command about food to now include the meat of animals. Noah also offers a burnt animal sacrifice (Gen. 8.20) and God responds with a pledge not to kill all living things again. God appears to be condescending to the human need for a sacrificial outlet but then also setting about to put an end to it.

The trajectory of these stories takes us from creation to redemption, from a discussion of the way things were meant to be originally to the kind of existence to which God is directing all things. Some of the Bible's best-loved images of peace and reconciliation involve carnivorous animals and

---

11 René Girard, *Violence and the Sacred*, trans. Patrick Gregory (Baltimore: Johns Hopkins University Press, 1977), 4.

humans in quiet repose with herbivores such as lambs and goats once at risk of being eaten or sacrificed (see Isa. 11.6). The story of Jesus and his institution of the Eucharist at the Last Supper culminates this. The Lamb of God is slain by humanity, offered to God as a sacrifice in the standard way in which we have come to be used to approving of our violence religiously; God rejects our sacrifice by raising him again; our violence is met with the risen Jesus' first word in John's Gospel: 'Peace . . .' The meal of peace that Christians share is a vegetarian one that presents meat (the body and blood of Jesus) using non-meat foods as another rejection of our violent association of sacrifice.[12] Just as the Old Testament taught that the life of the animal was in the blood, Jesus' life is now shared in the form of wine without requiring a death. Moreover, it is through bread, not meat, that we receive the spiritual food of Christ's body. The promise that there will be no more death in glory, it turns out, applies to more than humans. The end of all things is good news for animals too.

The end of meat is itself also good news for people. An economy of meat can be contrasted with an economy of vegetables, not having to do with the quality of the food itself, but with the labour it requires and the culture it produces. We have images of growth and harvest set against images of herding and slaughterhouses. The Old Testament scholar Walter Brueggemann (b. 1933) reflects along these lines in one of the biblical proverbs:

> Better is a dinner of vegetables where love is
> than a fatted ox and hatred with it.
>
> (Prov. 15.17)

Brueggemann confesses to deliberately overreading this text by seeing in it the way that beef represents the hustled, busy lives and frayed nerves that are necessary to bring it to a table. (It goes without saying that eating beef may not mean these things in all settings; sometimes they are a matter of scale.) Vegetables with love signal a healthy alternative to hectic affluence that instead points to enjoyment of one's neighbour. There is a wholesome focus on one's body and a communal, celebrative setting in which God's produce is most directly serving the benefit of people. Most of us would like to have it both ways: beef with love. But Brueggemann concludes:

> There are some things we cannot have without other things coming along. In the world of real productivity and real consumption, one cannot have

---

12 See Stephen H. Webb, *Good Eating* (Grand Rapids: Brazos, 2001), ch. 6.

great roast beef without quarreling. You might like it that way, but you cannot have it.[13]

In related prayer with the title 'After Eating', Wendell Berry asks God, 'May I be worthy of my meat.' It's a prayer suited for *after* we eat because we may have just eaten meat in the awareness of its cost. Indeed, the cost of meat might simply be too great sometimes, hurting our bodies, our planet and our communal relationships. It's very hard to want things such as meat while also being honest about what comes along with them (strife, discord and economic strain). God's eschatological vision of peace eliminates all of it.

At this point, and in consideration now of the broader issue about humans amid the whole created order, it can be tempting to be moralistic about how Christians ought to think about non-human creation. But the real issue has to do with seeing things for what they really are – part of God's creative gift of the universe in which God delights and finds joy, which shows divine harmony, and for which God indeed has a hope and dream that he is working to bring about. In light of this, contemporary debates about animal rights and the moral status of non-human creatures are not unimportant, but they pale in their theological significance.

A more fruitful way forward is to develop Christian approaches to seeing all of creation sacramentally. The Eastern Orthodox theologian Alexander Schmemann (1921–83) argued strongly against seeing the world as sharply divided into categories like sacred and profane.[14] An overly exalted human transcendence set against the under-exalted non-human creation is something we should also resist. To Schmemann, it is wrong to imagine that some ordinary things (like bread or wine or water) are, in a sense, lifted out of their ordinary life for use by God for sacramental purposes (in the Eucharist or as holy water). The problem with this is that ordinary things must leave behind their ordinary lives in order to become something more, recruited to divine use. Material things, on this view, spend most of their time separated from any deeper spiritual significance. The better way of envisaging the sacramental character of things in the created order is to notice and appreciate when things become what they truly are and were always meant to be by being put to genuine service of God.

---

13 Walter Brueggemann, *Texts Under Negotiation: The Bible and Postmodern Imagination* (Minneapolis: Fortress, 1993), 88.

14 Alexander Schmemann, *For the Life of the World: Sacraments and Orthodoxy* (Crestwood, NY: St Vladimir's Seminary Press, 1988), 132.

This doesn't mean that created things like animals and plants have an obvious use and integrity simply 'on their own'. Things are not left alone by God. A Christian vision involves seeing all things as participants in worship: trees lifting their branches and tulips opening up are in fact praising God when they do this. Everything in creation, according to Schmemann, has sacramental potential – not in the sense that everything can potentially be lifted out of its ordinary life, but in the sense that everything God created is able to be used by God who discloses the true meaning and significance of all things through such use. All the world is holy and finds its true home in God.

Even so, Christianity isn't always and everywhere associated with this sacramental way of framing the spiritual nature of created things. In a widely cited 1967 article, 'The Historical Roots of Our Ecologic Crisis', Lynn White faulted Christianity for being (especially in its Western form) 'the most anthropocentric religion the world has seen'.[15] He argues that Christians have had several main ways of insisting on the separateness of humans from the rest of creation. Human beings are thought of as the recipients of God's creation and also as exalted above it. Since nearly the beginning, Christians retold the story of Adam in the light of Christ. According to White, the implication was that, despite becoming incarnate in the world, Christ the second Adam displays God's transcendence over nature, a transcendence in which the first Adam (and therefore all people) shares.

Transcendence can be a problem when it causes us to neglect our physical, material world in favour of more spiritual things. A sacramental revealing of the natural spirituality of all things is lost. The rest of creation, White would say, suffers diminished significance as humans are lifted out of it. On the other hand, a more 'worldly' theology of the Incarnation would emphasize Christ's continuing presence with creation or, as Schmemann contends, the sacramental character of all of creation is shown when things can be revealed to be what they truly are – God's creatures. This is a much more genuinely Christian version of transcendence, in fact. Things are not shown to be essentially one way or the other, either weighed down by material baggage or lightly floating away as so much of this baggage is left behind. Instead, like the movement of Christ toward and into the world, true transcendence should not be thought of as *above* but *deeper into*. Augustine described God as paradoxically closer to each

---

15 Lynn White, 'The Historical Roots of Our Ecologic Crisis', *Science* 155.3767 (10 March 1967): 1203–7.

of us than we are even to ourselves. This calls for attempts to discover God in his closeness rather than in remoteness. The consequences of these attempts enrich an ecological mindset that sees all of creation in the light of God's abiding presence in and to it.

White's own hope is that Christianity might learn from St Francis of Assisi rather than the dominant Western traditions that sometimes sought to suppress his humility and openness to God's creation. Francis was open to seeing the sun as his brother and the moon as his sister because all of creation is God's dwelling place. White approves of how Francis is said to have preached to the birds, encouraging them to praise God, to flap their wings in spiritual ecstasy and to chirp songs of rejoicing. When they do these things, they are acting in ways that are most in touch with their true nature.

We have only scratched the surface of the great challenges humans face living on our earth. The approach here has been to try to isolate some of the distinctly theological, and especially sacramental, corrections that might help to orient Christians toward understanding how we might inhabit a more faithful and responsible place.

Bibliography

Abraham, Susan. 'What Does Mumbai Have to Do with Rome? Postcolonial Perspectives on Globalization and Theology.' *Theological Studies* 69 (2008): 376–93.

Ariès, Philippe. *Western Attitudes toward Death from the Middle Ages to the Present*. Translated by Patricia Ranum. Baltimore: Johns Hopkins University Press, 1975.

Aristotle. *Nicomachian Ethics*, second edition. Translated by Terence Irwin. Indianapolis: Hackett, 1999.

Athanasius. *On the Incarnation*.

Augustine. *Confessions*. Translated by Henry Chadwick. Oxford: Oxford University Press, 1991.

Augustine. *On Christian Doctrine*.

Augustine. *The Trinity*. Translated by Edmund Hill, OP. New York: New City Press, 1991.

Bainton, Roland H. *Christian Attitudes toward War and Peace: A Historical Survey and Critical Re-evaluation*. Nashville: Abingdon, 1960.

Barth, Karl. *Church Dogmatics III.4: The Doctrine of Creation*. Edited by G. W. Bromiley and T. F. Torrance. London: T&T Clark International, 2004.

Barth, Karl. *Community, State, and Church*. Translated by G. Ronald Howe. Eugene, OR: Wipf & Stock, 2004.

Bell, Jr, Daniel M. *Just War as Christian Discipleship: Recentering the Tradition in the Church Rather Than the State*. Grand Rapids: Brazos, 2009.

Bellah, Robert. *The Broken Covenant: American Civil Religion in Time of Trial*. New York: Crossroad, 1975.

Berry, Wendell. *The Art of the Common-place: The Agrarian Essays of Wendell Berry*. Edited by Norman Wirzba. Washington, DC: Counterpoint, 2002.

Blount, Brian K. 'Reading Revelation Today: Witness as Active Resistance.' In *Resistance and Theological Ethics*. Edited by Ronald H. Stone and Robert L. Stivers. Oxford: Rowman & Littlefield, 2004 (155–172).

Bonhoeffer, Dietrich. *Ethics*. Translated by Neville Horton Smith. New York: Touchstone, 1995.

Boswell, John. *Christianity, Social Tolerance, and Homosexuality: Gay People in Western Europe from the Beginning of the Christian Era to the Fourteenth Century*. Chicago: University of Chicago Press, 1980.

Boswell, John. *Same-Sex Unions in Premodern Europe*. New York: Vintage, 1994.

Brueggemann, Walter. *Texts Under Negotiation: The Bible and Postmodern Imagination*. Minneapolis: Fortress, 1993.

Cardenal, Ernesto. *The Gospel in Solentiname*. Translated by Donald D. Walsh. Maryknoll: Orbis, 2010.

Catholic Catechism. New York: Image Doubleday, 1995.

Cavanaugh, William. 'Discerning: Politics and Reconciliation.' In *The Blackwell Companion to Christian Ethics*. Edited by Stanley Hauerwas and Samuel Wells. Oxford: Blackwell, 2004 (196–208).

Coakley, Sarah. 'Kenosis: Theological Meanings and Gender Connotations.' In *The Work of Love: Creation as Kenosis*. Edited by John Polkinghorne. Grand Rapids: Eerdmans, 2001 (192–210).

Cone, James H. *A Black Theology of Liberation*. Philadelphia: J. B. Lippincott, 1970.

Dawkins, Richard. *A Devil's Chaplain: Reflections on Hope, Lies, Science, and Love.* New York: Mariner, 2004.

Didache: <https://www.ccel.org/ccel/richardson/fathers.viii.i.iii.html>.

Dignitas Personae: <www.vatican.va/roman_curia/congregations/cfaith/docu ments/rc_con_cfaith_doc_20081208_dignitas-personae_en.html>.

Disney, Lindsey and Larry Poston. 'The Breath of Life: Christian Perspectives on Conception and Ensoulment.' *Anglican Theological Review* 92.2 (Spring 2010): 271–95.

Douglas, Mary. *Purity and Danger: An Analysis of Concepts of Pollution and Taboo.* Harmondsworth: Penguin, 1970.

Endo, Shusaku. *Silence: A Novel.* Translated by William Johnston. New York: Picador, 1969, 2016.

Engelhardt, H. Tristram. *The Foundations of Bioethics*, second edition. Oxford: Oxford University Press, 1996.

Epistle to Diognetus.

Evans-Pritchard, E. E. *Nuer Religion*. Oxford: Oxford University Press, 1956.

Fahey, Joseph J. *War and the Christian Conscience: Where Do You Stand?* Maryknoll: Orbis, 2005.

Feldman, David Michael. *Birth Control in Jewish Law: Marital Relations, Contraception, and Abortion*. New York: New York University Press, 1968.

Figgis, John Neville. *Political Thought from Gerson to Grotius: 1414–1625*. New York: Harper, 1960.

Fletcher, Joseph. *Situation Ethics: The New Morality*. Philadelphia: Westminster, 1975.

Furnish, Victor Paul. 'The Bible and Homosexuality: Reading the Texts in Context.' In *Homosexuality in the Church: Both Sides of the Debate*. Edited by Jeffrey S. Siker. Louisville: Westminster John Knox, 1994 (18–35).

Gill, Robin. *A Textbook of Christian Ethics*, fourth edition. New York: Bloomsbury Academic, 2014.

Girard, René. *I See Satan Fall like Lightning*. Translated by James G. Williams. Maryknoll: Orbis, 2001.

Girard, René. *Violence and the Sacred*. Translated by Patrick Gregory. Baltimore: Johns Hopkins University Press, 1977.

Gregory of Nyssa: The Life of Moses. Edited and translated by Abraham Malherbe and Everett Ferguson. Classics of Western Spirituality. New York: Paulist, 1978.

Hallie, Philip. *Lest Innocent Blood Be Shed*. New York: Harper & Row, 1979.

Harris, Sam. *The Moral Landscape: How Science Can Determine Moral Values.* London: Free Press, 2010.

Hart, David Bentley. 'A Gift Exceeding Every Debt: An Eastern Orthodox Appreciation of Anselm's Cur Deus Homo.' *Pro Ecclesia* 7.3 (1998): 333–49.

Hauerwas, Stanley. 'Abortion Theologically Understood.' *The Hauerwas Reader.* Edited by John Berkman and Michael Cartwright. Durham, NC: Duke University Press, 2001 (603–22).

Hauerwas, Stanley. *In Good Company: The Church as Polis.* Notre Dame: University of Notre Dame Press, 1995.

Hauerwas, Stanley. *The Peaceable Kingdom: A Primer in Christian Ethics.* Notre Dame: University of Notre Dame Press, 1983.

Hauerwas, Stanley. *Vision and Virtue: Essays in Christian Ethical Reflection.* Notre Dame: University of Notre Dame Press, 1981.

Hauerwas, Stanley and Richard Bondi. 'Memory, Community and the Reasons for Living: Theological and Ethical Reflections on Suicide and Euthanasia.' *Journal of the American Academy of Religion* 44.3 (Sept. 1976): 439–52.

Hays, Richard. *The Moral Vision of the New Testament: Community, Cross, New Creation.* San Francisco: HarperCollins, 1996.

Hill, Wesley. *Washed and Waiting: Reflections on Christian Faithfulness and Homosexuality.* Grand Rapids: Zondervan, 2010.

Hovey, Craig. *What Makes Us Moral? Science, Religion and the Shaping of the Moral Landscape: A Christian response to Sam Harris* (London: SPCK, 2012).

Huebner, Harry J. *An Introduction to Christian Ethics: History, Movements, People.* Waco, TX: Baylor University Press, 2012.

Hume, David. 'On the Naturalness of Suicide.' In *Life and Death.* Edited by Louis Pojman. Boston: Jones & Bartlett, 1993 (142–6).

Instone-Brewer, David. *Divorce and Remarriage in the Bible.* Grand Rapids: Eerdmans, 2002.

Jennings, Willie James. 'Being Baptized: Race.' In *The Blackwell Companion to Christian Ethics,* second edition. Edited by Stanley Hauerwas and Samuel Wells. Oxford: Blackwell, 2011 (277–89).

Jennings, Willie James. *The Christian Imagination: Theology and the Origins of Race.* New Haven: Yale University Press, 2010.

Jenson, Robert W. 'On the Ascension.' In *Loving God with Our Minds: The Pastor as Theologian.* Edited by Michael Welker and Cynthia A. Jarvis. Grand Rapids: Eerdmans, 2004 (331–40).

Jenson, Robert W. *Systematic Theology,* vol. 2: *The Works of God.* Oxford: Oxford University Press, 1999.

John Paul II. *Evangelium Vitae:* <http://w2.vatican.va/content/john-paul-ii/en/encyclicals/documents/hf_jp-ii_enc_25031995_evangelium-vitae.html>.

Kant, Immanuel. *Zum ewigen Frieden: ein philosophischer Entwurf.* 1795.

Kass, Leon R. 'The Wisdom of Repugnance.' *New Republic* (2 June 1997): 17–26.

Lee, Justin. *Torn: Rescuing the Gospel from the Gays-vs.-Christians Debate.* New York: Jericho, 2012.

Leithart, Peter J. 'Response to "To Set Our Hope on Christ"': <https://www.firstthings.com/blogs/leithart/2005/06/to-set-our-hope-on-christ>.

Levine, Baruch A. *Numbers 1–20: The Anchor Bible.* New York: Doubleday, 1993.

Luther, Martin. *The Christian in Society I, Luther's Works, vol. 44.* Translated by W. A. Lambert. Philadelphia: Fortress, 1966.

Luther, Martin. *On the Bondage of the Will* (1525). In *Martin Luther: Selections from His Writing.* Edited by John Dillenberger. New York: Anchor Books, 1962.

Luz, Ulrich. *Matthew 8–22.* Translated by James E. Crouch. Minneapolis: Fortress, 2001.

McCabe, Herbert. *The Good Life: Ethics and the Pursuit of Happiness.* Edited by Brian Davies. New York: Continuum, 2005.

McFague, Sallie. *Models of God: Theology for an Ecological, Nuclear Age.* Philadelphia: Fortress, 1987.

McGee, G. and A. Caplan. 'The Ethics and Politics of Small Sacrifices in Stem Cell Research.' *Kennedy Institute of Ethics Journal* 9.2 (1999): 151–8.

Mattison III, William C. *Introducing Moral Theology: True Happiness and the Virtues.* Grand Rapids: Brazos, 2008.

Meilaender, Gilbert. *Faith and Faithfulness: Basic Themes in Christian Ethics.* Notre Dame: University of Notre Dame Press, 1991.

Meilaender, Gilbert. 'The Point of the Ban: Or, How to Think about Stem Cell Research.' *The Hastings Center Report* (January/February 2001).

Milbank, John. *Being Reconciled: Ontology and Pardon.* London: Routledge, 2003.

Milbank, John. *The Word Made Strange: Theology, Language, Culture.* Oxford: Blackwell, 1997.

Milgrom, Jacob. *Leviticus 17–22: Anchor Bible.* New York: Doubleday, 2000.

Miranda, José Porfirio. *Marx and the Bible: A Critique of the Philosophy of Oppression.* Maryknoll: Orbis, 1974.

Moltmann, Jürgen. *The Trinity and the Kingdom: The Doctrine of God.* Translated by Margaret Kohl. Minneapolis: Fortress, 1993.

Murdoch, Iris. *The Sovereignty of Good.* New York: Routledge, 2002.

Nelkin, Dana Kay and Samuel C. Rickless. 'So Close, Yet So Far: Why Solutions to the Closeness Problem for the Doctrine of Double Effect Fall Short.' *NOÛS* 49.2 (2015): 376–409.

Niebuhr, Reinhold. *An Interpretation of Christian Ethics.* New York: Harper & Row, 1935.

Niebuhr, Reinhold. *Why the Christian Church Is Not Pacifist.* London: Student Christian Movement, 1940.

Noll, Mark A. *The Civil War as a Theological Crisis.* Chapel Hill: The University of North Carolina Press, 2006.

Nussbaum, Martha C. *Hiding from Humanity: Disgust, Shame, and the Law.* Princeton: Princeton University Press, 2004.

Origen. *Homilies on Joshua.* Translated by Barbara J. Bruce. Washington, DC: Catholic University of America Press, 2002.

Origen. *On First Principles*. Edited by G. W. Butterworth. New York: Harper & Row, 1966.

Perry, John. 'Vocation and Creation: Beyond the Gentile–Homosexual Analogy.' *Journal of Religious Ethics* 40.2 (2012): 385–400.

Peters, Ted. *Playing God? Genetic Determinism and Human Freedom*. London: Routledge, 2003.

Plato. *The Republic*. Translated by Richard W. Sterling and William C. Scott. New York: Norton, 1985.

Pobee, John S. *Toward an African Theology*. Nashville: Abingdon, 1979.

Pui-lan, Kwok, Don H. Compier and Joerg Rieger, eds. *Empire and the Christian Tradition: New Readings of Classical Theologians*. Minneapolis: Fortress, 2007.

Rachels, James. 'Active and Passive Euthanasia.' In *Euthanasia: The Moral Issues*. Edited by Robert M. Baird and Stuart E. Rosenbaum. Buffalo: Prometheus, 1989 (45–51).

Ramsey, Paul. *Basic Christian Ethics*. Louisville: Westminster John Knox, 1950.

Ramsey, Paul. *Fabricated Man: The Ethics of Genetic Control*. New Haven: Yale University Press, 1970.

Reed, Philip A. 'The Danger of Double Effect.' *Christian Bioethics* 18.3 (2012): 287–300.

Schmemann, Alexander. *For the Life of the World: Sacraments and Orthodoxy*. Crestwood, NY: St Vladimir's Seminary Press, 1988.

Senior, Donald. *Why the Cross?* Nashville: Abingdon, 2014.

The Sheperd of Hermas.

Soskice, Janet Martin. 'Monica's Tears: Augustine on Words and Speech.' *New Blackfriars* 83.980 (Oct. 2002): 448–58.

St. Anselm: Basic Writings. Translated by S. N. Deane. La Salle, IL: Open Court, 1962.

Stassen, Glen H. 'The Fourteen Triads of the Sermon on the Mount (Matthew 5: 21–7:12).' *Journal of Biblical Literature* 122.2 (2003): 267–308.

Stout, Jeffrey. *Democracy and Tradition*. Princeton: Princeton University Press, 2004.

Stringfellow, William. *An Ethic for Christians and Other Aliens in a Strange Land*. Reprint. Eugene, OR: Wipf & Stock, 2004.

Tertullian. *On the Prescription of Heretics*. In *Ante-Nicene Fathers*, vol. 3. Edited by Allan Menzies and James Donaldson. New York: Charles Scribner's Sons, 1903.

Thomas Aquinas. *Summa Contra Gentiles*. Edited by Joseph Kenny. New York: Hanover House, 1955–7.

Thomas Aquinas. *Summa Theologica*. Translated by Fathers of the English Dominican Province. Allen, TX: Christian Classics, 1981.

Tran, Jonathan. 'The Wound of Tradition.' In *The Hermeneutics of Tradition: Explorations and Examinations*. Edited by Craig Hovey and Cyrus P. Olsen. Eugene, OR: Cascade, 2014 (226–52).

Trocmé, André. *Jesus and the Nonviolent Revolution*. Edited by Charles E. Moore. Maryknoll: Orbis, 2003.

Tutu, Desmond. *No Future without Forgiveness.* New York: Doubleday, 2000.

Virilio, Paul. *The Original Accident.* Cambridge: Polity, 2007.

Volf, Miroslav. *The End of Memory: Remembering Rightly in a Violent World.* Grand Rapids: Eerdmans, 2006.

Walker, Margaret Urban. *Moral Repair: Reconstructing Moral Relations after Wrongdoing.* Cambridge: Cambridge University Press, 2006.

Webb, Stephen H. *Good Eating.* Grand Rapids: Brazos, 2001.

Wells, Samuel. *Improvisation: The Drama of Christian Ethics.* Grand Rapids: Brazos, 2004.

Wells, Samuel and Ben Quash. *Introducing Christian Ethics.* Oxford: Blackwell, 2010.

White, Lynn. 'The Historical Roots of Our Ecologic Crisis.' *Science* 155.3767 (10 March 1967): 1203–7.

White, Mel. *Stranger at the Gate: To Be Gay and Christian in America.* New York: Simon & Schuster, 1994.

Yoder, John Howard. 'Armaments and Eschatology.' *Studies in Christian Ethics* 1.1 (1988): 43–61.

Yoder, John Howard. *For the Nations: Essays Public and Evangelical.* Grand Rapids: Eerdmans, 1997.

Yoder, John Howard. *The Politics of Jesus: Vicit Agnus Noster,* second edition. Grand Rapids: Eerdmans, 2002.

Yoder, John Howard. Review of *The Scapegoat* by René Girard. *Religion and Literature* 19.3 (Fall 1986): 89–92.

Yoder, John Howard. 'Walk and Word: The Alternatives to Methodologism.' In *Theology Without Foundations: Religious Practice and the Future of Theological Truth.* Edited by Stanley Hauerwas, Nancey Murphy and Mark Nation. Nashville: Abingdon, 1994 (77–90).

Further reading

Introduction

Gilligan, Carol. 'A Different Voice in Moral Decisions.' In *Speaking of Faith: Global Perspectives on Women, Religion and Social Change.* Edited by Diana Eck and Devaki Jain. Philadelphia: New Society, 1987. A classic account of different modes of moral reasoning used by men and women.

Williams, Rowan. 'Making Moral Decisions.' In *The Cambridge Companion to Christian Ethics.* Edited by Robin Gill. Cambridge: Cambridge University Press, 2001. Good for laying out the complex nature of moral decision-making.

1 The Bible

Green, Joel B., ed. *Dictionary of Scripture and Ethics.* Grand Rapids: Baker Academic, 2011. A good resource with short articles on issues of interpretation and concrete ethical issues.

2 Following Jesus

Verhey, Allen. *Remembering Jesus: Christian Community, Scripture, and the Moral Life.* Grand Rapids: Eerdmans, 2002. Exemplary integration of New Testament studies and some key contemporary moral themes.

3 Some key theological themes

Athanasius. *On the Incarnation.* Orthodox statement of the doctrine of incarnation.

Girard, René. 'The Triumph of the Cross.' In *I See Satan Fall like Lightning.* Translated by James G. Williams. Maryknoll: Orbis, 2001. A concise presentation of central Girardian ideas structured as a reflection on Colossians 2.14–15.

Milbank, John. 'Can Morality Be Christian?' In *The Word Made Strange: Theology, Language, Culture.* Oxford: Blackwell, 1997. A difficult but rewarding reading that distinguishes Christian ethics from what generally passes for 'morality' in culture.

4 Classical roots

Aristotle. *Nicomachean Ethics.* The classic virtue ethics text.

McCabe, Herbert. *The Good Life: Ethics and the Pursuit of Happiness.* Edited by Brian Davies. New York: Continuum, 2005. Clear and deep elaboration of happiness as the human end.

Mattison III, William C. *Introducing Moral Theology: True Happiness and the Virtues.* Grand Rapids: Brazos, 2008. A reader-friendly approach to the virtues for a contemporary audience.

Plato. *The Republic.*

Wells, Samuel. *Improvisation: The Drama of Christian Ethics.* Grand Rapids: Brazos, 2004. An imaginative implementation of the ethics of virtue through the practices of improvisational drama.

5 Modern options

Fletcher, Joseph. *Situation Ethics: The New Morality.* Philadelphia: Westminster, 1975. A text loved and hated, but important either way.

Hauerwas, Stanley. *Vision and Virtue: Essays in Christian Ethical Reflection.* Notre Dame: University of Notre Dame Press, 1981. Hauerwas's first collection of essays contains important critiques of Fletcher in chapter 1.

Meilaender, Gilbert. 'Moral Theory: Rules, Virtues, Results.' In *Faith and Faithfulness: Basic Themes in Christian Ethics.* Notre Dame: University of Notre Dame Press, 1991. A profound Christian response to consequentialism.

6 Contemporary challenges

Bonhoeffer, Dietrich. *Ethics.* Translated by Neville Horton Smith. New York: Touchstone, 1995. An important challenge to the very idea of ethics that also addresses specific issues such as suicide and truth-telling.

Jennings, Willie James. *The Christian Imagination: Theology and the Origins of Race.* New Haven: Yale University Press, 2010. Deeply important for understanding race theologically and historically.

Murdoch, Iris. *The Sovereignty of Good.* New York: Routledge, 2002. The importance of vision for morality.

7 Baptism and identity

Barth, Karl. *Community, State, and Church.* Translated by G. Ronald Howe. Eugene, OR: Wipf & Stock, 2004. Significant essays on the Church's relation to the world and civil government.

Epistle to Diognetus. Early insights into how Christians saw themselves within the world.

Yoder, John Howard. *For the Nations: Essays Public and Evangelical.* Grand Rapids: Eerdmans, 1997. A theology accused of withdrawing from worldly matters disagrees.

8 Mercy and peace

Tutu, Desmond. *No Future without Forgiveness.* New York: Doubleday, 2000. A modern classic from the best authority on Christian reconciliation.

Volf, Miroslav. *The End of Memory: Remembering Rightly in a Violent World.* Grand Rapids: Eerdmans, 2006. A strong theological statement about the goal of remembering wrongs that is aware of its critics.

Walker, Margaret Urban. *Moral Repair: Reconstructing Moral Relations after Wrongdoing*. Cambridge: Cambridge University Press, 2006. A practical and profound guide to difficult tasks.

9 Justice from above (order)

Bainton, Roland H. *Christian Attitudes toward War and Peace: A Historical Survey and Critical Re-evaluation*. Nashville: Abingdon, 1960. Presents a helpful typology of holy war, just war and pacifism.

Bell, Jr, Daniel M. *Just War as Christian Discipleship: Recentering the Tradition in the Church Rather Than the State*. Grand Rapids: Brazos, 2009. Situates just war within church practices.

Girard, René. *Violence and the Sacred*. Translated by Patrick Gregory. Baltimore: Johns Hopkins University Press, 1977. Explores the meaning of sacrifice across cultures and literature.

O'Donovan, Oliver. *The Just War Revisited*. Cambridge: Cambridge University Press, 2003. A dense, detailed and responsible treatment that argues for the crucial role of theology.

10 Justice from below (liberation)

Cahill, Lisa Sowle. 'Gender and Christian Ethics.' In *The Cambridge Companion to Christian Ethics*. Edited by Robin Gill. Cambridge: Cambridge University Press, 2001. Surveys Christian views on gender in the Bible, throughout Christian history and in modern times.

Cardenal, Ernesto. *The Gospel in Solentiname*. Translated by Donald D. Walsh. Maryknoll: Orbis, 2010. Transcriptions of conversations about Gospel readings involving Nicaraguan peasants, artists and others.

Cone, James H. *A Black Theology of Liberation*. Philadelphia: J. B. Lippincott, 1970. The classic statement of black theology.

Jennings, Willie James. 'Being Baptized: Race.' In *The Blackwell Companion to Christian Ethics*, second edition. Edited by Stanley Hauerwas and Samuel Wells. Oxford: Blackwell, 2011.

Parsons, Susan Frank, ed. *The Cambridge Companion to Feminist Theology*. Cambridge: Cambridge University Press, 2002.

Parsons, Susan Frank, ed. *Feminism and Christian Ethics*. Cambridge: Cambridge University Press, 1996.

11 Sexuality

Bennett, Jana Marguerite. *Water Is Thicker Than Blood: An Augustinian Theology of Marriage and Singlehood*. Oxford: Oxford University Press, 2008.

Furnish, Victor Paul. 'The Bible and Homosexuality: Reading the Texts in Context.' In *Homosexuality in the Church: Both Sides of the Debate*. Edited by Jeffrey S. Siker. Louisville: Westminster John Knox, 1994. A competent treatment of the relevant Bible passages.

Instone-Brewer, David. *Divorce and Remarriage in the Bible.* Grand Rapids: Eerdmans, 2002.

12 Vulnerable life

Disney, Lindsey and Larry Poston. 'The Breath of Life: Christian Perspectives on Conception and Ensoulment.' *Anglican Theological Review* 92.2 (Spring 2010): 271–95. A good overview of the many Christian views throughout history.

Hauerwas, Stanley. 'Abortion Theologically Understood.' *The Hauerwas Reader.* Edited by John Berkman and Michael Cartwright. Durham, NC: Duke University Press, 2001. Locates the abortion debate within the church community rather than in secular discourse.

Meilaender, Gilbert. 'The Point of the Ban: Or, How to Think about Stem Cell Research.' *The Hastings Center Report* (January/February 2001). Dated by now, but a rich example of moral reasoning about research on human embryos that challenges consequentialism.

13 Challenges posed by science and technology

Hovey, Craig. *What Makes Us Moral? Science, Religion and the Shaping of the Moral Landscape: A Christian response to Sam Harris* (London: SPCK, 2012). My response to a prominent New Atheist who claims that science is all we need to be moral.

Northcott, Michael S. 'Ecology and Christian Ethics.' In *The Cambridge Companion to Christian Ethics.* Edited by Robin Gill. Cambridge: Cambridge University Press, 2001. A concise account of how some of the major theological ideas help Christians think about the ecological crisis and living on our planet.

Peters, Ted. *Playing God? Genetic Determinism and Human Freedom.* London: Routledge, 2003. A careful examination.

Index

abortion 15, 28, 30–2, 99, 124, 237–48, 266
Abraham, Susan 128–9
addiction 4
adoption 171, 222, 227
adultery 97–9, 104, 223, 231
Alison, James 170
Ambrose 191
animals, non-human 22, 89, 108, 111, 217, 253, 258, 270–4
Anselm of Canterbury 168–74
anthropology, challenge to modern ethics 101
apartheid 172, 183
apocalypse 144; apocalyptic expectation 161–4
Aquinas, Thomas 89–94, 108–13, 123–30, 142, 150, 174, 195–6, 213, 244, 270
Arendt, Hannah 166
Ariès, Philippe 250–1
Aristotle 82–93, 95, 108, 110, 113, 123, 125, 129, 150, 270; see also new Aristotelianism
Athanasius of Alexandria 38–40
atomic bombing of Japan 194, 196
atonement 47, 56
Augustine, St 4–5, 25–6, 29, 49, 78–9, 82–3, 89–90, 94, 110, 127, 129, 185–6, 191–2, 195, 219, 221, 227, 270, 274

baptism 137–57, 211–12, 214, 220, 227–8, 234, 268
Barth, Karl 106, 157, 209, 220–2
Beatitudes 13, 14, 40
Bell, Daniel 192
Bentham, Jeremy 103, 197n11
Berry, Wendell 14, 273
biotechnology 267–8, 269
black theology 207–10, 277

body of Christ 2, 142
Bonhoeffer, Dietrich 6, 18, 89, 114, 117–20, 125–6, 209, 253–4
Boswell, John 236
Brueggemann, Walter 272–3

Cain and Abel 18, 67, 146, 164–5, 271
capitalism 155, 201, 269
Cardenal, Ernesto 204–5
catechumenate 141
categorical imperative 100
Cavanaugh, William 145–6, 195
celibacy 26, 230, 236
character 88–9
children see family
Church, as polis 54, 138, 149, 162
circumcision 137, 152, 205, 235
citizenship 144–51
civil disobedience 151–7
class 199–205
clean/unclean 44–6, 214, 231–2
Clement of Alexandria 141, 185, 240
cloning 109, 257–8, 263–6
Coles, Romand 131
colonialism 127, 206; see also postcolonial theory
communitarianism 149–50
concupiscence 219
Cone, James 208–10, 215
consequentialism 102–7, 116–17, 258
Constantine 186, 191, 204
contraception 99
Cook, James 101
crucifixion 62–9

death, culture of 247
deontology 96–102
deterrence 181–2
Deuteronomic theology 186–8
discipleship 36–54

disgust 109–10
divorce 7, 25, 29, 219, 223–4, 228
Docetism 58
doing vs being 6; *see also* virtues
dominion 22, 224, 270
double effect 196–7, 244–5, 255

ecofeminism 217
egalitarian view of gender 212–14; *see
    also* equality
egoism 103
election 140–1
embryos *see* stem cells
empiricism 80, 88, 259–63
ends rather than means, principle of 257,
    264–5
Engelhardt, H. Tristram 98, 101
Enlightenment ethics 95–6, 101–3,
    122–7, 145, 149, 217, 262; *see also*
    universal ethics
ensoulment 239–40
Enuma Elish 145–6
environmental stewardship 22, 258,
    269–75
equality 31, 45–6, 154, 207–8, 212, 217
Eucharist *see* sacrament
eugenics 263–4
eunuchs 228–33
euthanasia 249–56
Evans-Pritchard, E. E. 260–1
evil 3–5, 41, 81–3, 115–19, 160, 163, 185;
    intrinsically evil acts 99
exegesis 28
experience 27; *see also* praxis

facts and values, distinction between *see*
    moral realism
faith, leap of 116
family 224–30; *see also* marriage
feminist theology 213–17
Figgis, John 195
Fiorenza, Elisabeth Schüssler 213–14
Fletcher, Joseph 103–5, 124
foetus, moral status of 30–1, 239–44,
    248, 266
forgiveness 164–70

Francis of Assisi, St 275
freedom 17, 55, 96, 106–7, 120, 123, 146,
    194, 211–12, 264
friendship 105, 120, 171, 225, 227
Furnish, Victor Paul 233–4

Gandhi 154, 210
genetic engineering 257, 263–6
Gill, Robin 28–9
Girard, René 67–8, 155–6, 183–4, 271
Gregory of Nyssa 53, 240

Hallie, Philip 132–3
Hanukkah 152
happiness 81–94
Harris, Sam 105, 247, 259–60, 262
Hauerwas, Stanley 92, 105, 123–6, 131–2,
    241–3
Hays, Richard 238, 242
Hegel, Georg Wilhelm Friedrich 115, 125
hermeneutic of suspicion 215
Hippolytus of Rome 142
Historic Peace Churches 162
Hobbes, Thomas 145
homosexuality 111, 230–7
Hooker, Richard 111
Human Genome Project 263
Hume, David 259, 266–7
hypostatic union 57

ideology 201–2
idolatry 33, 126, 152, 187, 201, 216, 232
in vitro fertilization (IVF) 22, 244–6
incarnation/the Incarnation 56–62
Industrial Revolution 201–2
intention 46, 52, 99, 194–7, 245–6
intersex 228–33

Jennings, Willie James 128–31, 206, 208,
    211–12
Jenson, Robert 1
Jesus Christ, moral example of 43–9; *see
    also* crucifixion, discipleship, incarna-
    tion, resurrection 69–73
John of Damascus 89
John Paul II 238, 247

Jubilee year 41–2
Judas 62, 152, 253-4
Just War Theory 127, 191–7
justice 177–217

Kant, Immanuel 94–6, 100–2, 122,
    124–5, 264–5
Kass, Leon 109–10
Kierkegaard, Søren 114–20, 124–6
King, Jr., Martin Luther 70, 154
kingdom of God 37–8, 40–2, 159,
    199–200, 222–3

Land, Richard 192
law 95
Lessing, Gotthold 149–50
liberalism 121–3, 241
liberation 16, 198–217; *see also* freedom
liberation theology 201–5; *see also* praxis
liturgy 15–16, 21, 92, 147–8, 175–6, 249
Locke, John 145
Logos 36, 79
love, erotic 226
Lubac, Henri de 146
Luther, Martin 13, 29, 97, 112, 210
lying *see* truthfulness

McCabe, Herbert 86
McFague, Sallie 216–17
MacIntyre, Alasdair 95, 102, 114, 117,
    122–31
male images of God 215–17
Marcion of Pontus 33–4
marriage 98, 215, 219–30, 233–6; *see also*
    divorce, remarriage
martyrdom 68, 92–3, 104, 142, 145
Marx, Karl 201–3
Maximus the Confessor 146, 240
Meilaender, Gilbert 105–7, 248
meta-ethics 95–113
Milbank, John 48, 71
Mill, John Stuart 103
Miranda, José Porfirio 203
Moltmann, Jürgen 57–8, 170
moral realism 259–63
moral relativism 116, 120–6, 149

narrative 16–17, 24–5, 113
nationalism 3, 192
natural law 3, 107–13, 213
new Aristotelianism 120–6
New Atheists 105, 259
Niebuhr, Reinhold 159–63, 209
Nietzsche, Friedrich 71–2, 123, 177–8
Noll, Mark 123
non-resistance 161–2
non-violence 66, 155–6, 158, 190,
    210–11
Nussbaum, Martha 109

Origen of Alexandria 18–46, 146, 185–6
original sin 146, 219

parables 37–40
Passover 23
patriarchy 212, 224
peace 158–76; *see also* non-violence
Pelagius 49
penance 172, 183, 192–3
personhood 241
Peters, Ted 267
Philo of Alexandria 33, 240
physician-assisted suicide 252–6
Plato 78–83
playing God 107, 257, 267–8
Pobee, John 26
polygamy 25–6, 225
postcolonial theory, theology and ethics
    114, 126–9, 132
postmodern ethics 101–2
praxis 40, 204, 207
procreation 25, 111, 218–19, 222, 231, 234
promise-keeping 100–1
proportionality 194–5
public and private ethic 91, 159–61
public nature of ethics 91–2
public theology 150
punishment 29, 47, 62–3, 153, 164–5,
    169–84

race 128, 205–12, 215
Ramsey, Paul 161–2, 267–8
reason 91, 97, 100–3, 111–12, 122

reconciliation 148–9, 158, 164–5, 170–6, 182–3, 206–7
redistribution (almsgiving) 42, 203
Reformation 100, 230
relativism *see* moral relativism
remarriage 7, 29; *see also* divorce
restorative justice 183
resurrection 63–73
riches *see* wealth
Roe v. Wade 241
rules 96–9, 103–5, 117, 123–4; *see also* deontology

sacrament 227–8, 258, 268, 273–5
sacrifice/self-sacrifice 62–9, 72
salvation, as gathering 146–8
scapegoat mechanism 67–8, 183–4
Schmemann, Alexander 273–4
secularism 96, 100–2, 149, 182, 264; *see also* universal ethics
sexuality 26, 218–36
shalom 158
Shepherd of Hermas 200, 204
sin 4–6, 15, 18, 56, 61, 65, 77, 83, 94, 146–7; as disordered desire 219; as privation 4–5, 83; as sickness 5–6, 46–7, 249–50
singleness 219–24
situation ethics 104, 124
slavery 41, 122–3, 208–10
Socrates 80–2, 119
sola scriptura 13, 29
Sophists 80
Soskice, Janet 83
stem cells 243–4, 264–5
story *see* narrative
Stringfellow, William 155
suffering 187–8, 190, 248, 251–2, 255–6
suffering servant 25
suicide 110, 252–6, 266–7
supersessionism 35, 140

tattoos 33, 232
technology 3, 22, 245, 252, 257–75
teleological suspension of the ethical 116
telos 84–5, 89–90, 93, 113, 130

Ten Commandments 19, 51, 96–7, 138–9
Tertullian 28, 78–9, 89, 141, 186, 240
Thoreau, Henry David 14
toleration 121, 125
torture 98
tradition 27, 29, 96, 98–101, 121–33
traducianism 240–1
Trinity 216–18
Trocmé, André 132–3
Troeltsch, Ernst 148
Truth and Reconciliation Commission 183
truthfulness 6, 85, 89, 93, 99, 104, 118–19
Tutu, Desmond 172, 183

universal ethics 96, 124, 127–9; *see also* Enlightenment ethics; Kant
utilitarianism 103–5, 182

vengeance 72, 169, 182
violence 31, 66–8, 93, 102, 127–8, 142, 145–6, 152–9, 163, 170, 179, 183–6, 189–91, 210–11, 270–2; *see also* non-violence
Virilio, Paul 246
virtues 84–7; theological 93
vision, moral significance of 124
Volf, Miroslav 167–8

Walker, Margaret Urban 166–7, 172–3
war 28–9, 184–97; *see also* Just War Theory
wealth 42–3, 161, 178–9, 198, 200–5
Wesley, Charles 56
Wesley, John 192
White, Lynn 274
whiteness 208–11
Wilson, E. O. 260
witness, public 149–51
Wittgenstein, Ludwig 98, 150
women, as witnesses to Christ 214
worship 69–73

Yoder, John Howard 71, 125–6, 149–50, 156, 162–3

Zealots 152